Praise for *Globalizati*

"Not a week goes past without a new book on glo
have long set in. But this collection, bringing tog
pology and marrying them beautifully with h.
unique and invaluable insights. No serious student of globalization can a.......
to ignore it."

Jagdish Bhagwati, Professor, Columbia University,
author of *Free Trade Today*

"At last a book which assesses the impact of globalization on the neglected but
crucial topic of culture and education. What does it mean to be young in a
world which is increasingly connected through technology, trade, and population movements but where the gulf between rich and poor, between good
schools and bad, or between cultures is apparently growing? The product of
collaboration among distinguished scholars, this impressive collection provides
much-needed insights, analysis, and answers."

Margaret MacMillan, Provost, Trinity College,
Toronto, Ontario

"A brilliant collection of essays about the urgency of rethinking educational
change, both its challenges and opportunities. In a world of increasingly coor-
dinated markets and rising populations of migrants, state educational policies
strain to develop the philosophical and material resources that can address cultural and economic differences without, one hopes, confusing equality with
homogeneity. This book is a major contribution toward wresting democratic
futures from an uneven present."

Doris Sommer, Ira Jewell Williams Jr. Professor of
Romance Languages and Literature, Harvard University

"A book of serious scholarship written by leading authorities in their fields.
Although each chapter stands on its own, the whole book adds up to an
account of the impact of globalization on education, which is much greater
than the sum of its parts."

George Walker, Director General,
International Baccalaureate Organization

"This book comprehensively explores the challenges that globalization poses to
educators. The fate and future of the planet's children rest on the ability of education to meet those challenges. The contributors, experienced educators themselves, have thought freshly and deeply on the cultural implications of the globalizing process."

Arthur Schlesinger, author of *A Thousand Days:
John F. Kennedy in the White House*

"This book is unlike any other because it marries what we know and think about globalization to a fascinating account of the development of young people. The authors proclaim the message that globalization is a powerful tool for enlarging human capacity but that this potential can be realized only if our techniques and systems of education change drastically. It's a message which all those who care about the future of our species should heed."

Lord Skidelsky, founder and Chairman,
Centre for Global Studies, Warwick University

GLOBALIZATION

GLOBALIZATION

CULTURE AND EDUCATION
IN THE NEW MILLENNIUM

Edited by

Marcelo M. Suárez-Orozco
and
Desirée Baolian Qin-Hilliard

UNIVERSITY OF CALIFORNIA PRESS

BERKELEY   LOS ANGELES   LONDON

THE ROSS INSTITUTE

Chapter 10, *"How Education Changes:*
Considerations of History, Science, and
Values," is © 2004 by Howard Gardner.

University of California Press
Berkeley and Los Angeles, California

University of California Press, Ltd.
London, England

© 2004 by the Regents of the University of California

Library of Congress Cataloging-in-Publication Data

Globalization : culture and education in the new
millennium / edited by Marcelo M. Suárez-Orozco
and Desirée Baolian Qin-Hilliard.
        p.   cm.
"Published in association with the Ross Institute."
Includes bibliographical references and index.
ISBN-13 978-0-520-24125-1 (pbk. : alk. paper)
ISBN-10 0-520-24125-8 (pbk. : alk. paper)
    1. Globalization.   2. Education.   3. Culture.
I. Suárez-Orozco, Marcelo M., 1956–   II. Qin-
Hilliard, Desirée Baolian, 1972–

JZ1318.G57925   2004
303.48'2—dc22   2003061084

Manufactured in the United States of America
14   13   12   11   10   09   08 07
12   11   10   9   8   7   6   5   4

The paper used in this publication meets the minimum
requirements of ANSI/NISO Z39.48-1992(R 1997)
(Permanence of Paper). ∞

For Courtney Ross-Holst

Contents

Preface

Virtually all aspects of modern life—our jobs, our culture, our relationships with one another—are being transformed by the profound forces of globalization. Goods and people flow across national borders, and data and information flash around the world, at an ever accelerating rate.

Not only has globalization become the central issue of our time, but it will define the world our children inherit. So those concerned about the future must ask, how are our primary and secondary schools preparing today's students to be successful citizens in a global society?

That was the question posed one crisp fall week last year at a seminar in Cambridge, Massachusetts, hosted by Harvard University and the Ross Institute. The participants who gathered to exchange ideas included an array of international academics from various scholarly disciplines, a group of senior education and immigration policy makers from Sweden, a contingent of teachers and administrators from the Ross School, and several European high-tech executives. The ensuing exchanges between participants of such diverse backgrounds and points of view suggested to all that a major conversation on a topic of critical significance to the future of our children is long overdue.

This book grew from the Harvard-Ross Seminar on Education for Globalization and broadens that conversation. It is intended as a tool for anyone—parent, educator, scholar, public official, or informed citizen—interested in how education must adapt in a fast-changing world. It reflects the latest research and thinking from many fields—psychology, neuroscience, economics, anthropology, history, and education, among others. This diversity of disciplines highlights the complexity of the issues facing our schools, and the reality that no single field in isolation can address these issues.

The changes that must be made to precollegiate education cannot be overestimated. Businesses around the world have been undergoing profound change for more than two decades to adapt to new technologies and an increasingly interconnected global economy. Many universities are beginning to adopt similarly dramatic change. But most primary and secondary schools are still operating on a model that assumes time stopped in the early industrial age.

Precollegiate schools have barely begun tapping the potential of modern technology. The most advanced technology in use in many classrooms is the lightbulb. School buildings often resemble factories—kindergartners enter at one end; move slowly down the hall, having subject after subject applied; and spill out years later at the other end of the building with a diploma stamping them as educated.

What educators and policy makers need are models that can more readily take advantage of the challenges and opportunities offered by globalization. Knowledge today is spreading faster than at any time before in human history. Complex issues are cutting across traditional academic disciplines. Advances in communications let students anywhere in the world access the best teachers and newest ideas. Students have opportunities once unimaginable to collaborate with peers from other countries in order to gain insight and understanding about those cultures. These new opportunities suggest to me that educators are more relevant to the project of education than ever before: to scaffold new ways of knowing, to help children and youth reach higher and more complex levels of understanding, and to guide students to achieving greater appreciation for cultural complexity and diversity.

A dozen years ago, when the Ross School was launched in an effort to create a new model for education in a global society, we had more questions than answers. We never imagined that today we would be working with a school in Stockholm on how to better educate their students, most of whom are immigrants and refugees from the Middle East and North Africa. As the scholarship in this book demonstrates, answers about how precollegiate education must adapt to globalization are beginning to emerge. We ignore them at our peril.

Students who are not prepared for a lifetime of learning, who cannot adapt to new technology, or who cannot synthesize knowledge from multiple disciplines, often in multiple languages, will face diminishing economic opportunity and general well-being. Those unable to appreciate other cultures will be left out of important affairs or, worse, will too quickly turn to hostility. We already see these factors at work in the growing inequality between rich and poor and the proliferation of cultural conflict around the world.

For too long, education reform has been devoted to fixing breakdowns on the existing education assembly line. That must end. We need instead to shift our focus to rethinking and reshaping education, immediately. Globalization isn't sitting still; neither can our schools.

Courtney Ross-Holst
September 2003

Acknowledgments

This book would not have been possible without the help and support of many dedicated individuals and organizations. We would like to name and thank those who were involved in different phases of this collective effort.

The project leading to this book started with the 2002 Retreat on Globalization and Education, cochaired by Marcelo M. Suárez-Orozco and Howard Gardner and held at the Pocantico Conference Center of the Rockefeller Brothers Fund in Tarrytown, New York. That initiative was generously funded by Jerry Murphy, former dean of the Harvard Graduate School of Education, and by the David Rockefeller Center for Latin American Studies at Harvard University. We are grateful to Judy A. Clark, associate director of the Pocantico Programs, for the many courtesies she extended to us during our stay in Tarrytown. Participants of the Pocantico retreat included David Bloom (Harvard University), Jerome Bruner (New York University), John H. Coatsworth (Harvard), Peggy Dulaney (Synergos), Paul Farmer (Harvard), Swanee Hunt (Harvard), Ellen Lagemann (then president of the Spencer Foundation, now dean of the Harvard Graduate School of Education), Richard Murnane (Harvard), Pedro Noguera (Harvard), Gary Orfield (Harvard), Alejandro Portes (Princeton University), Lauren Resnick (University of Pittsburgh), Courtney Ross-Holst (Ross School and Ross Institute), Alan

Ruby (Atlantic Philanthropies), Saskia Sassen (University of Chicago), Richard Shweder (University of Chicago), Doris Sommer (Harvard), Lawrence Summers (president of Harvard University), Jim Trefil (George Mason University), Sherry Turkle (Massachusetts Institute of Technology), and George Walker (director general, International Baccalaureate).

The book is based on papers presented at a subsequent scholarly encounter building upon our work at the Pocantico Retreat. The Harvard-Ross Seminar on Education for Globalization was held from October 28 to November 1, 2002, at the Harvard Graduate School of Education. The seminar was made possible by generous support from Courtney Ross-Holst, founder and chair of the Ross School and Ross Institute of New York. We would like to thank the invited speakers: Antonio Battro, David E. Bloom, John H. Coatsworth, Howard Gardner, Henry Jenkins, Carola Suárez-Orozco, Sherry Turkle, and James L. Watson. Their inspiring contributions and the ideas and exchanges they generated constitute the heart of this volume. We are particularly grateful to Jagdish Bhagwati, university professor, Columbia University, who took the time to present to the seminar his influential and often controversial ideas in a special keynote address. We are also thankful to Tami Katzir, Gil Noam, Sue Grant Lewis, Vivian Louie, and Mica Pollock of the Harvard Graduate School of Education; Sunaina Maira of the University of California at Davis; and Nicholas Negroponte, founding director of MIT's Media Lab, for their roles as seminar discussants. They raised important, sometimes unsettling questions, pushing the invited speakers to think more clearly about the data and ideas under discussion.

Teachers and administrators from the Ross School—Darby Benedict, Sally Booth, Steve Coleman, Donna Dunson, Paul Flagg, Paul Linnehan, Debra McCall, Richard Normann, Kenneth Sacks, Chrissie Schlesinger, Patti Silver, and Li Zhang—participated in the Harvard-Ross Seminar with great enthusiasm and provided us with insightful feedback. A group of policy experts from Europe, including Anders Lönnberg, Kenneth Abrahamsson, Per Engback, Åsa Fasth, Peter Holmstedt, Björn Jakobson, Jan-Erik Sahlberg, and David Samuelsson, also joined the seminar and provided us with astute perspectives on globalization and education in the European context. Red Burns, of the Interactive Telecommunications Program (ITP) at New York University, also joined us as a special guest. We would also like to thank Harvard doctoral students Ana Romo (History Department), Stephen Chow, Jen de Forest, Girija Kaimel, Tere Sorte-Marti, Kim Sheridan, Caihong Wei, and Rebecca Zichlin (Graduate School of Education) for attending the seminar and contributing to the exchange of ideas. We are grateful to Mary Patricia Harmon, Adriana Katzew, and Josephine Louie, all doctoral students at the Harvard Graduate School of Education, for taking detailed notes during each session of the seminar.

The contributions made by all participants were critical in helping us provide systematic feedback to the seminar speakers so as to help them turn their presentations into the chapters of this book. Katie McNulty of the Ross Institute and Jeanne Alberts of the David Rockefeller Center for Latin American Studies at Harvard did an exemplary job assisting, with precision and diplomacy, in managing the seminar's complex logistics. Dean Ellen Condliffe Lagemann graciously welcomed all participants, as well as Harvard president Lawrence Summers, to a reception in honor of the Harvard-Ross Seminar in her new Cambridge home. Naomi Schneider nurtured the development of this manuscript with her legendary insight and professionalism. We would like to thank Carola Suárez-Orozco, Mark Verheyden Hilliard, Irina Todorova, Vivian Louie, Robert L. Hilliard, and Howard Gardner for their generous and incisive comments on earlier drafts of our introduction. Finally, we are happy to thank the National Science Foundation, Spencer Foundation, William T. Grant Foundation, and Provost's Fund for Interfaculty Collaborations at Harvard University for their generous support of various phases of this work.

ONE

Marcelo M. Suárez-Orozco and
Desirée Baolian Qin-Hilliard

GLOBALIZATION

Culture and Education in the New Millennium

INTRODUCTION

Globalization defines our era. It is "what happens when the movement of people, goods, or ideas among countries and regions accelerates" (Coatsworth, this volume). In recent years, globalization has come into focus, generating considerable interest and controversy in the social sciences, humanities, and policy circles and among the informed public at large (see, for example, Appadurai 1996; Bauman 1998; Baylis and Smith 1997; Bhagwati 2002; Castles and Davidson 2000; Giddens 2000; Hardt and Negri 2000, Inda and Rosaldo 2001; Jameson and Miyoshi 1999; King 1997; Lechner and Boli 1999; O'Meara, Mehlinger, and Krain 2000; Sassen 1998; Singer 2002; Tomlinson 1999). From terrorism to the environment, HIV-AIDS to Severe Acute Respiratory Syndrome (SARS), free trade to protectionism, population growth to poverty and social justice, globalization seems deeply implicated in nearly all of the major issues of the new millennium.

While globalization has created a great deal of debate in economic, policy, and grassroots circles, many implications and applications of the phenomenon remain virtual terra incognita. Education is at the center of this uncharted continent. We have barely started to consider how these accelerating transnational dynamics are affecting education, particularly precollegiate education. Instead, educational systems world-wide continue mimicking and often mechanically copying from each other and borrowing curricula (from trivial facts about history in middle school to trigonometry in high school), teaching methods ("chalk and talk"), and assessment tests (short answer and regurgitation). These practices would have been familiar to our forebears going to school two generations ago (Suárez-Orozco and Gardner 2003). Yet youth in school today, whether in Bali, Beijing, Beirut, Berlin, Boston, or Buenos Aires, will encounter a vastly different world from that of our grandparents.

Throughout most human prehistory and history, the vectors that organized and gave meaning to human lives and human imaginaries were structured primarily by local geography and topology, local kinship and social organization, local worldviews and religions. Even a few hundred years ago, a minute in human evolutionary time, the lives of our ancestors were largely shaped by local economies, local social relations, and local knowledge. Prior to the transoceanic explorations and conquests, villagers were likely to be born, raised, and schooled (however shortly), to work, marry, reproduce, and be buried in the same locale. They were largely oblivious to changes taking place even a few hundred miles away. Then "the village was practically the beginning and end of his or her world: visitors were rare, few travelers passed by, and excursions from the village would, in all likelihood, have only been to the nearest market town. . . . Contact with the outside world would have been the exception rather than the rule" (Held 2000).

Today the world is another place. While human lives continue to be lived in local realities, these realities are increasingly being challenged and integrated into larger global networks of relationships. The forces of globalization are taxing youth, families, and education systems world-wide. All social systems are predicated on the need to impart values, morals, skills, and competencies to the next generation (see Gardner, this volume). The main thesis of this book is that the lives and experiences of youth growing up today will be linked to economic realities, social processes, technological and media innovations, and cultural flows that traverse national boundaries with ever greater momentum. These global transformations, we believe, will require youth to develop new skills that are far ahead of what most educational systems can now deliver. New and broader global visions are needed to prepare children and youth to be informed, engaged, and critical citizens in the new millennium. This book has been developed around the idea that education will need both rethinking and restructuring if schooling is to best prepare the children and youth of the world to engage globalization's new challenges, opportunities, and costs.

Education's challenge will be to shape the cognitive skills, interpersonal sensibilities, and cultural sophistication of children and youth whose lives will be both engaged in local contexts[1] and responsive to larger transnational processes. We claim that two domains in particular will present the greatest challenges to schooling worldwide: the domain of *difference* and the domain of *complexity*.

The Domain of Difference

One of the paradoxes of globalization is that *difference* is becoming increasingly normative. Globalization and massive migrations are changing the ways we experience national identities and cultural belonging (see C. Suárez-Orozco, this volume). At the beginning of the twentieth century, W. E. B. Du Bois announced that "the color line" would define the social agenda for the United States. At the beginning of the twenty-first century, that line is complicated by the increasingly fluid political and cultural borders that once separated both nation-states and the people within them. These external and internal borders are increasingly becoming noisy and conflictive areas where cultural communication and miscommunication play out in schools, communities, and places of work and worship.

Globalization decisively unmakes the coherence that the modernist project of the nineteenth- and twentieth-century nation-state promised to deliver—the neat fit between territory, language, and identity (see Suárez-Orozco and Sommer 2002). Consider the following depiction of one of France's largest cities:

> To enter the Rue Du Bon Pasteur in the heart of this Mediterranean port is to leave France. Or rather, it is to leave a France still fixed in the imagination of many, a land where French is spoken and traditions of a secular society are enforced. The Rue Du Bon Pasteur—the Street of the Good Shepherd—is a haven owned, operated, and populated by Arab Muslims. Arabic is spoken here. All the women cover their hair with

scarves. Men in robes and sandals sit together in cafes where they reach out to Arabia via satellite television. The kiosk on the corner sells a score of newspapers and magazines flown in daily from the Arab world. The Attaqwa mosque in the middle of the street calls so many worshippers to prayer every Friday that dozens of them are forced to lay out their prayer rugs on the street. That street reflects the political and social reality facing France. Demography has transformed the country, whose population is about 7 percent Arab and Muslim, the highest percentage in Western Europe. (Sciolino 2003)

As Clifford Geertz has poetically noted, "all modern nations—even Norway, even Japan—contradict themselves: They contain multitudes" (Shweder, Minow, and Markus 2002, back cover). These "multitudes" not only challenge the structure and practices of the nation state (see Shweder, Minow, and Markus 2002) but may also invigorate democracy's best promise when difference engenders serious engagement and debate.

Managing difference is becoming one of the greatest challenges to multicultural countries. From France to Sweden, Brazil to Bolivia, Indonesia to Malaysia, the work of managing difference calls forth a new educational agenda. Children growing up in these and other settings are more likely than in any previous generation in human history to face a life of working and networking, loving and living with others from different national, linguistic, religious, and racial backgrounds. They are challenged to engage and work through competing and contrasting models, such as kinship, gender, language (monolingual and multilingual), and the complicated relationships between race, ethnicity, and inequality, in new ways. It is by interrupting "thinking as usual"—the taken-for-granted understandings and worldviews that shape cognitive and metacognitive styles and practices—that managing difference can do the most for youth growing up today.

Take, for example, the widely shared Western idea that individuals ought to autonomously and freely enter marriage agreements predicated on individual agency and love. A Swedish youngster might find it odd, maybe even bizarre, that for her Kurdish classmate, the idea of "love marriage" would be culturally incomprehensible. Working through the cultural models and social practices that structure the idea of love marriage—a historically new and, until very recently, ethnographically rare practice—and the idea of "arranged marriage"—the preferred marriage practice found in most ethnographic and historical records—can open up more nuanced and sophisticated understandings of human nature and culture, history and kinship, social organization and values. If the child learns nothing else, she should know that there is nothing natural about love marriage!

Negotiating differences requires energy—the kind of energy that can be recycled and harnessed to bolster a cornerstone of human intelligence: the ability to consider multiple perspectives (Piaget 1936; Gardner 1999; Vygotsky 1978). Taking multiple perspectives, reversing mental routines, and articulating multiple hypotheses from a common set of facts and working through the logical and rational vectors that would best explain those preexisting facts are crucial features of human intelligence.[2] When distinct cultural models and social practices are deployed to address a common set of problems, youth gain the cognitive and metacognitive advantages inherent in examining and working on a problem from many angles. Freely, fully, and respectfully arguing within a framework of difference is likely to better equip youth to deal with the complexities of the day.

The Domain of Complexity

Globalization engenders complexity. Throughout the world it is generating more intricate demographic profiles (see C. Suárez-Orozco, this volume), economic realities (see Bloom, this volume; Coatsworth, this volume), political processes, technology and media (see Jenkins, this volume; Turkle, this volume; Battro, this volume), cultural facts and artifacts (see Watson, this volume; Jenkins, this volume), and identities (see Maira, this volume; C. Suárez-Orozco, this volume). Many countries are indeed undergoing intense demographic transformations. Sweden, a country of nine million people today, has a million immigrants, roughly half of them from the Muslim world (for other examples, see C. Suárez-Orozco, this volume). Economies likewise must adapt to the new, complex forces brought about by global capital. Local politics, too, are stretched in new ways—for example, when "absentee citizens" in the diaspora exercise political power in the communities they left behind.

Globalization's increasing complexity necessitates a new paradigm for learning and teaching. The mastery and mechanical regurgitation of rules and facts should give way to a paradigm in which cognitive flexibility and agility win the day. The skills needed for analyzing and mobilizing to solve problems from multiple perspectives will require individuals who are cognitively flexible, culturally sophisticated, and able to work collaboratively in groups made up of diverse individuals. In his contribution to this volume Howard Gardner claims that the complexity behind many of globalization's "big problems" requires deep disciplinary grounding *as well as* the ability to achieve multi-disciplinary understandings, collaborations, and solutions. "Trends in our increasingly globalized society," writes Gardner (this volume), "have brought interdisciplinary concerns to the fore. Issues like poverty reduction, anti-terrorism, privacy, prevention of disease, energy conservation, ecological balance—and the list could be expanded at will—all require input from and syntheses of various forms of disciplinary knowledge and methods. Educational institutions seek, in their ways, to respond to the demand for this kind of skill; and the more adventurous students are attracted to studies that call for a blend of disciplinary expertises." Multitasking, learning how to learn, learning from failures, lifelong learning, and the ability to master and move across domains now have a premium.[3]

An education for globalization should therefore nurture the higher-order cognitive and interpersonal skills required for problem finding, problem solving, articulating arguments, and deploying verifiable facts or artifacts to substantiate claims. These skills should be required of children and youth who will, as adults, fully engage the larger world and master its greatest challenges, transforming it for the betterment of humanity—regardless of national origin or cultural upbringing. This we term the convergence hypothesis: *globalization is de-territorializing the skills and competencies it rewards, thereby generating powerful centripetal forces on what students the world over need to know.*

In this book we examine how globalization is shaping the lives of the children of the world in and out of schools. Our aim is to stimulate new thinking, research, and policy work in a domain that remains largely ignored by scholars of education. Millions of children and youth are growing up in a world where global processes are placing new demands on educational systems that are traditionally averse to change (see Gardner, this volume). There is virtually no scholarship on globalization and precollegiate education.[4] While there is some research on policy, administration, and curriculum that address globalization and primary and secondary education worldwide (see, for example, Burbules and Torres 2000; Quashigah and Wilson 2001; Stromquist and Monkman 2000), generally these works fail to foreground how globalization is impacting the experiences of youth in and out of schools. Likewise, there is a small but growing literature on youth and globalization (see, for example, Amit-Talai and Wulff 1995; Bennett 2000; Jenkins 1992, 1998; Larson 2002; Maira and Soep, forthcoming). Alas, most of these works fail to emphasize the role of education and schools in the lives of youth.

A number of researchers have begun to systematically examine how globalization is changing the lives of youth in Latin America and the Caribbean (Welti 2002), in Arab countries (Booth 2002), in sub-Saharan Africa (Nsamenang 2002), and in Southeast Asia (Stevenson and Zusho 2002). More and more young people in these areas have access to global information; they copy the styles of U.S. teenagers (who themselves, as Jenkins [this volume] informs us, borrow from youth elsewhere), sing English-language songs, have more leisure opportunities for dating, and are more likely to be playing similar computer games. In many of these places, rural households shrink as a result of youth migrating to urban areas in search of work and other opportunities.[5] Gender roles are also transformed. While many observers see globalization as positive, promoting economic development and intercultural exchanges, there are also corrosive developments, such as globalization's threats to century-long traditions, religious identities, authority structures, values, and worldviews (see Arnett 2002; Brown, Larson, and Saraswathi 2002; Stevenson and Zusho 2002). It is increasingly obvious that in many corners of the world the winds of anti-globalization are blowing strong (Naidoo 2003; also see Watson, this volume).[6]

In the remainder of this introduction, we review some of the dominant themes in the scholarship on globalization and propose a tentative definition of the term. Then we examine the basic topics that unfold in the following chapters. We claim that four domains are at the heart of the new global impulses affecting youth and education worldwide: the globalization of economy and capital; the globalization of media, information, and communication technologies; large-scale immigration;

and the globalization of cultural production and consumption. Together these currents are reshaping the experiences of youth in and out of schools the world over. As a number of chapters in this book suggest, youth are active players in the making of new globalizing spaces in culture, economy, and society. The following chapters are devoted to exploring the complex psychological, educational, sociocultural, and historical implications of globalization for the future of today's children and youth.

INTERDISCIPLINARY REFLECTIONS ON GLOBALIZATION

Globalization is at the heart of any understanding of broad processes of social change taking place in disparate locales around the world. After September 11, 2001, some observers announced the end of globalization (Rugman 2001; Gray 2002). While globalization, especially when narrowly defined as free markets and free capital flows, has generated doubts (Sen 2000), it may be premature to dismiss its relevance for judicious social science, education, and policy work. First, it remains the case that the major predicaments of the future will not likely be contained within the boundaries and paradigms of the twentieth-century nation-state. The case of SARS forcefully illustrates this dynamic. Within a few months of its original appearance (probably in Guangdong Province in coastal China some time toward the end of 2002), it became a worldwide health threat with serious economic, social, and political consequences not only in Guangdong but also in Beijing and in places as far away as Canada and Chinese diasporas throughout the world.[7]

Second, despite the economic slowdown and new international travel barriers after September 11, the general momentum toward increasing global integration in economic, communications, and security matters will likely continue into the future.[8] As the Foreign Policy Association has recently suggested, after September 11 "being there" is likely to be replaced by continued and growing communication and exchanges via means such as international telecommunications and the Internet. The association also notes that "the new global emphasis on fighting terrorism on military, diplomatic, and economic fronts could serve to increase levels of international political engagement over the coming years. Nor can forward momentum in the global economy be ruled out. Even as nations are struggling to pull themselves out of recession, they are continuing to strengthen the mechanisms for global integration" (Foreign Policy Association 2002).

Third, in a number of significant cases, nation-states continue to regroup in fundamental ways on supranational lines. For example, the European Union (EU) has grown from an original six-country entity in the early 1950s (including Germany, France, Belgium, Luxembourg, Italy, and the Netherlands) to the formal creation of the European Economic Community (EEC) and European Atomic Energy Community (EURATOM) in 1958. By the 1970s, it had added Denmark, Ireland, and the United Kingdom. Greece, Spain, and Portugal became members in the 1980s, and Austria, Finland, and Sweden in the 1990s. By the year 2004, ten new members are to be added, including Cyprus, the Czech Republic, Estonia, Hungary, Latvia, Lithuania, Malta, Poland, the Slovak Republic, and Slovenia (see European Union 2002). Finally, the *potential* for globalization remains quite high (see Coatsworth, this volume).

But before scholars of education can begin to mine the analytic potential of this new work, it is necessary to attend to basic definitional and theoretical matters. The term *globalization* in its current usage is quite broad and lacks well-defined boundaries. Some simply equate globalization with free markets.[9] Others use the term interchangeably with such concepts as *transnationalism* or *postnationality.* Still others use the term as a proxy for *imperialism* or *neocolonialism.* In the popular mind, *globalization* is often a proxy for *Americanization.* Others use *globalization* to examine themes that in earlier scholarship came under the rubric of "development" or "world systems" theory.

Each scholarly discipline seems to privilege its own set of concerns. Anthropologists, for example, tend to approach globalization in relation to their inherent interest in culture (see Watson, this volume). Globalization tends to detach social practices and cultural formations from localized territories. One hundred years ago European and Euro-American anthropologists took long journeys to remote locations to study exotic social institutions and cultural beliefs. Today globalization delivers the "exotic" to the anthropologist's own backyard. Turkish cultural formations are in plain sight, as ubiquitous in parts of Frankfurt as they are in

Istanbul. Likewise, Mexican culture is now alive and well in New York—where by the year 2000 roughly half a million Mexican citizens resided, with well over 300,000 in New York City alone (Smith 2002). But globalization also delivers what is "mundane" in the anthropologists' backyard to remote and out of the way places.[10] This is sometimes referred to as the "Coca-colonization" or "McDonaldization" of the developing world (indeed as James Watson indicates in his chapter, McDonald's has emerged as the very incarnation of globalization in part because "on an average day the company serves nearly fifty million customers in over thirty thousand restaurants located in 118 countries. In the mid-1990s a new McDonald's opened somewhere in the world every eight hours"). A cursory look through the programs of the American Anthropological Association meetings of the past few years suggests just how globalization has become a central concern for anthropologists. Indeed, over the past decade anthropologists have developed a taste for such topics as transnationalism (see Basch, Schiller, and Blanc 1995; Gupta and Ferguson 1992; Mahler 1995), cultural hybrids and dualities (Canclini, 1995/1989; Inda and Rosaldo 2002; Zentella 2002), mass media (Michaels, 2002; Yang, 2002; Larkin, 2002), immigration (see M. Suárez-Orozco 1989, 1991, 1994, 1996, 1998, 1999, 2000; C. Suárez-Orozco and M. Suárez-Orozco 2001; and M. Suárez-Orozco and Páez 2002), and persisting cultural conflicts (Shweder 2000; Wikan 2000)—all brought about by globalization.[11]

Economists, in contrast, study globalization because of their interest in trade, financial markets, and transnational capital flows (see Bhagwati 2002; Burtless, Lawrence, Litan, and Shapiro 1998; Feldstein 2002; Stiglitz 2002; and Rodrik 1997). Arguments over the economic causes and consequences of globalization are lengthy and sometimes polarizing. A plurality of economists see globalization—especially free trade—as the path to development and growth (Bhagwati 2002; Feldstein 2002; Burtless et al. 1998). Harvard president Lawrence Summers, an economist and former U.S. secretary of the treasury, argued in the 2003 Godkin Lecture that "the rate at which countries grow is substantially determined by their ability to integrate with the global economy, their capacity to maintain sustainable government finances, and their ability to put in place an institutional environment in which contracts can be enforced and property right can be established" (see Abrams 2003). Many other leading economists seem to agree. Burtless, Lawrence, Litan, and Shapiro (1998) argue that increased "economic interlinkages" around the world have generated wealth and "helped promote capitalism and democracy" in such varied places as Asia, Latin America, and Africa. These scholars claim that globalization demonstrates "the virtues of trade and markets" while helping alleviate poverty and create new opportunities for economic growth and well-being. The insertion of China into the global economy has been hailed as a paradigm of the virtues of globalization in promoting both economic growth and human welfare: "In 1960, the average Chinese expected to live only 36 years. By 1999, the life expectancy has risen to 70 years, not far below the level of the United States. Literacy has risen from less than 50 percent to more than 80 percent" (Rodrik 2002, p. 30). Economists who celebrate the merits of globalization generally reject proposed "globaphobic" policies because they would interrupt the expansion of free markets and create unnecessary detours en route to development (Burtless et al. 1998). For some economists, *lack* of globalization, not globalization itself, is the cause of poverty and misery in the developing world.[12]

A small but influential group of economists, however, has been vocal in questioning the economic consequences of globalization (see, for example, Stiglitz 2002; Sen 2001; Rodrik 2002). These criticisms have tended to focus on (1) globalization's failure to generate economic growth in large sectors of the world, (2) its role in increased economic inequality within and across nations (see Bloom, this volume; Coatsworth, this volume), and (3) its role in the increasingly desperate fate of growing numbers of poor and disenfranchised people throughout the world: by 2002 "1.2 billion people around the world live[d] on less than $1 a day[, and] 2.8 billion people [more than 45 percent of the world's population] live[d] on less than $2 a day" (Stiglitz 2002, p. 25).[13]

These economists have also pointed out the unsavory fact that under globalization the fate of billions of people increasingly rests in the hands of the arbiters of global capitalism, especially the International Monetary Fund and financial interests in Wall Street, London, Geneva, and other global cities. These power brokers dictate the economic and social agendas of faraway countries with little accountability, huge asymmetries in decision-making powers, and a lack of concern for local institutional frameworks, needs, and priorities (Stiglitz 2002). Yet in the game of globalization, local factors may indeed be more important than ever before. Harvard economist Dani Rodrik (2002) has argued that free markets are not enough: "Economies that have performed well over the long term owe their success not to geography or trade, but to institutions that have generated market-oriented incentives, protected property rights, and enabled stability" (p. 29). Regardless of their beliefs about the economic consequences of globalization or their recipes for making globalization "work," nearly all respected economists agree that global "poverty is now the defining issue" (Rodrik 2002, p. 29). As the work of David Bloom (this volume) suggests, no serious debate on the economics of globalization and poverty can neglect the role of education in promoting development and well-being (see also Bloom and Cohen 2002).

Political scientists, for their part, have turned their attention to how globalization is challenging the workings of the state (Strange 1996; Waltz 1999; Berger and Dore 1996). Much of this scholarship focuses on the political consequences of global economic integration. Some have hypothesized that growing economic interdependence is inevitably generating certain similarities in the technologies, habits of work, and lifestyles that come to be privileged under globalization (Boyer 1996). These similarities would in turn seem to exert pressures on nation-states to "preserve distinctive social, political, and economic organizations" (Boyer 1996, p. 29). Some observers even "predict that the nation state will soon be obsolete and the government's room for maneuver will be limited" (p. 29). Yet other political scientists question the mechanistic assumption that growing economic interdependence leads to convergence in the political realm (Waltz 1999; Weiss, 1998).[14] While some political scientists see economic integration as the very essence of globalization, others have come to see growing inequality as its most profound legacy, which should reaffirm the centrality of politics over economics. As "the distribution of capabilities across states has become extremely lopsided, . . . the inequalities of international politics enhance the political role of one country. Politics, as usual, prevails over economics" (Waltz 1999, p. 11).

Globalization challenges the nation-state in other ways. Transnational nongovernmental organizations (NGOs) are increasingly vocal and effective in shaping political debates and choices around a host of issues (Mol 2001; Warkentin 2001; Nye and Donahue 2000). International institutional systems such as human, civil, and cultural rights regimes reach beyond the confines of individual nation-states (Nye 2001; Coleman and Porter 1999). For example, an Argentine torturer accused of committing crimes in his own country can be arrested in Mexico and tried for crimes against humanity in Spain, as happened in February 2001 (see Robben 2004).

Likewise war, famously defined as "the continuation of politics by other means," has since September 11 become thoroughly globalized. Both terrorism and the war on terrorism are global phenomena shifting from Kenya and Tanzania to New York and Washington and on to Bali, Saudi Arabia, and Morocco. Indeed, the attacks of September 11 seem to have ushered in a new globalized experiment in warfare, requiring transnational coordination and in the process creating unlikely partnerships. Al Qaeda itself is a paradigm of globalization—a network lacking any firm national or territorial base. It seems to be constituted of a set of loosely and rapidly changing interconnected financial, weapons-procuring, ideological, and religious networks, heavily reliant for its operations on globalization's new information, communication, and transportation technologies.[15] Al Qaeda's attacks generated a global response, bringing together such disparate nations as China, Russia, and the United States in a common cause. But in character with globalization's fluidity and speed of change, these alliances are fragile and constantly evolving, as the 2003 war in Iraq demonstrated when the European allies of the United States and the United Kingdom decided to take a different path in pursuing the UN objectives to disarm Iraq.

Another way globalization is reshaping the politics of the state is a result of large-scale immigration. Peoples in the diaspora—Mexicans in Los Angeles, Turks in Germany, or Algerians in France—have emerged as actors across national boundaries, shaping economic processes and the political agenda in both their countries of birth and their countries of choice. The power that diasporic communities exercise in their countries of origin has grown exponentially over the last few decades. Much of this flows from the fact that economic remittances from people in the diaspora have emerged as a critical source of foreign exchange for a growing list of countries, such as El Salvador, Haiti, the Dominican Republic, Mexico, and Tunisia. As a consequence, politics have new global dimensions. For example, Dominican politicos are fully cognizant that election campaigns in their country need to be waged in New York—where Dominicans are now the largest immigrant group— as well as in Santo Domingo.[16] Congressman Tip O'Neill's adage "All politics is local" is now somewhat anachronistic. Dual citizenship agreements—enabling one to maintain citizenship rights in more than one nation-state—are complicating and making more interesting the politics of belonging (see Castles and Davidson 2000).

While each discipline has generated its own idiosyncratic use of the term *globalization,* certain characteristics seem to converge. Most scholars who study globalization today would agree that it is best characterized as a set of processes that tend to de-territorialize important economic, social, and cultural practices from their traditional boundaries in nation-states. It involves a kind of "post-geography" (Bauman 1998).[17] In summary, for the purpose of this book, we approach globalization as the processes of change structured by four interrelated formations: (1) postnational forms of production and distribution of goods and services—fueled by growing levels of international trade, foreign direct investment, and capital flows; (2) information, communication, and media technologies that facilitate exchanges and instantaneously connect people across vast geographies and place a premium on knowledge-intensive work; (3) growing levels of worldwide migration; and (4) the resultant cultural transformations and exchanges that challenge traditional values and norms in both sending and receiving countries. These changes require new adaptations if youth are to interact in a civil and productive manner with those whose backgrounds may be extremely different from their own. Globalization is generating changes of a magnitude comparable to the emergence of agriculture ten thousand years ago or the industrial revolution two hundred years ago. It will demand fundamental rethinking of the aims and processes of education.

EDUCATION FOR GLOBALIZATION

In this book we examine the implications of the historical, cultural, technological, and demographic changes brought about by globalization for the experiences of children and youth in and out of schools. We start with a historical perspective. Without a historical narrative it is difficult to distinguish what might be new and a break from previous cycles of globalization from what mimics and repeats previous processes. What, if anything, is *new* about globalization?[18] A number of prominent scholars have claimed that globalization is best conceptualized as part of a long process of change—arguably centuries in the making (see, for example, Hardt and Negri 2000; Jameson and Miyoshi 1999; Mignolo 1998; Sen 2000). They remind us that certain features of globalization today are not necessarily new. Neither large-scale immigration nor international capital flows are unprecedented.

In the chapter "Globalization, Growth, and Welfare in History," Harvard historian John Coatsworth examines the implications of globalization for human welfare, productivity, and equity from a historical and regional perspective. Coatsworth identifies four distinct cycles of globalization in the Western hemisphere: (1) the opening of transoceanic conquest, communication, and trade from 1492 to 1565; (2) the kidnapping and forced migration of Africans and the subsequent establishment of slave plantations in the new world from 1650 to 1790; (3) the export-led growth in the Belle Epoque between 1880 and 1930; (4) and a new globalization cycle beginning in the mid-1980s.

Coatsworth argues that the current cycle of globalization, in regard to demographic and economic processes, is in fact quite weak as compared to previous cycles. For example, current migration flows are proportionally smaller than in previous periods: the foreign-born population of the Americas (including such varied countries as the United States, Argentina, and Brazil) a century ago was proportionally larger than at the turn of the millennium (Moya 1998). Furthermore, the current wave of globalization has been wanting in terms of economic growth in most Latin American countries. Over the last decade, growth has been elusive and inequality a constant and growing concern. Coatsworth's analysis suggests that globalization tends to exact short-term costs (paid in the currency of decreasing health and well-being and increasing inequality) while generating long-term growth especially in economic productivity. Coatsworth's arguments are sobering and highly relevant to today's debates about globalization. He also offers a provocative suggestion: in terms of both the economics and demographics of globalization, the current cycle has not reached the potential predicted from previous trends. If anything, in many regions of the world, globalization is more of a promise than a fait accompli. Finally, Coatsworth notes that education has a much more prominent role to play than in previous cycles of global change. Educators must develop an agenda to facilitate the incorporation of growing numbers of immigrant children worldwide and develop curricular and pedagogical programs to impart the cross-cultural skills children will need to thrive in their historical moment and emerge as agents of change to combat growing worldwide inequalities. Globalization without social justice hurts and threatens us all.

Whether one sees globalization as a promise yet to be realized or as a new international reality, surely economics are at the forefront of important changes worldwide. As Anthony Giddens noted in his BBC Reith Lectures, "the level of world trade today is much higher than it ever was before, and involves a much wider range of goods and services" (Giddens 2000, p. 27).[19] Poverty and inequality are the elephants in the globalization room (Naidoo 2003). While some regions of the world such as East Asia have "managed globalization" quite well (Yan 2002) and in so doing have achieved unprecedented economic growth and well-being, in other regions of the world the forces of globalization seem to have conspired to intensify patterns of inequality and human suffering (see Bauman 1998; Dussel 2000; Mittelman 2000; Nader 1993).[20]

What are the implications of these global economic dynamics for education? In his chapter, "Globalization and Education: An Economic Perspective," Harvard economist David Bloom argues that because of globalization, education is more important than ever before in history. He deploys a vast array of up-to-date data on the state of global education in much of the developing world. Bloom's materials prompt both optimism and caution. He claims that growing worldwide inequality, indexed by increasing gaps in income and well-being, generally mimics a continuing and growing global gap in education. While primary education enrollments have improved worldwide, consistency and quality of educational experiences remain "patchy." Furthermore, secondary education in developing countries remains quite weak.[21] Bloom argues that increasing efforts to improve basic education (both in quantity and quality) in developing countries, such as in sub-Saharan Africa and South Asia, will surely help narrow income gaps with developed countries. Education, he claims, is "clearly a strong trigger for positive development spirals." He cites estimates that in the developing world, each additional year of basic education corresponds to a rise of over 10 percent in the individual's earning power. Bloom concludes his chapter by reflecting on the challenges and opportunities brought about by globalization. These include a more competitive world economy, the increasing importance of cross-national communication, and the rapid speed of change. Bloom points out that globalization also brings about opportunities for education, particularly in the ways that new technologies can be put to work to improve both the quantity and quality of education worldwide—a theme further developed by Antonio Battro in his contribution to this volume.

The current cycle of globalization is in part the product of new global media, information, and communication technologies that instantaneously connect people, organizations, and systems across vast distances. While in 1980 there were only two million computers worldwide, in 1995 the number totaled more than 150 million, 90 percent being personal computers (Lopez, Smith, and Pagnucco 1995, p. 35). In 2000 eighty million new users logged on to the Internet for the first time (Foreign Policy Association 2002). The cost of telephone calls has plummeted, owing to satellite communication technology. For example, the price of a three-minute phone call from New York to London dropped from about $250 in 1930 to about $30 in 1970, and to less than 20 cents by the year 2000. In addition to creating and circulating images, information, and data, these technologies have the promise of freeing people from the constraints of space and time. These new technologies of globalization are rapidly and irrevocably changing the nature of learning, work, thought, entertainment, and the interpersonal patterning of social relations (Gardner, Csikszentmihalyi, and Damon 2001; Turkle 1997; Watson, this volume).[22]

The technologies of globalization present unique opportunities and challenges for education. In the chapter "Globalization, Digital Skills, and the Brain," Antonio Battro—the eminent Argentinean physician, psychologist, and brain scientist and one of the founders of the new field of mind, brain, and education—examines the extraordinary enabling potential that the digital world offers those with disabilities and children growing up in out-of-the-way places. Battro argues that the genius of computer technologies is their "friendliness." They open up new opportunities for education particularly among those who have traditionally been shut out, thus more fully developing their cognitive, emotional, and social potential. Battro claims that the ability to make a simple change in the state of a system, what he calls "the click option," is a universal skill that has both evolutionary and developmental origins. He refers to computer use among a hunting and gathering Bushman group in the Kalahari Desert. Battro claims that a universal "digital skill" develops quite early in life and that such "universal digital skills" have important implications for education, particularly in their potential revolutionary effect for special education and for children living in remote areas. For example, a brain-computer interface permits a patient who suffers from locked-in syndrome (i.e., is cognitively intact but seriously impaired in motor abilities) to communicate with others through the computer. In this case the computer is used as "a *functional prosthesis* or extension of the brain." Other examples track the enabling qualities of computers among deaf children in remote locations of Latin America. Computers allow hearing-disabled youth to become radio amateurs, something impossible in the past. Battro concludes that it is important for educators to fully mine the enabling potential afforded by the digital world.

However, it is also important for educators to note the potential challenges and "disabling" effect of computers. In "The Fellowship of the Microchip: Global Technologies as Evocative Objects," eminent Massachusetts Institute of Technology psychologist Sherry Turkle examines the phenomenological correlates of new information, communication, and media technologies as "carriers of ideas and habits of mind." Turkle offers careful analysis of the ambiguities and contradictions that computational and media technologies engender in human thought and affect. For example, while the Internet may offer people opportunities to become "fluent with the manipulation of personae," it can also lead to diminished comfort in the self, and the software's functional opacity may lead to disempowerment. Turkle uses the example of PowerPoint to illustrate the potential constraining effects of technologies on learning. PowerPoint encourages presentation of a point instead of conversation and argument over an issue. She argues that by using informational technologies, students get far more than content; these technologies "model styles of thought." Turkle concludes that it is critical for educators and policy makers to understand that computational technologies "both empower and limit this generation as they prepare for the responsibilities of global citizens."

Another issue raised by globalization is the impact of these new technologies on local cultures around the world. The new technologies of globalization generate images, powerful and seductive, of the good life and the good things that make the good life and circulate them worldwide, creating new globalized structures of desire, modernist longings, and with them, feelings of relative deprivation. Youth from China to Argentina flock to see the same movies, visit the same Internet sites, and often come to desire the same "cool" brand-name clothes, music, and lifestyles. One of the dominant discourses in the study of globalization is the "cultural homogeneity" hypothesis. It predicts that global processes of change enabled by new information and media technologies will inevitably lead to a more homogeneous world culture. Will the next generation of youth become global citizens eating McDonald's hamburgers, drinking Starbucks coffee, and using a globalized English to communicate with each other online? If that is the case, then the diversity in the cultures and experiences of youth may disappear. Two leading scholars of globalization and culture, Henry Jenkins and James Watson, complicate these ominous predictions by highlighting the critical role of local meaning-making systems in interrupting and reshaping global media and cultural exchanges, nearly always recasting them in autochthonous terms.

In "Pop Cosmopolitanism: Mapping Cultural Flows in an Age of Media Convergence," MIT communications scholar Henry Jenkins examines how the technologies of globalization are used to appropriate, decontextualize, recontextualize, and transform cultural images, facts, and artifacts and the resultant "new modes of creativity and expression" in disparate settings. He characterizes the current rapid exchanges of images, facts, and artifacts across national and cultural borders as a form of "media convergence." Jenkins notes that media convergence tends to be multidirectional, reflecting the circulation of products from West to East, as well as a continuous concomitant cultural flow from East to West.[23] There are of course flows of cultural products across other axes, such as within Asian countries. Jenkins argues that the meanings of cultural images and products exchanged typically undergo metamorphoses that are both "unpredictable and contradictory." For example, a teenager in the Philippines used Photoshop to create a series of images of *Sesame Street*'s Bert interacting with Osama bin Laden and posted them on his home page. These images were later used by anti-American Pakistani demonstrators who (unaware of the Bert image in the background) waved signs of bin Laden as CNN videotaped them. These phenomena, Jenkins concludes, offer a theoretical challenge to the widely popular "cultural imperialism" and the "cultural homogeneity" hypotheses.

In his chapter, "Globalization in Asia: Anthropological Perspectives," Harvard social anthropologist James Watson develops a study of globalization in Asian societies and especially its repercussions for cultural practices and changing youth experiences. Watson illustrates the rapid social and cultural transformations occurring in Asia today with examples from a variety of domains such as food, sports, television, movies, Internet technology, clothing, and other aspects of globalization that are subtly changing youth's daily lives. Watson disagrees with the widely shared notion that globalization is destroying cultural diversity by homogenizing cultural practices the world over. He concludes that local vectors always transform global products rendering them meaningful in terms of local sensibilities, social practices, and cultural models. For example, the film *Titanic* was the most popular movie in China in 1997 because the majority of moviegoers identified the tragedy of the film with their personal experiences during the Cultural Revolution. Watson argues that to capture cultural changes, it is important to distinguish between form and content. He concludes that "the sameness hypothesis is sustainable only if one ignores the internal meanings that people assign to cultural innovations."

Another novel feature of globalization is new patterns of large-scale immigration (see Basch et al. 1994; Castles and Davidson 2000; Portes and Rumbaut 2001; C. Suárez-Orozco 2000; C. Suárez-Orozco and M. Suárez-Orozco 2001; M. Suárez-Orozco and Páez 2002; M. Suárez-Orozco, C. Suárez-Orozco, and Qin-Hilliard 2001, vols. 1, 2, and 3).[24] Immigration generates new identities.[25] It is also a powerful metaphor for many of the processes that globalization seems to generate, such as feelings of cultural disorientation, anxiety, and confusion about rapidly changing roles, cultural scripts, and social practices; "identity threats"; and multiple identities (Arnett 2002). In some ways, to paraphrase Julia Kristeva (1991), globalization makes us all into dislocated "immigrants," just as it makes us all feel a bit like "strangers to ourselves." Two chapters deal with the issue of identity in the era of globalization, with a specific focus on the transformation brought about by large-scale immigration.

In the chapter "Formulating Identity in a Globalized World," Harvard cultural psychologist Carola Suárez-Orozco examines the impact of globalization and immigration on the vicissitudes of identity formation among youth. C. Suárez-Orozco contends that one of the challenges facing immigrant children in their adaptation to a new society is identity formation. Immigrant children face a complex task. They have to negotiate matters of identity while juggling multiple, often competing and clashing cultural codes. These include cultural models of the family and home, cultural models of the new country, and the larger globalized youth culture. Large-scale immigration is often unsettling and generates backlash among native citizens. Immigrant children often have to face what C. Suárez-Orozco terms "negative social mirroring" from members of the new country who may come to feel ambivalent, anxious, and xenophobic toward the new arrivals. Such social mirroring can have a negative impact on immigrant youth identity development. C. Suarez-Orozco argues that there is need to reframe the Eriksonian model of identity formation and development in light of new global forces and realities. Erikson (1968) proposed a stage-specific model of identity formation that involved giving up certain earlier "identifications" to achieve the autonomy, coherence, and independence that "identity" confers. C. Suárez-Orozco argues that in a global world, identity is no longer best conceived as an achievement that involves overcoming or giving up certain cultural identifications. Instead, youth who are players in a global stage must cultivate the multiple identities that are required to function in diverse, often incommensurable cultural realities. Rather than theorizing identity as oriented toward "either" the home culture "or" the host culture, many immigrant youth today are articulating and performing complex multiple identifications that involve bringing together disparate cultural streams. Increasingly immigrants refuse to give up their cultural sensibilities and particularities in favor of complete identification with the host culture. These psychosocial dynamics interrupt the predictions of the classic theory of immigrant assimilation—as a unilinear process of change with inevitable diminished ethnic identifications (M. Suárez-Orozco 2000). Hence C. Suárez-Orozco's critique of the stage model of identity formation has implications for both psychological and sociocultural theories of immigrant assimilation.

In her chapter, "Imperial Feelings: Youth Culture, Citizenship, and Globalization," cultural theorist Sunaina Maira explores the connections and disconnections between theories of globalization and the study of youth culture. Maira argues that there has been a strong "epistemological barricade" between these two areas of study, partially due to the traditional conceptions of youth as "inadequately formed adults." Following Appadurai's lead, Maira articulates the concept of "youthscape" as a framework for an interdisciplinary approach to research on youth and globalization (see also Maira and Soep, 2004). For Maira "youthscape" is "a site for local youth practices" that is "embedded within national and global forces." In her chapter she draws on recent field-based research with South Asian Muslim youth and their experiences with race and citizenship in the aftermath of September 11. Maira's analysis unfolds in the context of an effort to examine the youths' understandings and practices of "cultural citizenship," an aspect of the concept of youthscape she is attempting to develop. Maira discusses in detail two distinct types of cultural citizenship emerging from this site: "flexible citizenship," a national citizenship that youth construct through both transnational popular culture (from their countries of origin) and an emerging identity shaped by their work environments in the United States. For these youth, citizenship is "flexible, shifting, and contextual." The second type is what Maira terms "dissenting citizenship." These Muslim immigrant youth find themselves articulating a critique of U.S. race and ethnic relations in the aftermath of September 11, often raising their voices in the public sphere at a time when the Southeast Asian immigrant leadership chooses silence. Dissenting citizenship is "based on a critique and affirmation of human rights" even though it means that they must "stand apart" from other citizens in their new home. Maira's contribution is a detailed example of immigrant youth living in transnational youthscapes, articulating and performing the kinds of multiple identities postulated by Carola Suárez-Orozco as an increasingly common reality in the era of globalization.

Globalization means that the lives of children growing up today will be shaped in no small measure by global processes in economy, society and culture. Educational systems tied to the formation of nation-state citizens and consumers bonded to local systems to the neglect of larger global forces are likely to become obsolete, while those that proactively engage globalization's new challenges are more likely to thrive. In the final chapter of this volume, Harvard psychologist and education scholar Howard Gardner examines how education changes over time. Historically education has changed because of shifts in values (such as from religious to secular), scientific findings altering our understanding of the human mind (such as the development of psychometrics), or broader historical and social forces, such as globalization. Gardner argues that an important challenge posed by globalization for education is the tension between the glacial pace of institutional change in ministries of education and schools and the rapid social, economic, and cultural transformations taking place around them. Gardner suggests that precollegiate education will need to encompass the following skills, abilities, and understandings: (1) understanding the global system; (2) the ability to think analytically and creatively within disciplines; (3) the ability to tackle problems and issues that do not respect disciplinary boundaries; (4) knowledge of other cultures and traditions, which should both be an end in itself and a means to interacting civilly and productively with individuals from different cultural backgrounds— both within one's own society and across the planet; (5) knowledge of and respect for one's own cultural traditions; (6) fostering of hybrid or blended identities; and (7) fostering of tolerance and appreciation across racial, linguistic, national, and cultural boundaries.

This book is unlike anything written to date on the topic of globalization, culture, and education. First, it is based on commissioned, heretofore unpublished essays by scholars representing a wide array of social science and education scholarship, originally presented at a weeklong Harvard University workshop on education for globalization held in Cambridge, Massachusetts. The commissioned papers were developed around strict guidelines determined by our interest in sampling an array of disciplinary considerations (including anthropology, economics, education, history, media and communications, and psychology—both cultural and developmental) and regional concerns (including the United States, Latin America, Africa, and Asia). We invited senior scholars working in these domains to present at the workshop. We also wanted to examine how education has changed over the centuries. Because we sensed that a great deal of the current scholarship, policy, and popular debate on globalization lacks any historical depth, we invited a senior scholar in the field of history to develop an essay on the historical background of the current cycle of globalization. The original drafts of the papers were circulated to all presenters and participants ahead of time. The Harvard workshop was structured so as to encourage the invited scholars to make brief presentations on their previously circulated papers, with substantial time then devoted to commentary and conversation led by appointed discussants.[26] In addition to the invited scholars, the panels included a select group of seasoned teachers and administrators from the Ross School in New York. The Ross School is an example of just what is possible when the challenges of globalization are taken seriously in a precollegiate setting. The presence and perspective of the teachers was critical in grounding abstract conceptual and empirical discussions in real-life concerns facing teachers in classrooms. Also present was a small group of Harvard doctoral students, as well as a group of policy experts from Europe to offer a point of view on globalization that varies significantly from the American conception.

Harvard doctoral students and note takers were responsible for transcribing the themes emerging from the discussions after each presentation. On the basis of these transcripts, we provided detailed and extensive editorial feedback and suggestions to each author for revising his or her original paper for inclusion in this book. The chapters included surely benefited from this lengthy process by displaying better integration and coherence across domains and between chapters. The authors present original materials and identify new theoretical and empirical opportunities suggesting new areas in need of further scholarly work. Taken together, the various contributions can also be read as a plea for new collaborative and interdisciplinary work on the complex relationship between globalization and education. It is our intention that the book will help generate new ideas, new empirical data, and new conceptual work that will inform scholarly debate, public policy, and the general citizenry about changes and choices we face in schools, neighborhoods, communities, and countries around the world.

Globalization will continue to be a powerful vector of worldwide change. We need better understanding of how education will be transformed by globalization and how it, in turn, can shape and manage the course or courses of globalization. We need a major research agenda to examine how education most broadly defined can best prepare children to engage in a global world. We need better theoretical understandings of globalization's multiple faces—economic, demographic, social, and cultural. We need more dialogue between scholars, practitioners, and policy makers. This volume is a contribution to that vision.

NOTES

1. By "local context," we mean local values, worldviews, and realms of the sacred.

2. As in the classic Agatha Christie mysteries, a set of seemingly unrelated facts can be woven into multiple possible scenarios accounting for some pre-existing (mysterious) condition.

3. Whereas fifty years ago the typical successful professional spent most of his or her career within a single specialized domain and in many cases in a single corporation, today individuals are more likely to pursue multiple career pathways.

4. There is, however, a small corpus of work on globalization and collegiate education. Some of this scholarship focuses on the ways globalization is challenging the historic role of higher education. Shapiro (2002), for example, claims that globalization will reshape universities in the twenty-first century. He suggests that globalization will undo the "historical monopoly [of universities] over the provision, accreditation, and certification of higher education" (p. 12). Others examine how market forces and the new information, communication,

and media technologies will inevitably generate a new agenda and new priorities in higher education in an international context (see for example, Currie and Newson 1998; Green 2002; Shapiro 2002; Slaughter 1998 for issues related to the United States; Peach 2001 and de Wit 1995 for issues related to Europe; Waghid 2001 for Africa; Mok 2000 for Asia; Sabour 1999 for countries in the Middle East; and Gough 1999 for Australia). Green (2002) claims that colleges and universities will need to address new questions about "how to educate students who will contribute to the civic life, both locally and globally, and understand that the fate of nations, individuals, and the planet are inextricably linked" (p. 8). Likewise, Slaughter (1998) claims that globalization is reshaping higher education, especially the relationships between basic and applied research, discovery, innovation, and profit making. He claims that globalization is giving supremacy to the "technosciences" and uses the examples of telecommunications and biotechnologies as paradigms of the new agenda emerging in higher education worldwide. Universities are institutionalizing new priorities centering on technoscience because of its huge economic implications. At the same time, Slaughter sees a movement away from the university's traditional focus on the liberal and humanistic education of undergraduates. He argues that technoscience commands the greatest level of financial and symbolic support in universities because of new global market forces—"big technoscience" translates into "big money." Issues with high stakes for profit making such as the role of intellectual property are more visible, protected, and regulated than ever before. Therefore it is not surprising that universities are "increasingly working with industry on government-sponsored technoscience initiatives" (p. 57). Similarly, former Harvard president Derek Bok cautions against higher education institutions blurring the boundaries between the academic and the corporate worlds, creating problems such as secrecy and conflicts of interest (Bok 2003). Other scholars tend to focus on institutional and administrative considerations pertinent to higher education in the era of globalization (see Currie and Newson 1998). Yet others address how teacher education needs to be reconsidered and restructured to face the challenges of globalization (Kirkwood 2001; White and Walker 1999; McLaren and Farahmandpur 2001).

5. For example, Tashi Tenzing (2003) describes how globalization is changing the lives of young Sherpas at the foot of the Himalayas:

> Life for Sherpas has become increasingly complicated. Many of our young people are understandably tired of the hardship—the freezing winters and scarce food—and are no longer satisfied grazing yaks or growing potatoes in difficult terrain at high altitudes. The influx of Western tourists to Everest has exposed Sherpas to a new lifestyle, leading many to seek an easier, more cosmopolitan existence in the cities and abroad. Few people, especially working-age men, stay in the mountains. Indeed, I myself do not wish to make my livelihood, plowing high-altitude fields of barley. Indigenous crafts are dying out, and many Sherpa villages are now home only to the frail and elderly and the few relatives who remain to take care of them.
> (p. A27)

6. While everyone agrees that we must understand the sources of these reactions to globalization, there is little empirical understanding or theoretical framing of the conditions that generate and perpetuate anti-globalization attitudes

and practices. Is globalization locally perceived as an opportunity or a threat? Are the skills, habits of mind, and interpersonal sensibilities needed to thrive under globalization seen as compatible and easily integrated into local cultural structures, narratives, and rituals? Or are these seen as incompatible and threatening to local cultural and historical models and social practices? How are the media and popular culture implicated in the making of attitudes and perceptions toward globalization? What are the processes by which global formations are given local meanings, whether positive, neutral, negative, or mixed? What is the role of "localization"—the emergence of local isomorphs of global forms—in facilitating or impeding global understandings? Are new hybrid cultural practices (blending local meaning and global formations) facilitating or impeding the global challenge? What role do the media and popular culture play in the making of the global-local nexus? While the focus of this line of work falls on individuals who are directly involved with education, we propose to construe edcation quite broadly to include a range of stakeholders. Many of the chapters in this book address these and similar questions.

7. By the end of May 2003 it was estimated that "the economic damage caused by SARS could approach $100 billion, making it one of the costliest diseases to emerge in the past decade" (Aoki 2003, p. C1).

8. September 11 has so far failed to stop the momentum toward increased economic globalization, at least as indexed by international trade. "World trade is projected to grow by nearly 8% in the second half of this year (2002) and by 10% in the first six months of the next year" (Foreign Policy Association 2002, p. 10).

9. For example, the eminent Harvard economist Dani Rodrik defines globalization as "in essence, free trade and free flows of capital" (Rodrik 2002, p. 29).

10. Large-scale immigration amplifies the already powerful worldwide changes generated by globalization. The synergy between globalization and immigration explains why "New York culture" is alive in such Mexican states as Puebla and Guerrero. These regions of Mexico are being palpably transformed by the economic, social, and cultural adaptations of Mexican citizens in the diaspora. As Harvard historian John Coatsworth has noted, Mexican history today is being made in the United States (see Coatsworth 1998, pp. 75–78). The dimensions of these transformations are significant. For example, it is estimated that in the year 2002 Mexican citizens residing in the United States remitted to Mexico nearly 12 billion dollars in cash and other gifts. These immigrants are also changing their home communities via "social remittances"—i.e., new social practices and cultural models they acquire in the diaspora and remit back home (see Levitt 2001). These social remittances are changing an array of cultural formations such as gender relations, economic strategies at the household level, social ambitions and expectations, and the political process at the sending community level (see Smith 2002).

11. Anthropology's involvement with the study of cultural forms and their dispersal across time and space has a long history. Much of the early literature privileged the study of "culture contact" and "cultural borrowing" via trading, invasions, or conquest. Franz Boas's early efforts, which resulted in the establishment of American anthropology as a major scholarly discipline in the early

decades of the twentieth century, centered on theoretical debates over the "diffusion" (versus "multiple invention") of cultural forms (such as a fishing hook, folktale motif, or kinship term) across distinct "culture areas." This work was critical to the dismantling of earlier extravagant and racist theories of stages in the cultural evolution of societies.

12. Lawrence Summers used those same words in his keynote address at the Pocantico Retreat on Globalization and Education, held in Tarrytown, New York, in April 2002 and organized by Howard Gardner and Marcelo M. Suárez-Orozco, one of the events that led to this book.

13. Despite the triumphal free-market rhetoric of the 1990s,

> for most of the world's developing countries, the 1990s were a decade of frustration and disappointment. The economies of Sub-Saharan Africa, with few exceptions, stubbornly refused to respond to the medicine meted out by the World Bank and the IMF. Latin American countries were buffered by a never-ending series of boom-and-bust cycles in capital markets and experienced growth rates significantly below their historical averages. Most of the former socialist economies ended the decade at lower levels of per-capita income than they started it—and even in the rare successes, such as Poland, poverty rates remained higher than under communism. East Asian economies such as South Korea, Thailand, and Malaysia, which had been hailed previously as "miracles" were dealt a humiliating blow in the financial crisis of 1997. That this was also the decade in which globalization came into full swing is more than a minor inconvenience for its advocates. If globalization is such a boon for poor countries, why so many setbacks?
>
> (Rodrik 2002, p. 29)

14. In the case of China, a country greatly transformed by the economics of globalization, political processes have remained carefully managed and controlled so as to avoid globalization's spilling over into the political domain (Yan 2002).

15. It has proven an illusive target, challenging traditional military strategies predicated upon the defense and control of "space," either air, maritime, or territory.

16. Mexican politicians have taken longer to wake up to the new global game, but in late December 2000 newly elected President Vicente Fox spent a day at Mexico's busy northern border personally welcoming some of the immigrants returning home for Christmas, performing and telecasting a new strategic approach to *paisanos* living in the United States. Under the Fox administration the over eight million Mexican citizens living in the United States are no longer an afterthought. The rough formula: a million people in the diaspora translate to about a billion dollars in remittances sent home every year might help explain the newfound interest among Mexican politicians in cultivating ties with their brothers and sisters living in the United States.

17. While globalization is defined as economic, social, and cultural processes that are postnational, we do not mean to suggest that globalization augurs the demise of the state apparatus. Globalization certainly undermines the workings of the nation-state—from national economies to traditional ideas of citizenship and cultural production (see Castles and Davidson 2000; Sassen 1998). On one hand, the state apparatus does in some important ways appear somewhat irrelevant in the context of globalization—as, for example, when billions of dollars

enter and exit national boundaries. On the other hand, states are responding to globalization by hyperdisplays of power and theatrics. Arguably the most globalized spot in the world today—also, alas, the most heavily trafficked international border in the world—is the vast region that at once unites and separates the United States and Mexico. It is also the most heavily guarded border in history (Andreas 2000). The militarization of the border at a time of record border crossings suggests a process more complex than the simple erosion or demise of the nation-state. In the places that matter—that is, where states bump into each other—hyperpresence is the name of the game. This is the case in the United States, in post-Schengen Europe, and in Japan. (Per the Schengen agreement, there are no longer internal border controls among European Union member states. Hence, a French citizen needs no passport or visa to travel to Spain and vice versa). While internally Europe has become borderless, external controls—that is, keeping would-be migrants from entering Europe—have intensified. To claim that the state is waning is to miss one of the more intriguing paradoxes of state performance.

18. Is globalization simply "modernization"? Is it "Westernization" in fastforward? Is it "imperialism" now driven by the extraordinarily high octane of American hyperpower? Is it unfettered American capitalism sans frontiers? Alternatively, is it a phenomenon or a set of phenomena of a completely different order? Are these processes of change drastically different from what occurred in the world centuries ago?

19. Indeed, "a growing share of what countries produce is sold to foreigners as exports. Among rich or developed countries, the share of international trade in total output (exports plus imports of goods relative to GDP) rose from 27 to 39 percent between 1987 and 1997. For the developing countries, it rose from 10 to 17 percent" (World Bank 2001, p.1). Likewise, foreign-direct investment (i.e., firms making investments in other countries) overall "more than tripled between 1988 and 1998 from $192 billion to $610 billion" (World Bank 2001, p. 1). The most significant characteristic of economic globalization is "in the level of finance and capital flows. Geared as it is to electronic money—money that exists only as digits in computers—the current world economy has no parallels in earlier times" (Giddens 2000, p. 27). From the time the reader got up this morning to the time she goes to bed tonight more than a trillion dollars will have crossed national boundaries (Giddens 2000).

20. The last decade of the twentieth century witnessed vast but uneven economic growth and increasing inequality (World Bank 2001). According to Giddens, "the share of the poorest fifth of the world's population in the global income has dropped, from 2.3 percent to 1.4 percent between 1989 and 1998. The proportion taken by the richest fifth, on the other hand, has risen. In sub-Saharan Africa, 20 countries have lower incomes per head in real terms than they had in the late 1970s" (Giddens 2000, pp. 33–34). But how is globalization related to growing inequality? In his World Bank Presidential Fellows Lecture, Kumi Naidoo (2003) argues that "globalization is exacerbating global inequality, and its 'rules'—to the extent we can call them that—appear to be driven by the rich at the expense of the poor. The relentless lauding of so-called 'free-trade' in fact masks a set of double standards that protect certain markets

Table 1.1. CHANGES IN TECHNOLOGY
IN WORLD REGIONS

	Televisions per 1,000 Persons		Telephones per 1,000 Persons	
	1970	*1995*	*1975*	*1995*
Industrialized Countries	280	525	178	414
East Asia	5	255	4	49
Latin America & Caribbean	70	220	34	86
Southeast Asia & Pacific	5	155	2	29
Arab States	28	127	8	49
South Asia	1	60	2	16
Sub-Saharan Africa	1	33	6	12

SOURCE: United Nations Development Program (1998). *Human Development Report.* New York: Oxford University Press.

in wealthy countries and deny poor and developing countries the chance to benefit from the most promising segments of their own economies" (p. 2).

21. "Overall, the proportion of adolescents in secondary schools in developing countries rose from 23% in 1970 to 52% in 1997 (United Nations Educational, Scientific, and Cultural Organization 1999), but the proportion in developed countries is now above 90%" (Arnett 2002, p. 775).

22. Yet a paradox of globalization is that as it unites it also divides the world between those who can access and manipulate the new technologies and those who are left behind, "stuck," so to speak, in local tools and local contexts (Bauman 1998; also Table 1.1).

23. Other cultural theorists in the Americas have examined similar South-North back-and-forth cultural flows, exchanges, and transformations in music (Flores 2000), art (Canclini 1995), and religion (Levitt 2002).

24. Large-scale immigration is a world phenomenon that is transforming Africa, Asia, Europe, and the Americas. The United States is now in the midst of the largest wage of immigration in history. Nearly 30 percent of Frankfurt's population is immigrant. Amsterdam will be 50 percent immigrant by the year 2015. Leicester, England, is about to become the first city in Europe where "whites" will no longer be the majority. Japan, long held as the exception to the North American and European rule that immigrant workers are needed to maintain economic vitality, is now facing a future in which immigrants will be needed to deal with the country's aging-population problem (Tsuda 2003). Immigration and globalization upset the symbolic order of the nation, interrupt taken-for-granted social practices, reshape political processes, engender new cultural attitudes, and channel the new anxieties of long-time citizens. It has a democratizing potential, but the potential for friction is equally obvious. Immigration means that foreign languages, foreign social practices (sometimes practices deeply destabilizing to liberal democracies, such as female genital

mutilation among immigrants in Europe and the United States), and cultural models (such as marriage before legal adulthood) that generate anxieties and threaten the cultural imagination of the nation (Shweder, Minow, and Markus 2002). But at the same time the immigrants are needed. They are summoned to do the unpleasant jobs that over time have become culturally coded as "immigrant jobs" (the Japanese call them the "3 k jobs" for the Japanese words for "dirty, dangerous, and demanding"). Indeed, Western Europe faces one of the most delicious of paradoxes: while postfascist anti-immigrant sentiment continues to grow, according to Europe's leading demographers approximately fifty million new immigrant workers will need to be recruited over the next few decades to deal with the continent's peculiar demographic predicament—below-replacement fertility rates.

25. In the so-called "global cities" (Sassen 1998), foreign languages, habits, and sensibilities are thriving. Newcomers learn to live everyday life with divided linguistic and cultural identifications, and native citizens learn to expect it in others. As acknowledged by the U.S. Census Bureau, a growing number of Americans identify themselves in terms of multiple cultural, racial, and ethnic belongings. This, nevertheless, causes unease in the American landscape.

26. Another unique feature about the Harvard workshop is that an entire day was devoted to discuss just two presentations (one in the morning and one in the afternoon), allowing for a thorough analysis and discussion of the issues at hand.

REFERENCES

Abrams, S. (2003). Global interests linked to developing world. *Harvard Gazette,* April 10, p. 17.

Amit-Talai, V., and H. Wulff, eds. (1995). *Youth cultures: A cross-cultural perspective.* London: Routledge.

Andreas, P. (2001). *Border games: Policing the U.S.–Mexico Divide.* Ithaca, NY: Cornell University Press.

Aoki, N. (2003). SARS impact could hit $100b. *Boston Globe,* May 23, C1.

Appadurai, A. (1996). *Modernity at large: Cultural dimensions of globalization.* Minneapolis: University of Minnesota Press.

Arnett, J. J. (2002). The psychology of globalization. *American Psychologist* 57: 774–783.

Basch, L. N., G. Schiller, and C. Blanc (1994). *Nations unbound: Transnational projects, postcolonial predicaments and deterritorialized nations states.* Basel, Switzerland: Gordon and Breach Science.

Bauman, Z. (1998). *Globalization: The human consequences.* New York: Columbia University Press.

Baylis, J., and S. Smith (1997). *The globalization of world politics.* New York: Oxford University Press.

Bennett, A. (2000). *Popular music and youth culture: Music, identity and place.* London: Macmillan.

Berger, S., and R. Dore, eds. (1996). *National diversity and global capitalism.* Ithaca: Cornell University Press.

Bhagwati, J. (2002). Coping with antiglobalization: A trilogy of discontents. *Foreign Affairs* 81(1): 2–7.

Bloom, D. E., and J. E. Cohen (2002). Education for all: An unfinished revolution. *Daedalus* (summer): 84–95.

Bok, D. (2003). *Universities in the marketplace: The commercialization of higher education.* Princeton: Princeton University Press.

Booth, M. (2002). Arab adolescents facing the future: Enduring ideals and pressures for change. In *The world's youth: Adolescence in eight regions of the globe.* B. B. Brown, R. Larson, and T. S. Saraswathi, eds. New York: Cambridge University Press.

Boyer, R. (1996). The convergence hypothesis revisited: Globalization but still the century of nations? In *National diversity and global capitalism.* B. S. and R. Dore, eds. Ithaca: Cornell University Press.

Brown, B. B., R. Larson, and T. S. Saraswathi, eds. (2002). *The world's youth: Adolescence in eight regions of the globe.* New York: Cambridge University Press.

Burbules, N. C., and C. A. Torres (2000). From education in the enlightenment to globalized education: Preliminary thoughts. In *Globalization and education: Critical perspectives.* N. C. Burbules and C. A. Torres, eds. New York: Routledge.

Burtless, G., R. Z. Lawrence, R. E. Litan, and R. J. Shapiro, eds. (1998). *Globaphobia: Confronting fears about open trade.* Washington, DC: Brookings Institution Press.

Canclini, N. (1995) *Hybrid cultures: Strategies for entering and leaving modernity.* C. Chippari and S. López, trans. Minneapolis: University of Minnesota Press. (Original work published 1989).

Castles, S., and A. Davidson (2000). *Citizenship and migration: Globalization and the politics of belonging.* New York: Routledge.

Coleman, W., and T. Porter (1999). *International institutions, globalization and democracy: Assessing the challenges.* Paper presented at the 11th annual meeting of the Society for the Advancement of Socio-Economics, Madison, WI, July 8–11.

Currie, J., and J. Newson, eds. (1998). *Universities and globalization: Critical perspectives.* Thousand Oaks, CA: Sage Publications.

de Wit, H. (1995). Education and globalization in Europe: Current trends and future developments. *Frontiers: The Interdisciplinary Journal of Studying Abroad* 1. http://www.frontiersjournal.com/back/one/volone.htm.

Dussel, E. P. (2000). *Polarizing Mexico: The impact of liberalization.* New York: Lynne Rienner.

Erikson, E. (1968). *Identity: Youth and crisis.* New York: W. W. Norton.

European Union (2002). EU Commission Says 10 Countries Ready to Join EU in 2004. http://www.eurunion.org/news/press/2002/2002051.htm.

Feldstein, M. (2002). Argentina's fall: Lessons from the latest financial crisis. *Foreign Affairs* 81(2): 8–14.

Flores, J. (2000). *From bomba to hip-hop: Puerto Rican culture and Latino identity.* New York: Columbia University Press.

Foreign Policy Association (2002). Globalization's Last Hurrah? *Foreign Policy* (January–February) http://www.foreignpolicy.com/issue_janfeb_2002/global _index.html.

Gardner, H., M. Csikszentmihalyi, and W. Damon (2001). *Good work: When excellence and ethics meet.* New York: Basic Books.

Gardner, H. (1999). *Intelligence reframed.* New York: Basic Books.

Giddens, A. (2000). *Runaway world: How globalization is reshaping our lives.* New York: Routledge.

Gough, N. (1999). Globalization and school curriculum change: Locating a transnational imaginary. *Journal of Educational Policy* 14(1): 73–84.

Gray, J. (2002). The end of globalization. *Resurgence* 212 (May–June). http://resurgence.gn.apc.org/issues/gray212.htm.

Green, M. F. (2002). Going global: Internationalizing U.S. higher education. *Current* 444: 8–15.

Gupta, A., and J. Ferguson (1992). Beyond "culture": Space, identity, and the politics of difference. *Cultural Anthropology* 7: 6–23.

Hardt, M., and A. Negri (2000). *Empire.* Cambridge, MA: Harvard University Press.

Held, D. (2000). *A globalizing world? Culture, economics and politics.* London: Routledge.

Inda, J., and R. Rosaldo (2001). *Anthropology of globalization: A reader.* New York: Blackwell.

Jameson, F., and M. Miyoshi, eds. (1998). *The cultures of globalization.* Durham, NC: Duke University Press.

Jenkins, H. (1992). *Textual poachers: Television fans and participatory culture.* New York: Routledge.

King, A., ed. (1997). *Culture, globalization, and the world system: Contemporary conditions for the representation of identity.* New York: Cambridge University Press.

Kirkwood, T. F. (2001). Preparing teachers to teach from a global perspective. *Delta Kappa Gamma Bulletin* 67(2): 5–12.

Kristeva, J. (1991). *Strangers to ourselves.* New York: Columbia University Press.

Larkin, B. (2002). Indian films and Nigerian lovers: Media and the creation of parallel maternities. In *Anthropology of globalization: A reader.* J. Inda and R. Rosaldo, eds. New York: Blackwell.

Larson, R. W. (2002). Globalization, societal change, and new technologies: What they mean for the future of adolescence. *Journal of Research on Adolescence* 12(1): 1–30.

Lechner, F., and J. Boli, eds. (1999). *The globalization reader.* New York: Blackwell.

Levitt, P. (2001). *The transnational villagers.* Berkeley: University of California Press.

Levitt, P. (2002). Two nations under God? Latino religious life in the U.S. In *Latinos! Remaking America.* M. Suárez-Orozco and M. Páez, eds. Berkeley, CA, and Cambridge, MA: University of California Press and David Rockefeller Center for Latin American Studies, Harvard University.

Lopez, G. A., J. G. Smith, and R. Pagnucco (1995). The global tide. *Bulletin of the Atomic Scientists* 51(5): 32–39.

Mahler, S. (1995). *American dreaming: Immigrant life on the margins*. Princeton: Princeton University Press.

Maira, S., and E. Soep (2004). *Youthscapes: Popular culture, national ideologies, global markets*. Philadelphia: University of Pennsylvania Press.

McLaren, P., and R. Farahmandpur (2001). Teaching against globalization and the new imperialism: Toward a revolutionary pedagogy. *Journal of Teacher Education* 52(2): 136–150.

Michaels, E. (2002). Hollywood iconography: A Warlpiri reading. In *Anthropology of globalization: A reader*. J. Inda and R. Rosaldo, eds. New York: Blackwell.

Mignolo, W. (1998). Globalization, civilization processes, and the relocation of languages and cultures. In *The cultures of globalization*, F. Jameson and M. Miyoshi, eds. Durham, NC: Duke University Press.

Mittelman, J. (2000). *The globalization syndrome*. Princeton: Princeton University Press.

Mok, K. H. (2000). Reflecting globalization effects on local policy: Higher education reform in Taiwan. *Journal of Education Policy* 15(6): 637–660.

Mol, A. P. J. (2001). *Globalization and environmental reform: The ecological modernization of the global economy*. Cambridge, MA: MIT Press.

Moya, J. C. (1998). *Cousins and strangers: Spanish immigrants in Buenos Aires, 1850–1930*. Berkeley: University of California Press.

Nader, R., ed. (1993). *The case against free trade: GATT, NAFTA, and the globalization of corporate power*. New York: North Atlantic Books.

Naidoo, K. (2003). *Civil society, governance and globalization*. World Bank Presidential Fellows Lecture, presented at the World Bank Headquarters, Washington, DC, February 10.

Nsamenang, B. (2002). Adolescence in sub-Saharan Africa: An image constructed from Africa's triple inheritance. *The world's youth: Adolescence in eight regions of the globe*. In B. B. Brown, R. Larson, and T. S. Saraswathi, eds. New York: Cambridge University Press: 61–104.

Nye, J. S., and J. D. Donahue, eds. (2000). *Governance in a globalizing world*. New York: Brookings Institution Press.

Nye, J. S. (2001). Globalization's democratic deficit: How to make international institutions more accountable. *Foreign Affairs* 80 (July–August): 2–6.

O'Meara, P., H. Mehlinger, and M. Krain, eds. (2000). *Globalization and the challenges of the new century: A reader*. Bloomington: Indiana University Press.

Peach, M. (2001). Globalization of education in Spain: From isolation to internationalization to globalization. *Higher Education in Europe* 26(1): 69–76.

Piaget, J. (1936). *Origins of intelligence in the child*. London: Routledge and Kegan Paul.

Portes, A., and R. G. Rumbaut (2001). *Legacies: The story of the second generation*. Berkeley: University of California Press.

Quashigah, A. Y., and A. H. Wilson (2001). A cross-national conversation about teaching from a global perspective: Issues of culture and power. *Theory into Practice* 40(1): 55–64.

Robben, A. (2004). *Hitting where it hurts: The traumatization of Argentine society.* Philadelphia: University of Pennsylvania Press.

Rodrik, D. (1997) *Has globalization gone too far?* Washington, DC: Institute for International Economics.

Rodrik, D. (2002). Globalization for whom? *Harvard Magazine* 104(6): 29–32.

Rugman, A. (2001). *The end of globalization.* New York: Amacom.

Sabour, M. H. (1999). Globalization and school curriculum change: Locating a transnational imaginary. *Journal of Education Policy* 14: 381–395.

Sassen, S. (1998). *Globalization and its discontents: Essays on the new mobility of people and money.* New York: New Press.

Sciolino, E. (2003). A maze of identities for the Muslims of France. *New York Times*, April 9, international sec.

Sen, A. K. (2000). *Global Doubts.* Commencement address, Harvard University, Cambridge, MA. http://www.commencement.harvard.edu/sen.html.

Singer, P. (2002). *One world: The ethics of globalization.* New Haven: Yale University Press.

Shapiro, B. (2002). Higher education in the new century—Some history, some challenges. *Education Canada* 42(1): 12–15.

Shweder, R. (2000). What about "female genital mutilation"? *Daedalus* 129: 209–232.

Shweder, R, M. Minow, and H. R. Markus (2002). *Engaging cultural differences: The multicultural challenge in liberal democracies.* New York: Russell Sage Foundation.

Slaughter, S. (1998). National higher education policies in a global economy. In *Universities and globalization: Critical perspectives.* J. Currie and J. Newson, eds. Thousand Oaks, CA: Sage Publications.

Smith, R. (2002). Gender, ethnicity, and race in school and work outcomes of second-generation Mexican Americans. In *Latinos: Remaking America.* M. Suárez-Orozco and M. Páez, eds. Berkeley: University of California Press.

Stevenson, H. W., and A. Zusho (2002). Adolescences in China and Japan: Adapting to a changing environment. In *The world's youth: Adolescence in eight regions of the globe.* B. B. Brown, R. Larson, and T. S. Saraswathi, eds. New York: Cambridge University Press.

Stiglitz, J. (2002). *Globalization and its discontents.* New York, W. W. Norton.

Strange, S. (1996). *The retreat of the state: The diffusion of power in the world.* New York: Cambridge University Press.

Stromquist, N. P., and K. Monkman (2000). *Globalization and education: Integration and contestation across cultures.* Lanham, MD: Rowman & Littlefield.

Suárez-Orozco, C. (2000). Identities under siege: Immigration stress and social mirroring among the children of immigrants. In *Cultures under siege: Social violence and trauma.* A. Robben and M. Suárez-Orozco, eds. Cambridge, UK: Cambridge University Press.

Suárez-Orozco, C., and M. Suárez-Orozco (1995). *Transformations: Immigration, family life, and achievement motivation among Latino adolescents.* Stanford, CA: Stanford University Press.

Suárez-Orozco, C., and M. Suárez-Orozco (2001). *Children of immigration.* Cambridge, MA: Harvard University Press.

Suárez-Orozco, M. (1989). *Central American refugees and U.S. high schools: A psychosocial study of motivation and achievement.* Stanford, CA: Stanford University Press.

Suárez-Orozco, M. (1991). Migration, minority status, and education: European dilemmas and responses in the 1990s. *Anthropology and Education Quarterly* 22: 99–190.

Suárez-Orozco, M. (2000). Everything you ever wanted to know about assimilation but were afraid to ask. *Daedalus* 129: 1–30.

Suárez-Orozco, M. (1994). Remaking psychological anthropology. In *The making of psychological anthropology II.* M. M. Suárez-Orozco, G. Spindler, and L. Spindler, eds. Fort Worth, TX: Harcourt Brace.

Suárez-Orozco, M. (1996). Unwelcome mats. *Harvard Magazine* 98: 32–35.

Suárez-Orozco, M. (1998). *Crossings: Mexican immigration in interdisciplinary perspectives.* Cambridge, MA: David Rockefeller Center for Latin American Studies and Harvard University Press.

Suárez-Orozco, M. (1999). Latin American immigration to the United States. In *The United States and Latin America: The new agenda.* V. Bulmer-Thomas and J. Dunkerley, eds. Cambridge, MA: David Rockefeller Center for Latin American Studies and Harvard University Press.

Suárez-Orozco, M., and H. Gardner. (2003). Educating Billy Wang for the world of tomorrow. *Education Week,* October 22, pp. 34–44.

Suárez-Orozco, M., and M. Páez. (2002). *Latinos: Remaking America.* Berkeley: University of California Press.

Suárez-Orozco, M., and D. Sommer. (2002). Globalization, immigration, and transculturation. Unpublished Manuscript. Harvard University.

Suárez-Orozco, M., C. Suárez-Orozco, and D. Qin-Hilliard, eds. (2001). *Interdisciplinary perspectives on the new immigration: Vol. 1. Theoretical perspectives.* New York and London: Routledge.

Suárez-Orozco, M., C. Suárez-Orozco, and D. Qin-Hilliard, eds. (2001). *Interdisciplinary perspectives on the new immigration: Vol. 2. The new immigrant in the American economy.* New York and London: Routledge.

Suárez-Orozco, M., C. Suárez-Orozco, and D. Qin-Hilliard, eds. (2001). *Interdisciplinary perspectives on the new immigration: Vol. 3. The new immigrant in American society.* New York and London: Routledge.

Tenzing, T. (2003). For Sherpas, a steep climb. *New York Times,* May 29, A27.

Tomlinson, J. (1999) *Globalization and culture.* Cambridge: Polity Press.

Turkle, S. (1997). *Life on line: Identity in the age of the Internet.* New York: Touchstone.

Tsuda, T. (1996). *Strangers in the ethnic homeland: The migration, ethnic identity, and psychosocial adaptation of Japan's new immigrant minority.* Unpublished doctoral dissertation, University of California, Berkeley, Department of Anthropology.

Tsuda, T. (2003). *Strangers in the ethnic homeland: Japanese Brazilian return migration in transitional perspective.* New York: Columbia University Press.

United Nations Educational, Scientific and Cultural Organization (1999). *UNESCO Statistical Yearbook.* Lanham, MD: UNESCO, Berman Press.

Vygotsky, L. S. (1978). Mind in society: The development of higher psychological processes. Cambridge, MA: Harvard University Press.

Waghid, Y. (2001). Globalization and higher education restructuring in South Africa: Is democracy under threat? *Journal of Education Policy* 16(5): 455–464.

Warkentin, C. (2001). *Reshaping world politics: NGOs, the Internet, and global civil society.* Lanham, MD: Rowman & Littlefield.

Waltz, K. (1999). Globalization and governance. James Madison Lecture, Political Science Online. http://www.apsanet.org/PS/dec99/waltz.cfm.

Weiss, L. (1998). *The myth of the powerless state.* New York: Cornell University Press.

Welti, C. (2002). Adolescents in Latin America: Facing the future with skepticism. In *The World's Youth: Adolescence in Eight Regions of the Globe.* B. B. Brown, R. Larson, and T. S. Saraswathi, eds. New York: Cambridge University Press.

White, C., and T. Walker (1999). Technology, teacher education, and the postmodern: Encouraging the discourse. *Action in Teacher Education* 21(3): 45–56.

Wikan, U. (2000). Citizenship on trial: Nadia's case. *Daedalus,* 129: 55–76.

World Bank. (2001). Assessing globalization. Washington, DC. http://www1.worldbank.org/economicpolicy/globalization/key_readings.html. Accessed November 2002.

Yan, Y. (2002). Managed globalization: State power and cultural transition in China. In *Many globalizations: Cultural diversity in the contemporary world.* Peter Berger and Samuel Huntington, eds. Oxford, UK: Oxford University Press.

Yang, M. (2002). Mass media and transnational subjectivity in Shanghai: Notes on (re)cosmopolitanism in a Chinese metropolis. In *Anthropology of Globalization: A Reader.* J. Inda and R. Rosaldo, eds. New York: Blackwell.

Zentella, A. (2002). Latin languages and identities. In *Latinos: Remaking America.* M. Suárez-Orozco and M. Páez, eds. Berkeley: University of California Press.

TWO

John H. Coatsworth

GLOBALIZATION, GROWTH, AND WELFARE IN HISTORY

INTRODUCTION

Globalization is what happens when the movement of people, goods, or ideas among countries and regions accelerates. The world has experienced four major cycles of globalization since Italian sea captains flying the flags of Spain and Portugal initiated regular interoceanic travel in the fifteenth and sixteenth centuries. Each of these globalization cycles transformed entire societies in regions across the globe.

The first globalization cycle began in 1492 and lasted until the early 1600s. This cycle witnessed the conquest and colonization of American societies by Spain and Portugal and the creation of a vast trans-Atlantic trading system that had never existed before. It also included the establishment of regular trade between the Atlantic and Indian Oceans; the first trans-Pacific trade route, from Acapulco to Manila; and the first regular ocean commerce between Europe and East Asia.

The second cycle commenced in the late seventeenth century with the rapid growth of a second wave of European colonization that established the main slave colonies in the New World. It also included the development of European settlement colonies in North America and the shift in European strategy in the Indian Ocean from the maintenance of trading post empires to the creation of full-scale conquest colonies. This cycle ended with a series of major shocks in the early nineteenth century, including the wars of the French Revolution and Napoleon, which helped to set off the Haitian Revolution of 1791.

The third cycle began in the late nineteenth century with huge increases in international trade, capital, and technology flows, as well as mass migrations from both Asia and Europe to the Americas. This cycle also saw the last big scramble for conquest colonies by the European powers in Africa and Asia. It ended with the Great Depression of the 1930s.

The most recent cycle began with the liberalization of international trade after the Second World War and intensified after a further liberalization of global trade in manufactured goods after 1967. A number of East Asian countries began taking advantage of this big change immediately, but the more inward-looking countries of Latin America and South Asia stuck with more closed, protectionist strategies until the 1980s. In most of Latin America this last cycle did not effectively begin until after the economic and financial crisis of 1982, which undermined the inward-looking development strategies of the region's major economies.

Globalization cycles have produced immense and measurable increases in human productivity. In the long run, these productivity gains trickled through to improve everyone's living standards. During each cycle, however, the initial gains were unequally distributed. Short-term benefits generally went to tiny minorities. In some cases, the productivity gains came at the cost of immense suffering over many generations. Most of the societies that endured the miseries of globalization became more productive and wealthier than other societies that did not globalize. Eventually, many of these wealthier societies achieved higher living standards for all their citizens, but by the time they did so, those who had lived through the onset of globalization and paid the heavy price were long dead.

Understanding the contradictory effects of past globalizations may help contemporary societies maximize the benefits and mitigate the costs of the new cycle we are living through now. Moreover, the history of globalization has implications for the way we educate today's students about the world they will inherit. This chapter will focus mainly on Latin America, where the effects of globalization, both positive and negative, have been particularly strong over the past five centuries. It will first look at the huge demographic effects of the first three cycles. Second, it will survey the productivity advances that accompany globalizations. Third, it will analyze the gap between the productivity and welfare effects of each cycle. The chapter will conclude with some observations about globalization and education.

GLOBALIZATION AND POPULATION

The first major cycle of globalization was initiated by European traders who sailed south along the coast of West Africa looking for gold and eventually found their way around the Cape of Good Hope and into the Indian Ocean to trade for spices. Columbus's 1492 voyage then demonstrated that trans-Atlantic trade and communication could be feasible, though Columbus himself believed that the Atlantic and Pacific Oceans were the same and convinced himself that he had reached Asia. The globalization of the Americas began with Columbus's second voyage in 1494. While the first voyage of three small ships went to discover and explore, the second voyage consisted of an armada of warships and soldiers whose purpose was to conquer and subjugate. In this and subsequent expeditions, Spanish conquistadores attacked the larger Caribbean islands, established settlements, and enslaved the inhabitants. In 1519 they began a series of campaigns to overthrow and replace the Native American states on the mainland. The Aztec capital of Tenochtitlán (Mexico City) fell in 1521, the main Andean cities by 1537. Meanwhile, the Portuguese, who first landed on the coast of Brazil in 1500, had also begun to establish permanent settlements.

The demographic impact of the Iberian conquests on the native populations of the Americas overshadowed all other effects. The arrival of the Europeans brought the indigenous population into contact with lethal pathogens such as smallpox, pneumonia, influenza, and measles to which it had never before been exposed. Though by no means free of sickness, the Native Americans had few domesticated animals to carry and spread the diseases they did have (Diamond 1997). The catastrophic effects of the rapid epidemiological globalization of the Americas were magnified as a result of Spanish and Portuguese treatment of their indigenous subjects. The precontact population of the Americas probably stood at fifty million to seventy million, though estimates have ranged from less than twenty million to more than one hundred million and continue to be debated. By the early seventeenth century, the Native American population had fallen to less than five million (Cook, 1998; Deneven 1993; Newson 1985). Globalization killed more than 90 percent of the inhabitants of the Americas.

The second cycle of globalization in the Americas centered on the American tropics with the spread of sugar cultivation and plantation slavery, first to Brazil and then to the Caribbean. While the first cycle had produced devastating encounters between Europeans and Native Americans and thus to one degree or another involved the entire hemisphere, the second cycle affected mainly the tropical zones of the New World. Though more limited geographically within the Americas, the effects of this second cycle of globalization extended to Africa as well as Europe.

The demographic impact of the African slave trade was as significant as the conquest itself. Between 1500 and 1888, in the nearly four centuries of the trans-Atlantic slave trade, roughly 9 million Africans were kidnapped and shipped to the new world. Of that number, 1.3 million arrived between 1500 and 1700, an average of some 7,000 per year. In the eighteenth century, the peak era of African slavery in the Americas, more than 4 million slaves were forcibly transported. By the 1770s, over 50,000 slaves were arriving every year. Most of the slaves brought to the Americas were sold in the sugar-growing regions of Brazil and the British, Danish, Dutch, French, and Spanish West Indies (Eltis 2000).

Sugar production could not have developed in the Americas without the migration of a working population from outside the hemisphere. African slaves repopulated the Americas after the collapse of the Native American population. By the early sixteenth century, the first cycle of globalization had eliminated the Native American population of the Caribbean and greatly reduced those of Brazil and the other mainland colonies. Only slaves could have solved the New World's tropical labor shortage, because only slaves could have been forced to labor for subsistence wages in labor-scarce regions where land was abundant. Brazilian planters enslaved the Native Americans initially, but they died or escaped at such high rates that slave-hunting expeditions far into the interior could no longer replace them (Schwartz 1978). Sugar could have been produced by free wage laborers (and was later on), but the wage levels required to attract and transport free immigrants from

Europe to the disease-ridden tropical regions of the Americas far exceeded the cost of importing slaves from Africa. In the British West Indies, English colonists first populated Barbados, Nevis, and Saint Kitts but were dislodged by slave plantations whose owners could afford to bid up land prices because sugar production with African slaves proved to be more profitable than tobacco and indigo grown by free farmers (Klein 1986, p. 50).

More Africans migrated to the New World between 1492 and 1800 than Europeans (Eltis 2000, pp. 9–11). The Africans were not taken to the areas where the largest number of Native Americans died, such as the densely populated highlands of Mexico and Peru. The trans-Atlantic slave trade brought most of its human cargo to tiny patches of tropical coast scattered along a narrow strip of northeastern Brazil, the northern coast of South America, and a small number of the Caribbean islands. The slave colonies of the eighteenth century proved to be immensely productive, but at a fearsome price in death and misery.

The third cycle of globalization in Latin America occurred with the onset of export-led economic growth in the closing decades of the nineteenth century. The timing differed from place to place, but the process quickly assumed similar characteristics throughout Latin America. West European and U.S. demand for food and raw materials rose during the industrial revolution. Capital and technology from the developed countries enabled Latin America to build the railroads that made land and mineral wealth accessible to profitable exploitation. External public indebtedness financed the necessary infrastructure, including railroad subsidies. Foreign direct investment poured into mines and plantations, with immediate and impressive results: the onset of sustained increases in per-capita gross domestic product (GDP) for the first time since the conquest (in Mesoamerica and the Andes) and the introduction of sugar (in the tropics).

In a number of countries, most notably the southern cone (Argentina, Chile, and Uruguay) and Brazil, European laborers immigrated in huge numbers as demand for labor and real wages increased. In the Caribbean, contract laborers from India also came in large numbers (O'Rourke and Williamson 1999). The large-scale migrations to Latin America coincided with even larger flows into the northern United States.

The fourth cycle of globalization is also producing large-scale migratory flows. In the past two decades, as the chapter by Marcelo Suárez-Orozco and Desirée Baolian Qin-Hilliard shows clearly, the stream of immigrants, documented and undocumented, into the United States from Latin America has accelerated. Large numbers of people have also moved, or tried to move, from the European periphery—including the rapidly globalizing countries of Eastern Europe, North Africa, and the Middle East—to the high-wage economies of the European Union.

Thus, while the major demographic impact of the first cycle of globalization was to depopulate the Americas, that of the last three cycles has come through transnational migrations. The second cycle involved kidnapping and enslaving millions of Africans, many of whom perished en route to the Americas. Virtually none of these migrants ever returned to their homes in Africa. In the third cycle, however, migration was "free," that is, compelled mainly by market forces as Europeans (mainly) fled the poverty of their homelands. Substantial numbers became discouraged and returned to their homelands. High rates of return migration are also common in today's fourth cycle. Temporary, seasonal migrations also occurred in both the third and fourth cycles, as in the Italian "swallows" (*golondrinos*) who traveled to Argentina to work the wheat harvests in the early twentieth century, the Mexican braceros in the United States, and the "guest workers" in Europe after the Second World War.

The impact of globalization on human populations has varied enormously over time. The vast death toll of the American conquests has never been repeated, but globalization has always involved large-scale migrations of people from one continent to the other. Even when the migrations are not physically coerced, as in the Atlantic slave trade, the risks and traumas of mass migration still cause great dislocation and suffering.

GLOBALIZATION AND PRODUCTIVITY

Globalization and productivity go hand in hand. The conquest of the Americas yielded substantial, long-term benefits, though the human catastrophe of the postconquest century makes it impossible to weigh them against the millions who perished. As the indigenous population collapsed over the sixteenth century and into the seventeenth century, agricultural productivity and per-capita income rose. In Central Mexico and some of the more densely populated highland regions in the Andes, the people who survived the epidemics abandoned more marginal lands and resettled on the most fertile and best-watered terrain (Borah and Cook 1971–79; Gibson 1964). Frequently Spaniards and other outsiders grabbed the best of the lands left vacant after epidemics and resettled indigenous villagers as *peones* on their haciendas (Chevalier 1970). Whatever the process, the results were impressive. Total agricultural production fell as the death toll mounted, but per-capita output rose because agricultural production fell more slowly than the drop in the indigenous population.

The "Columbian exchange" of plant and animal species also contributed to rising productivity. Biodiversity rose in both the Old World and the New, but the increase was greater in the Americas. The Old World held twelve of the world's fourteen species of domesticated animals and some 500 of the 640 plant species cultivated by humans (Crosby 1972). Conquest and colonization brought the diversity and crop mix of New World agriculture closer to that of the Old. The Americas gave the Old World maize, potatoes, hot peppers, beans, peanuts, tomatoes, tropical fruits, and cacao, to mention the most exportable of its cultivated plants. European transplants to the New World included wheat and other grains, wine grapes, onions, sugar cane, fruit trees, and rice. Greater diversity increased the options available to farmers, and thus agricultural productivity, on both sides of the Atlantic (Crosby 1972).[1]

The introduction of domesticated animals in the New World also produced benefits. Though the explosive multiplication of hoofed animals (ungulate eruptions) damaged crops and even entire ecosystems, the long-term impact of introducing domesticated animals was positive. The new animals transformed both agricultural practices and dietary standards, especially in Mesoamerica, where the pre-Hispanic population had suffered from a shortage of protein. The Europeans brought horses, oxen, donkeys, cattle, sheep, goats, pigs, chickens, and a variety of other animals, including silkworms and pets of all kinds. In the context of rapid depopulation, the fact that animals required more land but less labor to produce equivalent nutritional benefits may even have helped to improve resistance to disease by raising nutrition levels.

The European conquest and colonization had other productivity-enhancing effects. The Spaniards and the Portuguese introduced new tools and technologies as well as new institutions and methods of organizing economic activity. The Americas imported sailing ships, wheeled vehicles, iron and steel making, deep-shaft mining, and the chemistry of tanning leather and making soap, along with money and commercial credit. The opening of long-distance trade also contributed to productivity advance.

During the second globalization cycle, tropical plantations produced enormous short-term economic gains. The first truly "global" economic enterprise was the New World sugar plantation on which European owners forced African slaves to produce an Asian crop in the American tropics for export to European consumers. At first only the Portuguese exported substantial quantities of sugar, up to nine thousand tons per year by the early 1600s. Slave-worked sugar plantations did not become dominant in the Caribbean until late in the seventeenth century. The transition began in the 1640s, when the Dutch facilitated the transfer to the Caribbean of slaves, plants, technology, and equipment from the territories in northeast Brazil, which they had seized temporarily (1630–1654) from Portugal. By the 1740s, both British Jamaica (exporting thirty-six thousand tons per year) and French Saint Domingue (sixty-one thousand tons) produced more than Brazil (twenty-seven thousand tons). The other British, Dutch, French, and Danish islands were not far behind (Klein 1986; Higman 1996; Schwartz 1985).

The productivity of the sugar colonies, especially in the Caribbean, made these regions among the richest in the world. The consumption of sugar rose rapidly in Europe, so prices and profits stayed high despite the increasing supply in the eighteenth century. The per-capita GDP of the sugar islands exceeded that of the thirteen British North American colonies until well into the nineteenth century (Eltis 1995). Even Spanish Cuba, which produced more tobacco than sugar until the end of the eighteenth century, had a higher GDP per capita than the United States until at least the 1830s (Balbín, Salvucci, and Salvucci 1993).

After roughly 1800, however, slavery in Latin America ceased to be associated with economic growth and commercial success. Only its revival in the southern United States made it seem feasible as a modern institution in a modernizing society. In Latin America, slave plantations gained ground for a time only in Brazil and Cuba, but economic stagnation rather than economic growth was the result.[2] In their eighteenth-century heyday, however, the slave plantation colonies of tropical America provided a dramatic example of rapid and for a time sustained economic growth that raised their economies to unprecedented heights of productivity.

Globalization in the late nineteenth and early twentieth centuries also transformed entire economies in relatively short periods of time, but the economic achievements of this cycle proved to be more durable than the first two cycles. In Latin America the breadth and depth of globalization in the Belle Epoque far exceeded those of the current globalization cycle. For example, foreign trade represented a much higher proportion of total GDP in the 1910s in most Latin American countries than today (Bulmer-Thomas 1994). Foreign investment, measured either as an annual flow of new resources or as the value of existing foreign-owned assets, weighed much more heavily in the economies of Latin America a century ago than today (Twomey 1998). This suggests how great the potential may be for achieving a far higher degree of integration into the global marketplace than Latin America has managed to achieve since the most recent cycle of globalization began in the early 1980s. In East Asia, where the third cycle was weaker and the current, fourth cycle somewhat stronger than in Latin America, most countries have already opened their economies and developed their export industries to a degree unprecedented in their histories. Unlike the success stories in Latin America, however, those in such Asian countries as China, Japan, Korea, and Taiwan depended much less on immigration and foreign direct investment. This is also true of the South Asian economy, dominated by India, which opened later and still exports a meager proportion of its GDP.

Since the financial and economic collapse of the early 1980s, Latin America has embarked on a new cycle of globalization. The growth performance of the Latin American economies during the fourth globalization cycle has been generally disappointing, however. The late-twentieth-century globalization cycle is at such an early phase of its development that it could still be blocked by inertia or even reversed by a return to inward-looking pre-1982 strategies. Market pressures and elite policy preferences push toward globalization, but the political viability of elected governments that embrace globalization in the twenty-first century will depend critically on the magnitude and distribution of the costs and benefits.

Most of the major economies in Latin America did not embrace more open, market-oriented strategies until the mid-1980s or later. Those that globalized early, such as Chile, did not start growing rapidly until the mid-1980s anyway. Unfortunately, the countries that waited until after the 1982 crisis to change strategy did not experience a shift to high rates of sustained growth, though Argentina, Brazil, the Dominican Republic, and Mexico did achieve short-lived spurts of growth in the 1990s. In many countries globalization was hampered by incomplete reforms that stopped far short of using the external sector, and export growth in particular, as an engine to drive productivity advance.[3] Regional trade blocks, such as MERCOSUR or the reviving Central American Common Market, lacked the dynamism that closer ties to the vastly larger North American market might have provided.

Even though the Latin American economies have not managed to return to the high growth rates of the pre-1930 era, the overall twentieth-century performance of the major economies roughly matched the per-capita GDP growth rate of the United States (about 1.6 percent per annum for the century as a whole; see the estimates in Maddison 1994). This rate translates into an impressive and unprecedented quadrupling of GDP per capita in the past one hundred years. To put it differently, the major economies of this region had a GDP per capita equivalent to roughly one fourth the U.S. level in 1900 and in 2000 (Coatsworth 1998). The twentieth century thus ended with the Latin American economies facing exactly the same relative gap between their performance and that of the United States as they faced at the beginning.

THE COSTS OF GLOBALIZATION

The human costs of the first two globalization cycles were enormous. They included the death of over 90 percent of the Native American population and the kidnapping, enslavement, and forced migration of millions of Africans. The benefits of the improvements in productivity after the Spanish conquest did not reach the indigenous populations of the Americas, either because death occurred too swiftly or because the conquerors and their descendants imposed rules that concentrated the private gains in the hands of European and creole minorities. The same was true for the slave colonies, where mortality rates both in the Atlantic crossing and after arrival in the New World remained so high and fertility rates so low that the African-origin population of Latin America did not begin to grow by natural increase until after abolition.

It is true that the nutrition and longevity of indigenous populations born generations after the conquest and of the descendants of African slaves long after abolition were higher than before globalization in each case, but these later improvements scarcely compensate for the human cost of conquest and slavery. Moreover, the productivity gains achieved in the first two globalization cycles were exhausted once each cycle had run its course. By the early 1700s, the economic growth of the mainland colonies of Spain had ceased and did not resume until the third cycle began in the 1870s. In the slave plantation regions of the Americas (except for the United States), productivity changes turned negative once sugar prices began falling in the early nineteenth century. By this time, the main sugar economies had already stopped growing.

Historians and economists have debated for decades about the links, if any, between slave plantation agriculture and long-term economic retardation. Whatever the nature of those linkages may be, it is clear enough that neither slavery nor sugar cane cultivation contributed to economic growth or development in Brazil or the Caribbean in the long run. The much debated issue of how much, if at all, slavery contributed to the industrial revolution in Britain or the United States, in contrast, has now shifted back toward earlier views that assigned slavery and slave profits a significant and positive role. If this is true, then the separation between winners and losers in the second cycle of globalization is both temporal and geographic. The industrial revolution has never reached most of the former slave plantations zones of the Americas (Solow and Engerman 1987).

The human costs of the third cycle of globalization, between 1880 and 1930, as in earlier periods, were not negligible. These included a long list of human and environmental problems, ranging from the massive, unplanned, and unhealthy proliferation of urban settlements to massive air and water pollution, extensive deforestation, and the unregulated depletion of nonrenewable natural resources. The onset of export-led economic growth also produced a kind of inequality shock, from which the region has yet to recover. The first and most visible disaster occurred wherever economic growth, strong governments, and railroad construction came together in prolonged assaults on the traditional, sometimes undocumented property rights of indigenous villagers and poor peasants, from Mexico in the north to Bolivia in the south. Railroads opened vast tracts of land to profitable commercial exploitation (Coatsworth 1974). As formerly isolated but productive land became accessible, waves of usurpation by powerful outsiders, usually with local collaborators, hit region after region. The ownership of land, and thus of income from agriculture, became far more concentrated than ever before. In a number of countries, most notably Mexico, this abrupt redistribution of assets provoked political and social unrest. The Mexican Revolution began in western Chihuahua, where elite land grabbing inspired by railroad construction provoked the victims to take up arms (see Katz 1998; for a Brazilian example, see Diacon 1991).

A second dimension of this third-cycle inequality shock affected labor-scarce regions where export producers imposed and governments enforced coercive systems of forced labor, indenture, and even slavery to facilitate export production. These included the imposition of rural pass books and vagrancy statutes that permitted local authorities, in Cuba, Guatemala, and parts of the Andes, to force unwilling workers to labor on export plantations (Bauer 1979). In the henequen-growing areas of Mexico, new forms of slavery were introduced, abetted by the Díaz regime when it captured Yaqui Indian rebels in Sonora on the U.S. border and shipped them to Yucatán for sale on the docks to local planters (Wells 1985). Coercive forms of *enganche,* or indenture, also developed in southern Mexico, Central America, and parts of the Andes. Migration, population growth, and reforming governments helped to end such practices, but only after decades of abuse in many cases.

Third, industrial and mining development required ever larger or "lumpier" investments. Productivity and wages rose, but returns to scarce, often foreign capital rose faster. The wage gap between unskilled and skilled workers also tended to grow, as demand for the latter out-paced supply in the early decades of economic growth. This is a common feature of early growth spurts in many regions of the globe. In Latin America the migration of rural unskilled workers to the cities kept unskilled wages low. In some countries, notably Argentina, Brazil, Chile, and Uruguay, immigration from Europe tended to further dampen unskilled wage rates relative to skilled wages, though real wage levels in absolute terms increased.

Finally, the failure of many Latin American governments to invest adequately in the development of human resources also tended to exacerbate initially and then to prolong the income inequalities that still make this region the most unequal in the world.

Sustained economic growth from the 1870s to the 1920s did contribute to incremental improvements in all the conventional indicators of human development—longevity, health, education, and the like. Life expectancy in Latin American increased from less than forty years to over sixty-five in the late twentieth century. Infant mortality rates dropped from three hundred to four hundred per one thousand live births in 1900 to less than fifty. Illiteracy fell from over 80 to nearly 10 percent.[4] These achievements required substantial investments in human capital, made all the more difficult by rates of population growth that accelerated to peaks in the 1950s and 1960s in many countries. Nonetheless, progress in most countries of Latin America, particularly in nations historically divided by ethnicity and race, has lagged behind the region's economic capacities and the minimum requirements for modern economic progress. Part of the explanation for this historic failure probably lies in the relatively low cost of the skills and technology Latin America began importing at the end of the nineteenth century. Many liberal policy makers, whose ideological forebears had insisted a few decades before on education as crucial for national development, now looked to foreign investment and European immigration as the keys to economic modernization.

CONCLUSIONS: GLOBALIZATION AND EDUCATION

The three past cycles of globalization analyzed in this chapter all shared certain characteristics that also mark the contemporary globalization process. First, each cycle of globalization raised the productivity of the affected economies. Openness to external trade, capital, technology, ideas, and immigrants has usually promoted economic growth, while less integrated or closed economies have tended to grow more slowly. A second commonality is the tendency for tiny minorities—Spanish conquerors, slavocracies, export oligarchies, and foreign investors—to reap the lion's share of the short-term benefits of globalization. Third, all three past globalizations in Latin America coincided with a sharp decline in living standards for most people and a sharp rise in inequality. Finally, globalization cycles produced long-term benefits that eventually spread throughout entire societies. Only in the third of the three past globalizations, however, did improvements in living standards continue after the cycle itself had ended.

The contradictory history of the past cycles of globalization discussed in this chapter form part of a larger pattern of change in human societies. Advances in productivity, which are crucial for improving human welfare in the long run, often impose terrible human costs at first. This has been true not only in globalization cycles but in other periods of economic progress as dissimilar as the transition to sedentary agriculture from hunting and gathering, on one hand, and the first decades of the industrial revolution, on the other.

The profoundly contradictory history of past globalizations makes it crucial that policy makers, producers, citizens, and especially educators undertake conscious efforts to better understand and manage globalization processes in the future. This observation suggests at least three conclusions.

First, education can play an important role in managing the flow of immigrants into host societies. Past cycles, especially the third, provide valuable lessons. Third-cycle migratory flows provoked nationalist and even nativist reactions in many host countries. In both Argentina and the United States, for example, educational reformers at the turn of the twentieth century focused their attention on assimilating immigrant children through new primary school curricula emphasizing acquisition of basic skills in the dominant language and rote learning of appropriately uplifting national myths and symbols. Educating immigrant children as well as adults to become loyal citizens preoccupied education policy makers in the major host countries for decades.

While similar pressures have developed in the United States and Western Europe during the current, fourth cycle of globalization, new transport and communications technologies now make the repressive assimilationism of the early twentieth century impossible. Immigrants from Latin America to the United States, for example, communicate continuously with family and friends in their native countries, remit massive amounts of funds to support their families and communities, and return for visits far more frequently that ever before. The impact of immigrants on the United States (and Western Europe) is matched by the impact of these same migrants and former migrants on their home countries. In these circumstances, nativist calls for forced assimilation in schools, or in society at large, are doomed to failure.

As cheap travel and instantaneous communication allow more immigrants (and their offspring) to retain ties to their former homelands, the number of individuals who are affectively or legally transnational, with formal and emotional ties to more than one society, is likely to increase. In the era of belligerent and defensive nationalisms, "divided" (or worse yet, multiple) loyalties often seemed almost treasonous. In the twenty-first century, such qualities represent valuable human capital.

Second, the contemporary globalization cycle both produces and requires greater cross-cultural skills. Since travel and communication are now much less costly in comparison to wage and income levels, the intergenerational loss of linguistic, cultural, and social skills among immigrants and their descendants is rapidly diminishing. Once the graveyard of languages, the United States has experienced a resurgence of interest in "heritage" languages among third- and later-generation citizens. The loss of language and other skills among the immigrants themselves and their children is declining. At the same time, the demand for language instruction among nonimmigrants and the frequency of foreign travel by U.S. citizens is much greater than in the third cycle. The global marketplace now rewards those who maintain or acquire the capacity to "perform" in more than one cultural setting. Encouraging all students to recognize and value the intercultural sophistication that many immigrant children routinely display has already become an important pedagogical tool. Educators in K–12 schools need the flexibility to tailor the learning experience both to foster and to make maximum use of the cultural resources represented in each class.[5]

Third, education is enormously important in combating the inequalities that tend to be exacerbated by globalization processes. Educational historians and analysts continue to debate the effectiveness of education in raising students' productivity (and thus their wage levels) in the economy. Economists often argue that large-scale immigration of relatively unskilled workers tends to keep wages near the bottom of the income scale, but many also conclude that the overall impact (which includes lower inflation and longer periods of low unemployment) is positive. Most argue that education increases mobility in the job market. And education that includes completing a four-year college degree enhances lifetime earnings significantly. One of the few ways to reduce the inequality effects of globalization is to provide high-quality education to immigrants and the native born alike.

Despite all the best efforts of enlightened policy makers and educators, globalization will continue to impose costs and bestow benefits unequally and unfairly. Education is not the whole answer to this historically intractable problem, but it is a significant part of the answer.

NOTES

1. The dietary effects also appear to have been positive, though overdependence on corn in Italy and potatoes in Ireland caused severe problems well into the nineteenth century (see Crosby 1972, pp. 183–185; Warman 1988).

2. Cuban GDP per capita was only slightly higher in 1850 than in 1750 (Balbín et al. 1993; on Brazil see the estimates in Maddison 1994).

3. One measure of an economy's globalization is the ratio of exports to GDP. In Argentina and Brazil that ratio in 2001 still hovered between 5 and 10 percent. In Chile and Mexico the ratio stood at over 25 percent.

4. The Mexican case is typical (see Instituto Nacional de Estadística, Geografía e Informática 1985).

5. Needless to say, the imposition of standardized tests that force schools to follow rigid curricular guidelines undermines the capacity of schools to do this.

REFERENCES

Balbín, P. F., R. J. Salvucci, and L. K. Salvucci (1993). El caso cubano: exportación e independencia. In *La independencia Americana: consecuencias económicas*, L. Prados de la Escosura and S. Amaral, eds. Madrid: Alianza Universidad.

Bauer, A. J. (1979). Rural workers in Spanish America: Problems of peonage and oppression. *Hispanic American Historical Review* 59(1): 34–63.

Borah, W., and S. F. Cook (1971–79). *Essays in population history:* Vol. 3. Berkeley: University of California Press.

Bulmer-Thomas, V. (1994). *The economic history of Latin America since independence.* Cambridge, UK: Cambridge University Press.

Chevalier, F. (1970). *Land and society in colonial Mexico: The great hacienda.* Berkeley: University of California Press.

Coatsworth, J. H. (1974). Railroads, landholding and agrarian protest in the early Porfiriato. *Hispanic American Historical Review* 54(1): 48–71.

Coatsworth, J. H. (1998). Economic and institutional trajectories in nineteenth-century Latin America. In *Latin America and the world economy since 1800.* J. H. Coatsworth and A. M. Taylor, eds. Cambridge, MA: David Rockefeller Center for Latin American Studies and Harvard University Press.

Cook, N. B. (1998). *Born to die: Disease and New World conquest, 1492–1650.* Cambridge, UK: Cambridge University Press.

Crosby, A. W., Jr. (1972). *The Columbian exchange: Biological and cultural consequences of 1492.* Westport, CT: Greenwood Press.

Diacon, T. (1991). *Millenarian vision, capitalist reality: Brazil's Contestado Rebellion, 1912–16.* Durham: Duke University Press.

Diamond, J. (1997). *Guns, germs, and steel: The fates of human societies.* London: Jonathan Cape.

Deneven, W. M., ed. (1992). *The native population of the Americas in 1492.* 2d ed. Madison: University of Wisconsin Press.

Eltis, D. (1995). The total product of Barbados, 1664–1701. *Journal of Economic History* 55(2): 321–336.

Eltis, D. (2000). *The Rise of African slavery in the Americas.* Cambridge: Cambridge University Press.

Gibson, C. (1964). *The Aztecs under Spanish rule: A history of the Indians of the Valley of Mexico, 1519–1810.* Stanford, CA: Stanford University Press.

Higman, B. W. (1996). Economic and Social Development of the British West Indies, from Settlement to ca. 1850. In *The Cambridge Economic History of the United States.* S. L. Engerman and R. E. Gallman, eds. Cambridge, UK: Cambridge University Press.

Instituto Nacional de Estadística, Geografía e Informática (1985). *Estadísticas históricas de México:* Vol. 1. Mexico City.

Katz, F. (1998). *The life and times of Pancho Villa.* Stanford, CA: Stanford University Press.

Klein, H. (1986). *African slavery in Latin America and the Caribbean.* Oxford, UK: Oxford University Press.

Maddison, A. (1994). Explaining the economic convergence of nations, 1820–1989. In *Convergence of productivity: Cross-national studies and historical evidence.* W. J. Baumol, R. R. Nelson, and E. N. Wolff, eds. Oxford, UK: Oxford University Press.

Newson, L. A. (1985). Indian population patterns in colonial Spanish America. *Latin American Research Review* 20(3): 41–74.

O'Rourke, K. H., and J. G. Williamson. (1999). *Globalization and history: Evolution of a nineteenth-century Atlantic economy.* Cambridge, MA: MIT Press.

Schwartz, S. B. (1978). Indian labor and New World plantations: European demand and Indian responses in Northeastern Brazil. *American Historical Review* 83: 43–79.

Schwartz, S. B. (1985). *Sugar plantations in the formation of Brazilian society: Bahia, 1550–1835.* Cambridge, UK: Cambridge University Press.

Solow, B. L., and S. M. Engerman, eds. (1987). *British capitalism and Caribbean slavery: The Legacy of Eric Williams.* Cambridge, UK: Cambridge University Press.

Twomey, M. (1998). Patterns of Foreign Investment in Latin America in the Twentieth Century. In *Latin America and the world economy since 1800.* J. H. Coatsworth and A. M. Taylor, eds. Cambridge, MA: David Rockefeller Center for Latin American Studies and Harvard University Press.

Warman, A. (1988). *La historia de un bastardo, maiz y capitalismo.* Mexico: Instituto de Investigaciones Sociales, UNAM: Fondo de Cultura Economica.

Wells, A. (1985). *Yucatán's gilded age: Haciendas, Henequen and International Harvester, 1860–1915.* Albuquerque: University of New Mexico Press.

THREE

David E. Bloom

GLOBALIZATION AND EDUCATION

An Economic Perspective

INTRODUCTION

As much as the living are to the dead.

Aristotle, when asked how much educated
men were superior to those uneducated

The role of education in promoting development has been the subject of much discussion in recent decades. In 1948 the Universal Declaration of Human Rights proclaimed free and compulsory education to be a basic human right. In 1990 the World Conference on Education for All, held in Jomtien, Thailand, pledged to provide primary education for all by 2000; this pledge was reaffirmed in Dakar, Senegal, in 2000. In 2000 the United Nations Millennium Development Goals promised universal *completion* of primary education by 2015. And in 2002 the Plan of Implementation that emerged from the World Summit on Sustainable Development in Johannesburg highlighted the central role of education in promoting good health, environmental protection, and sustainable development.

Much progress has been made in implementing these international commitments. Many developing countries can now boast 100 percent primary school enrollment rates, and access to secondary education has risen sharply in most areas. However, 113 million primary school–aged children (nearly all of them in developing countries) remained out of school in 2000 (Bloom and Cohen 2002), and improvements in enrollment rates have not always been matched by advances in educational quality.

In today's globalizing world the governments of developing countries are faced with a plethora of demands on their time and resources. Managing debt burdens, dealing with international donors and financial institutions, tackling health crises such as HIV-AIDS and tuberculosis, protecting the environment, and promoting domestic industry to help producers penetrate export markets are just a few of the major issues landing daily on policy makers' desks. Developing an integrated set of priorities in a rapidly changing economic environment is becoming increasingly complex.

Education has the potential to make these tasks easier in a number of ways. First, a strong educational system can help create a deep pool of resources from which competent policy makers will emerge. The ability to grasp, absorb, and select from a large number of facts; aptitude for flexible, creative thinking; skills in working with others to achieve goals; and a determination to get results all can be developed by a good education. Second, education has powerful effects on human development—weak human capabilities are the source of many of the problems policy makers are confronted with. Knowledge promotes health-seeking behavior and good health, not to mention good doctors and medical staff. It can also help improve women's status in society. Poverty, too, is easier to escape if people can learn new skills and work productively with others. And third, economic development in a global market is easier if a country's workforce both is productive and has the mental agility to retrain for new industries as old ones become defunct and new opportunities arise.

This chapter looks at the links between education and economic development in a globalizing world. The first part of the chapter will outline a historical perspective on economic development and education. The second part will focus more narrowly on the process of globalization, assessing its benefits and the problems it brings and looking at it from the perspective of the developing country. Part three will assess the state of education in the developing world. As we will see, primary education has spread widely in many areas. But while enrollment rates have risen, quality remains inconsistent, and secondary education enrollment lags far behind. The fourth part of the chapter summarizes the reasons for the growing importance of education in today's globalizing world and examines the special pressures globalization is exerting on educational systems. The final part will outline some of the challenges and opportunities facing education in developing countries in the light of globalization. If developing countries are to begin to catch up with developed economies, an effective response will be critical.

HISTORICAL PERSPECTIVES

Why are some countries richer than others? This is one of the oldest questions in the field of economics. Adam Smith's *The Wealth of Nations,* published in 1776, both posed the question and provided one of the most resonant and enduring responses. Smith's answer focused on the accumulation of physical capital (including tools, equipment, factories, and infrastructure to make better use of natural resources) and technology. Investment in physical capital, Smith argued, would lead to improved productivity and income growth. Increased division of labor and greater specialization, moreover, would boost trade between individuals, firms, and countries.

Current statistics show, however, that income differences across countries are larger than capital and technology differences. Factors beyond those Smith described, therefore, also appear to be at work. In the early 1950s, the economist T. W. Schultz expanded the concept of capital to include human capital, which represents the skills acquired by people through education, training, and on-the-job learning. This broader notion of capital helped explain more of the income differences between countries, but it, too, did not offer a complete explanation.

In the 1970s the idea of endogenous economic growth gained prominence, introducing the notion of feedback between income and capital accumulation. As Smith suggested, capital accumulation leads to income growth. But the reverse is also true. As incomes grow, people and firms have more money to invest in capital and technology. This investment leads to further income growth. Endogenous growth creates the possibility that small initial capital differences could magnify the size of small initial income differences, which would in turn further widen the capital differences. This idea explains yet more of the variation across countries in income per capita, although significant disparities nevertheless remain.

In recent years, of course, globalization (which is really an old phenomenon)[1] has come to center stage. Smith himself perceived the benefits of international economic integration, positing that trade was essential to increasing the division of labor and, as a consequence, to promoting economic growth. "As it is the power of exchanging that gives occasion to the division of labor," he wrote, "so the extent of this division must always be limited by the extent of that power, or, in other words, by the extent of the market." London and Calcutta, he continued, "carry on a very considerable commerce with each other, and by mutually affording a market, give a good deal of encouragement to each other's industry" (Smith 1776, pp. 121, 123). By expanding the market, globalization therefore provides incentives for greater refinement and division of labor and for further trade.

Globalization refers to the process whereby countries become more integrated via movements of goods, capital, labor, and ideas. International trade and capital mobility are the main channels through which globalization is occurring. Globalization is changing the basis of the world economy from industry to knowledge. The success of East Asia, largely built on international trade, has prompted many, including the World Bank and the International Monetary Fund, to argue that global integration is key to reducing the income differentials between countries. As we will see, this view is controversial, but there is no doubt that it has been extremely influential in the past two decades.

International migration is an important aspect of globalization that has once again come to the fore. A recent United Nations report (United Nations Population Division 2002) estimates that 175 million people are now living in countries other than where they were born, with 40 percent of these living in developing countries. The presence of large immigrant populations requires a sensitive and effective response from school systems, so that these populations can quickly gain the skills that are increasingly valued in a globalized economy. In highlighting both the identity conflicts and the broader concerns that arise in first- and second-generation immigrants, Carola Suárez-Orozco (2002) implicitly reminds us that revamped education systems will need to take careful account of immigrants' situations. Of significant importance, too, are the "social remittances" that immigrants send to their home countries (Levitt 1996).

The importance of both globalization and education to understanding economic performance has long been recognized by economists. Policy makers' interest in the two areas has been uneven, however. In the last century, some countries (particularly those in East Asia) opened up their economies to world trade, while others (for example, Russia, Eastern European countries, Burma, and China) closed them. Some invested in education, but some could not afford to or chose not to. Still others perceived an educated populace as a threat to their power. In the next two sections, we will look at globalization and education and assess their role in promoting development.

THE PROCESS OF GLOBALIZATION

Global integration has been facilitated by a number of measures adopted by a sufficient number of countries to form a critical mass. Tariffs and quotas on imports have been reduced. Barriers to capital mobility have been lowered. State-owned industries have been privatized and foreign firms allowed to invest in them. Regional and global alliances and agreements, from the European Union (EU) to the World Trade Organization, have worked to increase trade between countries by lowering tariffs, restricting countries' abilities to shelter domestic industries, relaxing border controls, and in the case of the EU, creating a unified currency. The growth of the Internet, falling transport costs, and improvements in telecommunications have also helped speed up global integration. Ideas can now spread more quickly and deals can be more swiftly closed.

Globalization offers great potential for developing-country economies. As East Asia has shown, integration with the global economy can broaden markets and allow nations to become richer through exports. Faster and cheaper transport and communication reduce the cost of both exports and imports, so industries can import the technology and tools they need to upgrade their own products and move into higher-value, more dynamic areas. East Asia's economies began by exporting low-value, labor-intensive goods such as toys and textiles.

They invested the profits in upgrading the physical and human capital at their disposal and are now exporting high-value goods such as cars, semiconductors, and household appliances. Quality of life improvements in the region have been unprecedented (Bloom, Rosenberg, Weston, and Steven 2002).

Globalization has also increased the global pool of foreign direct investment (FDI), which offers further opportunities for countries to improve productivity and expand their industrial capacity. Foreign firms can create jobs; import new technology, knowledge, and skills; and provide business to local suppliers. FDI has been important for many developing countries. India's thriving software industry has been driven partly by FDI from firms like Sun Microsystems, Microsoft, and Intel, which, attracted by India's well-educated, inexpensive labor force, have invested substantial resources in the now booming cities of Bangalore and Hyderabad.

East Asia and, more recently, India, China, and some parts of Eastern Europe have benefited greatly from globalization, but other regions have suffered. Inequality between countries is rising, with the World Bank estimating that more than half of poor countries lost ground to the United States (the world's biggest economy) between 1985 and 1997 (World Bank 1999). Less than a quarter narrowed the gap. Increasing inequality has led to concerns that the process of globalization is now favoring rich countries rather than poor. Violent demonstrations in Seattle, Genoa, and London and more peaceful protests at the World Summit on Sustainable Development in Johannesburg have pushed these concerns onto policy makers' radar screens.

Many of these concerns are legitimate. The benefits of globalization *have* gone disproportionately to wealthy countries. Poverty in some areas *is* increasing. Africa in particular has suffered: the region's economic growth was negative in the 1990s; foreign debt equals about 80 percent of its GDP; and the continent's trade accounts for just 2 percent of the world total, whereas its share of the world's population is 10 percent (Bloom, Weston, and Steven 2002). Even within rich countries, many people have reason to be unhappy. Global trade means industries often have to compete with cheaper products produced elsewhere, which can lead to business closures and job losses. While this potentially provides benefits to workers in countries where labor is cheap, low-skilled workers in rich countries inevitably suffer. The determination of U.S. steelworkers and European farmers to keep their industries from being opened up to global competition shows that resistance to globalization is not limited to international nongovernmental organizations and developing countries.

Perceptions of the unfairness of globalization could eventually become a threat to global integration itself. Already, countries such as Zimbabwe, where liberalization of the economy in the early 1990s did not have the desired effect, have reverted to protecting some of their industries (Bloom, Weston, and Steven, 2002). And it is likely that resentment over rising inequality is one of the factors behind the increasing turbulence in much of the Muslim world: although global barriers to the movement of goods and capital have been lowered, labor mobility has become, if anything, more difficult in recent years. With many young people forced to remain in struggling countries where job opportunities are scarce, the risk that unemployment will lead to unrest grows.

The international policy community has begun to acknowledge the concerns over globalization. The Millennium Development Goals focus on reducing poverty via the channels of education, health care, and reduced gender inequality. Debt relief is under way in many countries. The World Summit on Sustainable Development in August 2002 endorsed the New Partnership for Africa's Development, drawn up by African leaders as a road map out of the continent's troubles. However, more will be needed than international agreements. Poverty and inequality must be tackled from the grass roots, and education provides one tool for addressing these problems.

THE STATE OF EDUCATION

Global income inequality is mirrored by global inequality in education. Obviously, primary and secondary education is both more readily available and generally of better quality in developed countries. As the human development answer to Adam Smith's question suggests, educational differences exacerbate the economic differences between countries. The economist Amartya Sen, whose thinking has been instrumental in advancing the human development argument, has suggested that the economic success of Japan in the last 150 years was driven by the nation's focus on expanding education before economic development was under way. The contrasting fortunes of China and India add further weight to this theory. On one hand, India's "massive negligence of school education," Sen argues, meant that the country was ill prepared for economic expansion.[2] The spectacular success of China's economy, on the other hand, since it turned to a more market-oriented system in 1979, was built on a highly literate population nurtured by a strong basic education system (Sen 1999, pp. 42–43). The success of Ireland, too, in the last decade has been partly founded on its early and deep commitment to education.

This section looks first at primary education, then at secondary education. The third of the United Nations' Millennium Development Goals focuses on primary schooling. By 2015, the goal promises, "all children everywhere will be able to complete a full course of primary education" (World Bank Group 2000; the goals make no mention of secondary education).

As Figure 3.1, taken from the Millenium Development Goals Web site, shows, progress toward universal primary school enrollment is patchy. Central Asia and Latin America have seen impressive rises in attendance rates since 1990. Progress in South Asia and Africa, in contrast, has been much slower. Absolute enrollment rates, moreover, vary widely between continents. Rates of around 60 percent in sub-Saharan Africa compare unfavorably with the average for high-income countries of over 95 percent. Although the gap here is narrowing, which may have long-term positive effects on economic differences, the gap between South Asia and Latin America has actually increased in recent years.

Differences in quality of education are also wide but are difficult to measure. *Completing* primary schooling is certainly key, however, and the third Millennium Development Goal aims to ensure that all children do so. As Figure 3.2 shows, Africa and Asia are by no means certain to reach the completion target. The world's poorest regions—sub-Saharan Africa and South Asia—have the most ground to make up. According to the United Nations, seventy-six developing countries have enough schools to educate all primary school–age children, but only

East Asia & Pacific

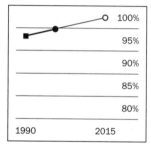

Europe & Central Asia

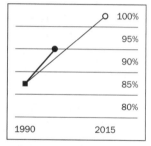

Latin America & the Caribbean

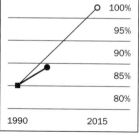

Middle East & North Africa

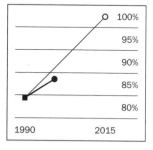

South Asia

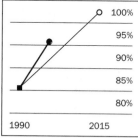

Sub-Saharan Africa

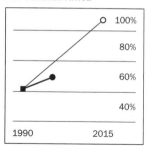

High-Income countries

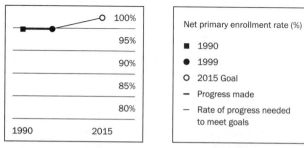

Net primary enrollment rate (%)

■ 1990

● 1999

○ 2015 Goal

— Progress made

— Rate of progress needed
    to meet goals

Figure 3.1. Uneven progress toward universal enrollment in primary schools. (*Global Economic Prospects,* cited in World Bank Group, Millennium Development Goals, www.developmentgoals.org [accessed September 15, 2003].)

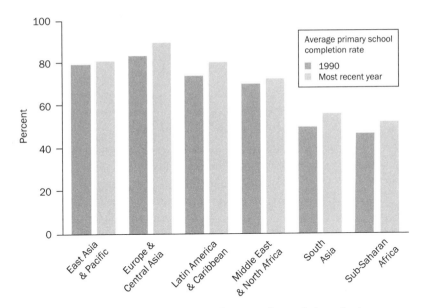

Figure 3.2. Slow progress toward universal completion of primary schooling. World Bank Group, Millennium Development Goals.

twenty-seven of those keep all their pupils for the duration of the course. More alarmingly, some countries have seen declines in completion rates (World Bank Group 2000).

Literacy rates offer some encouraging signs that quality has improved, though there are wide gender disparities. Table 3.1 shows wide gender differences in all areas outside Europe, Central Asia, and Latin America. Even East Asia, a development success story, has far more literate men than women. Again, the poorest regions fare the worst, although improvements in recent decades have been significant.

While primary enrollment has improved, then, consistency and quality remain low in many places. Rote learning, outdated curricula, unmotivated teachers, and infrastructure difficulties are just a few of the problems besetting educational systems in developing countries. We know, moreover, that primary education alone is insufficient in today's economy. A recent report by the World Bank/UNESCO Task Force on Higher Education and Society suggested that "higher education is to a knowledge economy as primary education is to an agrarian economy and secondary education is to an industrial economy" (Task Force on

Table 3.1 MALE AND FEMALE
ADULT LITERACY RATES

	Literacy Rate, Adult Male (% of males aged 15 and older)			
	1970	*1980*	*1990*	*1999*
East Asia & Pacific	69	80	87	92
Europe & Central Asia	95	97	98	98
Latin America & Caribbean	77	82	86	89
Middle East & North Africa	44	56	67	75
South Asia	45	52	59	66
Sub-Saharan Africa	39	49	60	69

	Literacy Rate, Adult Female (% of females aged 15 and older)			
	1970	*1980*	*1990*	*1999*
East Asia & Pacific	42	57	71	78
Europe & Central Asia	90	92	94	95
Latin America & Caribbean	70	77	83	87
Middle East & North Africa	17	28	41	53
South Asia	18	25	34	42
Sub-Saharan Africa	18	28	40	53

SOURCE: World Bank, *World Development Indicators*, 2001. Washington, DC.

Higher Education and Society 2000). Although globalization is advancing some developing countries toward industrialization and still others toward knowledge-based industries, many still fit the description of agrarian economies. If the predominantly agrarian countries are to progress from that state, they need to invest in secondary and tertiary, as well as primary, education.

Secondary education in developing countries is even weaker than primary schooling. According to a recent UNICEF report (UNICEF 2002), only around half of secondary school–aged children in developing countries are enrolled in secondary education. In the least-developed countries, less than a quarter are enrolled. Again, gender disparities are huge in some areas: South Asia has 52 percent of its boys in secondary education but only 33 percent of girls. In the Middle East and North Africa, rates are 64 percent and 55 percent, respectively. Sub-Saharan Africa is struggling to get both boys and girls into secondary school—

Table 3.2 AVERAGE YEARS OF SCHOOLING
IN POPULATIONS OVER AGE TWENTY-FIVE

	1960	2000
All Developing Countries	1.8	4.9
Middle East & North Africa	1.1	5.1
Sub-Saharan Africa	1.4	3.8
Latin America & Caribbean	3.1	5.7
East Asia & Pacific	2.3	6.5
South Asia	1.3	4.2
Advanced Countries	7.0	9.8
Transitional Economies	7.2	10.0

SOURCE: Barro, R. J., and J.-W. Lee. (2000). *International data on educational attainment: Updates and implications.* National Bureau of Economic Research working paper series. no. 7911. Table 3.

28 percent of boys and just 22 percent of girls are enrolled. Enrollment rates are rising, fast in some areas, but the developing world lags far behind industrialized countries.

While data on completion rates in secondary education are patchy, those on the number of years children attend school are available and are presented in Table 3.2. Between 1960 and 2000 high-income countries and what came to be known as "transitional economies" built on an already high average. The developing country average, meanwhile, more than doubled over the forty-year period but remained low, at just 4.9 years. Sub-Saharan Africa and South Asia are the most underperforming regions, with averages of 3.8 and 4.2 years, respectively.[3]

Basic education, then, shows wide variations across the world. Although much progress has been made, particularly in primary education, the poorest areas—South Asia and sub-Saharan Africa—have the worst educational records. Moreover, differences between rich and poor are growing.

Demographic trends are likely to make catching up even more difficult. Although UN projections include few dramatic changes in the global school-age population over the next half century as a whole, they predict large increases in the countries that can least afford it (Bloom and Cohen 2002). The school-age population in the least-developed countries will grow by 71 percent between 1995 and 2030. Based on enrollment statistics alone, if universal primary education is to be achieved by 2015, primary schools in developing countries will have an estimated 170 million more children to absorb than in 2000—an increase of nearly a third (Bloom and Cohen 2002). Sub-Saharan Africa and South Asia, the two regions with the lowest current enrollment figures, will account for over 80 percent of this increase.

In the face of these demographic realities, the task of increasing access will be daunting. Although many developing countries have the schools to educate many more children than they currently do, most are nevertheless failing to provide a full course of either primary or secondary education. Policy makers must focus on increasing access to education—and improving educational quality—at all levels, and on promoting incentives for students to complete their schooling.

WHY EDUCATION IS MORE IMPORTANT THAN EVER

The opportunities and the threats posed by global integration place a premium on education via three main channels.

The first channel enables students, and ultimately nations, to operate more effectively in the increasingly competitive global economy. Competing in global markets and attracting foreign investment require high productivity, as well as the flexibility to use new technology to upgrade to higher-value goods and services. Education both raises people's productivity and provides a foundation for rapid technological change. It also nurtures creativity and the generation of new ideas. Each year of schooling in developing countries is thought to raise individuals' earning power, which is closely linked to productivity, by about 10 percent (Sperling 2001; Psacharopoulos and Patrinos 2002). East Asia's well-educated populations were able to continually improve productivity while maintaining the flexibility to diversify production and move up the export value chain.

The second channel lies in bringing nations closer together and increasing the importance of cross-national communication. Increased trade and international mobility mean countries are becoming ever more interdependent, economically, socially, and politically. Interaction with people from other countries and cultures is becoming more common in many fields. As Suárez-Orozco and Gardner (2002) have argued,

Children growing up today will need to develop—arguably more than in any generation in human history—the higher order cognitive and inter-personal skills to learn, to work, and to live with others, which are increasingly likely to be of very different racial, religious, linguistic, and cultural backgrounds.

And Henry Jenkins (this volume) points out that widespread cross-cultural interchange, taking place at many levels of society, creates a "teachable moment" that allows students to reflect on other cultures and on the view of other cultures that global capitalism both provides and distorts.

A good education promotes a nonparochial attitude, facilitates communication and understanding, and encourages people to broaden their knowledge and their experiences—all of which can speed up the process of globalization. Children need to develop the knowledge and skills to deal with issues that go beyond their countries' borders and their everyday existence—such as environmental degradation, international migration, and international security.

The third channel through which globalization affects education is the increasing speed of change. New skills are required if people are to respond to new threats and new opportunities. Increased mobility and trade mean a higher rate of transmission of infectious diseases, which can threaten economic growth. Diseases like HIV-AIDS, for example, can have serious economic consequences if allowed to get out of control, as well as hindering poverty reduction efforts even in low-prevalence countries (Bloom, River Path Associates, and Sevilla 2002). Education is a key determinant of health status and the best inhibitor of HIV transmission. In general, better-educated people are much more aware of the risks of HIV-AIDS and partake in less risky behavior than do less educated people. Conversely, diseases such as HIV-AIDS impede the schooling of many children. Families affected by the disease sometimes have to withdraw children from school to care for sick relatives, conserve household resources, or earn additional income. HIV-AIDS is an expensive illness to treat and it reduces people's ability to work; it therefore makes families poorer and less able to invest in their children's education. Efforts to increase the quantity of education, then, may be hampered by the vicious spiral triggered by AIDS.

Increases in trade also test societies' tolerance levels and can threaten social stability. By their nature, programs to open up economies generally increase the volume of imports into a country. This exposes the domestic industries that are uncompetitive, causing them to lay off workers. The tariffs recently imposed by the United States on steel imports are an attempt to protect its uncompetitive steel industries, which are threatened by more cheaply produced steel made elsewhere. Retraining programs are clearly vital for steelworkers laid off as a result of increased global competition. A strong education in childhood, however, that equips people with the cognitive skills necessary to quickly picking up new tasks and adjusting to new jobs will put future workers in a stronger position to cope with the structural changes that many economies will experience in conjunction with ongoing globalization processes (Bloom, River Path Associates, and Sevilla 2002).

Education by itself is not sufficient for economic development, but it is in most cases necessary. Although Cuba and Kerala, India, have shown that strong education systems do not always promote economic growth, in most cases only countries with vast mineral deposits have enjoyed rapid income growth without a well-educated populace. Neither is integration into the global economy sufficient for growth. Jamaica, for example, has both a well-educated population and an open economic policy. It does not, however, have a flourishing economy (Bloom, Rosenberg, et al. 2002). Many other countries, such as Malawi and Zimbabwe, have seen declines in economic performance since they opened up to global markets.

The United Nations Conference on Trade and Development and UN Development Program's Global Program on Globalization, Liberalization, and Sustainable Human Development highlight the importance of adopting a balanced approach to development (Agosín, Bloom, and Gitli 2002). Countries that have liberalized in recent decades without simultaneously paying attention to human development and growth promotion policies have performed disappointingly. Indeed, in many cases their economies have shrunk and poverty rates increased (Agosín, Bloom, and Gitli 2002).

The Global Program advocates instead a "three spheres" approach to development (see Figure 3.3), in which a balanced approach to the three areas of liberalization, economic growth, and human and social

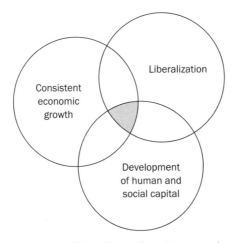

Figure 3.3. The "three spheres" approach to development proposed by the Global Program on Globalization, Liberalization, and Sustainable Human Development.

capital development replaces a focus on liberalization alone. Proactive policies, the program argues, are needed in each of the three spheres if positive results are to be achieved. Policy makers should attempt to trigger virtuous development spirals in which actions in one sphere set off beneficial effects in others.

The human and social capital development sphere is critical. Human development, in which education plays such a central role, is the fundamental goal of the development process. But it is also a vital *means* to broader development and economic growth. Strategic action to promote improvement in human capabilities is likely to enhance economic growth and liberalization.

Education is clearly a strong trigger for virtuous development spirals. Education promotes income growth, which in turn promotes further investment in education. The spirals catalyzed by education are interrelated with those sparked by globalization. Globalization, as we have seen, encourages specialization and thus greater earning opportunities. A well-educated population can speed up specialization and increase income gains. Those countries that take advantage of the opportunities offered by globalization and education for rapid growth are the ones most likely to succeed.

Globalization, then, is increasing the importance of education. The increasing competitiveness of the world economy, the growing interdependence of countries, and the strengthening links between human development and economic growth all mean education is coming to the fore. The final section of the chapter will outline some of the new challenges and opportunities offered by globalization to developing countries' educational systems.

CHALLENGES AND OPPORTUNITIES

Globalization poses many challenges for education but also creates new opportunities. This section addresses the major challenge of increasing educational quality and outlines some opportunities technology provides for addressing this challenge.

Demand for education is growing. Realizing that success in today's economy depends greatly on an individual's education, more and more parents are sending their children to school. Urbanization, which is increasing in many countries as families move to cities to take advantage of greater economic opportunities, means that children are less often needed to work in agriculture, in most cases making them more available for schooling. Demographic trends, moreover, promise to expand the absolute numbers of children who need to be educated.

Expansion of education threatens to dilute its quality. Already, rote learning and a lack of well-qualified teachers mean many children receive only the rudiments of an education. But with more children enrolling in school and schoolteacher numbers failing to keep up, greater resources to pay and train teachers, along with more efficient use of existing resources, will be essential to maintaining and improving standards. Countries must strike a balance between improvements in quality and quantity. A study in Tamil Nadu, India, for example, found that while enrollment rates in primary and secondary school rose by 35 percentage points from 1977 to 1992, teacher numbers rose by just 4 percent (Duraisamy, James, Lane, and Tan 1997). Good facilities, from books to buildings, are important for improving quality. But effective people are even more crucial: teacher salaries and training should be at the center of educational reform efforts, since success in reversing the brain drain of developing-country teachers is contingent on improved working conditions.

Governments attempting to improve quality also need to consider curriculum reform. One of the goals of modern education must be to help individuals see where they fit into the world. Communities and nations are still important, but awareness of global society is also needed. In an increasingly globalized economy, everyone's actions have effects on others, and responsibility for one's actions now extends beyond the local community and beyond national borders. The effects of many environmental problems, for example, are felt across the globe, even if the source of those problems is limited to a small area. Understanding these new realities is a first step to improving them— and education plays a vital role in creating this understanding at an early age.

Curricula in many countries have failed to keep pace with the changes brought about by globalization. There are a number of reasons for this, including limited resources, low numbers of teacher, time pressures on educators, and entrenched work practices. Curriculum designers face the ongoing challenge of adapting course content to a society's needs. For example, increased international communication increases the need not only for global awareness but for language skills as well. At the same time, domestic issues, from infectious diseases to environmental hazards to sustainable use of natural resources, are constantly changing and are very often country specific. Lessons from other countries can bolster developing-world educational systems, but maintaining and nurturing local knowledge, and strengthening local cultures, is also critical for addressing a country's needs. In the face of globalization-induced curricular homogenization, Suzanne Grant Lewis has emphasized the importance of maintaining the ability of local and national communities to bolster and validate "local knowledge," local languages, and local culture. A common model for education throughout the world would make such attention challenging, to say the least.[4]

Involving multiple stakeholders—including teachers, parents, and businesses—in framing curricula can provide an important forum for assessing what children should learn. And learning from curriculum reform implemented elsewhere—taking advantage of the opportunities for international knowledge sharing facilitated by globalization—can help educators avoid pitfalls and adapt new approaches.

The need to improve quality has sometimes interacted with increased globalization by creating the possibility that foreign corporations might play a significant role in running the schools in a developing country. The motivations for such a change could be benign and, indeed, beneficial: a poor country can benefit from close contact with developed-world practices. Just as likely, however, are the downsides that this phenomenon could present: that foreign investors will be seeking short-term profits and that their interests will clash with the host country's. A broader concern relates to the international homogenization of culture and language that may be further abetted by foreign participation in a country's education system.[5]

The technological improvements that globalization has accelerated present opportunities for improving quality. Improved communications, for example, can facilitate knowledge transfer between countries and between schools. Policy makers can therefore learn from experiences elsewhere, and teachers can garner knowledge from others. Use of online teaching materials and lesson plans can help ease teachers' workload. Teaching via audio and video, gathering knowledge via the Internet, and collective problem solving using online tools offer great potential for creating enthusiasm among both students and teachers.[6]

Technology can also boost the quantity of education. Online teaching materials or videoconferencing facilities can help increase access to education without diluting quality, reaching people who live far from the nearest school. Satellite schools, where students watch and interact in lessons delivered in the school at the hub of a network, also offer potential for improving access—combining use of new technology with human interaction provides a solid grounding for participation in a globalized economy. The Plan of Implementation from the August 2002 World Summit on Sustainable Development highlighted the urgency for developing countries to connect to the Internet. Clearly, as the plan acknowledges, providing reliable sources of electricity and then installing computers is an expensive and lengthy process for many developing countries, but the Internet may offer a cost-effective means of compensating for a lack of qualified teachers. If it does, it will end up saving rather than costing money.

In short, globalization brings with it both opportunities and threats. Countries must endeavor to use the former to counter the latter. Both the promise and the problems can best be addressed by an educated citizenry at the national level. Policy makers should therefore attempt to promote virtuous spirals, in which investment in education creates a pool of knowledgeable, skilled individuals who are able to make the most of the benefits while tackling the threats. In bringing educational systems up toward the levels of the developed world, long-term, consistent, and focused efforts will be needed.

CONCLUSIONS

Education is a vital factor in determining a country's wealth. The extent of integration into the global economy is also important. The combination of education and globalization can be extremely powerful. Companies that build on a well-educated workforce to trade successfully in global markets can act as a powerful spur to economic development.

Much has been achieved in promoting access to education across the world. But if countries are to benefit from the many opportunities offered by globalization while avoiding the threats, much work remains to be done. Quality should be at the forefront of educators' plans, but increased quantity of education is also essential.

In today's globalized economy, primary education is insufficient for robust and sustained economic development. The economic opportunities of globalization come with new and increasingly complex economic and welfare problems. The solutions to these problems require an informed citizenry and a strong technical base. A drive for improving and expanding secondary education is therefore the next big challenge. Many countries, particularly in Latin America and Central Asia, have shown that rapid progress can be made. A renewed focus is needed if the lagging areas are to catch up.

NOTES

The author is grateful to David Canning, Joel Cohen, Howard Gardner, Suzanne Grant Lewis, Martin Malin, Larry Rosenberg, Marcelo Suárez-Orozco, Mark Weston, and participants in the Harvard-Ross Seminar on Education for Globalization for many helpful discussions and comments.

1. There have been previous surges of global interconnectedness, most recently in the Belle Epoque, from 1880 to 1930. These periods led to increases in inequality. For a review of such cycles in relation to growth and equality, see Coatsworth, this volume.

2. India's successful software industry has been built on the strength of its tertiary educational systems rather than primary and secondary schooling.

3. These data do not show how completion rates may have changed in recent years. Since the data in the table characterize all adults over age twenty-five, they would not reveal whether there had been recent changes, even if they were substantial.

4. Based on comments at October 2002 seminar, Harvard Graduate School of Education.

5. James L. Watson (this volume) offers a fascinating world tour showing the dissemination and transformative power of U.S. culture. In addition, his description of the extent to which the accoutrements of "modern" life have reached working-class people and some segments of rural societies has clear links to the parallel issues that arise in redesigning the education systems of developing countries.

6. Sherry Turkle (this volume) presents a cautionary analysis of students' use of computer programs, from PowerPoint to computer games, noting some of the generally unseen constraints that these global technologies may be imposing on minds throughout the world.

REFERENCES

Agosín, M., D. E. Bloom, and E. Gitli (2002). Globalization, liberalization and sustainable human development: Analytical perspectives. Geneva: United Nations Conference on Trade and Development/UN Development Program (UNCTAD/UNDP). Draft available at http://www.unctad.org/en/docs/poedmm125.en.pdf.

Bloom, D. E., and J. E. Cohen (2002). Education for all: The unfinished revolution. *Daedalus* (summer): 84–95.

Bloom, D. E., River Path Associates, and J. Sevilla (2002). Health, wealth, AIDS and poverty. Manila: Asian Development Bank. http://www.adb.org/Documents/Reports/Health_Wealth/Default.asp.

Bloom, D. E., M. Weston, and D. Steven (2002). Continental drift: Globalization, liberalization and sustainable human development in sub-Saharan Africa. In *Making global integration work for poor people*. M. Agosín, D. E. Bloom, G. Chapelier, and J. Saigal, eds. Geneva: UNCTAD/UNDP.

Bloom, D., L. Rosenberg, M. Weston, and D. Steven (2002). Economic growth, liberalization and sustainable human development in Asia: Learning from the miracle workers. In *Making global integration work for poor people*. M. Agosín, D. E. Bloom, G. Chapelier, and J. Saigal, eds. Geneva: UNCTAD/UNDP.

Levitt, P. (1996). Social remittances: A conceptual tool for understanding migration and development. Harvard Center for Population and Development Studies. Working paper series no. 96.04. October.

Psacharopoulos, G., and H. Patrinos (2002). *Returns to investment in education: A further update.* Policy Research Working Papers. Washington, DC: World Bank.

Sen, A. (1999). *Development as freedom.* Oxford, England: Oxford University Press.

Sperling, G. (2001). Educating the world. *New York Times,* November 22.

Smith, A. (1776). *The wealth of nations.* London: Penguin Books.

Suárez-Orozco, C. (2002). Globalization and immigration: The role of social mirroring in the remaking of identity. Paper presented at Harvard-Ross Seminar on Education for Globalization, Harvard Graduate School of Education, Cambridge, MA, October.

Suárez-Orozco, M., and H. Gardner (2002). Education for globalization. Working paper presented at Pocantico Conference, Tarrytown, NY, April.

Task Force on Higher Education and Society (2000). Higher education in developing countries: Peril and promise. Washington, DC: World Bank.

UNICEF (2002). *The state of the world's children 2002.* Geneva.

United Nations Population Division (2002). International migration 2002. October. Press release available at http://www.un.org/esa/population/publications/ittmig2002/press-release-eng.htm.

World Bank (1999). *World development indicators, 1999.* Washington, DC.

World Bank Group (2000). Millennium Development Goals. http://www.developmentgoals.org.

FOUR

Antonio M. Battro

DIGITAL SKILLS, GLOBALIZATION, AND EDUCATION

INTRODUCTION

We are entering a new stage of the history of education. Our challenge today is to educate millions of children and adults with diverse needs in different locales, and we do not know how to face such a qualitative change of scale. Education as a process is "scale-sensitive." For example, every teacher knows that there is a limit to the number of students she can handle; a reduced seminar is much better than a large class, that learning disabled children benefit more from personalized tutoring, that there is an optimum in the physical size of the classroom, that simultaneous translation in a very large audience is not always the best way to communicate, and that videoconferences are more effective for small groups than for a large class. We must understand these limitations in order to cope with the massive change of scale, not only for better administration of resources but also for better education for all. In a sense, the education of future generations will entail trade-offs not only between quality and quantity but also between global and local issues. Information and communication technologies may come to the rescue of some of these problems. The good news is that these technologies are surprisingly well suited to our developing brains and minds, in the most diverse settings and cultures. In this chapter I analyze some of the psychophysical reasons of this remarkable fact, the neurocognitive foundations of the digital skills.

THE CLICK OPTION, THE UNIVERSAL BASIS OF THE DIGITAL SKILLS

My thesis is that the impressive global impact of digital technologies on human society, and particularly on education, is related to the universal capacity of the mind/brain to make very simple decisions. *The ability to decide to produce a simple change of state in a system* is what I call the *click option.* The procedures for expressing a click option can be extremely varied, but the result is always the same: a voluntary change of state in some artificial system (yes/no, on/off, 1/o) as the result of a personal decision, the outcome of a desire, wish, impulse, or simple reaction. Such systems or artifacts have evolved from simple machines activated by a mechanical trigger to the modern computer capable of responding to all sorts of actions, from the artificial traps used by hunter-gatherers to the handheld wireless computers of today.

We need to develop a network of increasingly complex *skills* in order to participate in the global digital network. Kurt W. Fischer and Thomas R. Bidell (1998) define *skill* as "the capacity to act in an organized way in a specific context" (Fischer & Bidell 1998, p. 478). Furthermore, "skills are both action-based and context-specific" and are "culturally defined" (p. 479). Like other human skills, digital skills develop "not only through self-regulation but also through mutual regulation" as "people build skills to participate with other people directly in specific contexts for particular sociocultural systems" (p. 479). By pushing a button, pressing a key, or touching an icon on a display, any person can change a feature of a proximal or distal environment. With a simple click on a computer we can send a message, print a drawing, hear music, see a video, control a robot, or take cash from a bank terminal. This elementary ability to make a click is the *basic component* of a skill that is found in all cultures and in all individuals, whatever their age and socioeconomic background, who are exposed to this kind of digital device. I suspect that without this basic digital ability it would be impossible to have reached the current level of globalization in our societies. This is, incidentally, one of the great advantages of computer technologies in education.

It is important to affirm that the click option is the basic unit of the digital skill, but it is a necessary, not a sufficient, condition for that skill. For instance, typewriting is not per se a digital skill in the full sense of the term. Of course we must train children to be comfortable with the computer keyboard. However, in order to become digital a skill must go beyond the simple motor task of hitting keys with precision and speed. Schools commonly start with handwriting before introducing typewriting, but this seems to be only a pedagogical tradition or convention. No one would prevent a child who is motor disabled from learning to write with a computer, but many educators seem to consider it a "forbidden experiment" to generalize this methodology to all children. I think, instead, it would be a good practice in the digital era to enforce writing skills with the help of a computer. The important analog skills of drawing and handwriting will not be delayed or impaired because we train the child to write with a word processor. On the contrary, they will support each other.

The digital revolution has also "opened" the human brain for observation and action. In fact, the new methods of brain imaging are the direct result of the ever increasing computer power that permits an accurate view not only of the anatomical details of the living brain but also of its chemical composition, as well as the identification of the functional changes embodied in neuronal networks of enormous complexity during the most diverse perceptual, motor, and cognitive tasks (Posner and Raichle 1994; Spelke 2002). By analogy to the World Wide Web (www), we could speak of a *brain wide web* (bww) with multiple cortical and subcortical subsets, some of them highly modular and stable and others more flexible and plastic, genetically programmed by the biological evolution of our species or epigenetically embodied in the cultural evolution and the educational development of the individual (Huttenlocher 2002).

Reciprocally, the www can be interpreted as the "nervous tissue" of globalization: it is modular and distributed, for it works at the same time at the local and the global level by reaching a restricted group of persons, a local community, and a very large and unpredictable audience connected to the Web. Any journalist who writes in a modern newspaper accessible on the Web knows how incredibly far his text can reach. I write a column every Sunday in *La Nación* of Buenos Aires and receive hundreds of e-mails, mostly from teachers in Argentina and abroad whom I have never met in person (Battro 2002b). The Web can process information sequentially or simultaneously, do serial or parallel processing. In fact, it allows us to deal with many active links at the same time, similar to the way the cerebral cortex activates many areas simultaneously during a particular task or takes one piece of information at a time. The Web works with sensors and motors, memories and representations, like the brain that controls our senses, muscles, images, emotions, and thoughts. Finally, on the Web we deal with the continuous and the discrete, the analog and the digital worlds. Our brain does the same.

TO CLICK OR NOT TO CLICK

In fact each click unfolds a new dimension in the virtual space of the digital world. If we have only one button to push or one lever to press, the option is called unary. If we have two, the options are binary; three, ternary; and so on. In mathematical logic these options form propositional, or Boolean, lattices. The simplest one is the unary lattice: the superior node is A or not A (tautology: $A \vee \sim A$), and the inferior is A and not A (contradiction: $A \cdot \sim A$); in between we find the node A and the node not A ($\sim A$). The practical alternative is "to click (A) or not to click ($\sim A$)." This network has four nodes and four links. The figure below represents the unary lattice in a prepositional format.

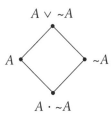

Remarkable is that with two options, A and B, we obtain a lattice with sixteen nodes; with three options, A, B, and C, a lattice with 256 nodes; and so forth. This growth is exponential (McCulloch 1965). This simple mathematical fact explains the incredible power of the click option. On the screen of our computer we have several options (links)

represented by buttons, words, and icons, and the combinations of these options rapidly become astronomical. This is the reason why we feel immersed (and sometimes lost) in an "ocean of possibilities" when we navigate the Web or use a word processor, a computer-aided design tool, or the like. It is worth mentioning that Jean Piaget—well before computers were introduced in schools—wrote two books on the logic of these formal operations, one dedicated to the sixteen binary operations, the other to the 256 ternary operations (Piaget, 1949, 1952). For Piaget and Bärbel Inhelder "the role of *possibility* is indispensable to the hypothetico-deductive or formal thinking" (Gruber and Voneche, 1977, p. 823).

For us too, the digital virtual space is unfolding a new dimension with each click, opening a new world of possibilities to explore. We can say that the elementary click option generates a *network of click options*. But we must develop some specific digital skills in order to work with a computer in the real world. I think we can do it with certain ease, at all ages, because the new digital skills are based on the old click options that we can trace in the evolution of our species and in the development of the individual.

AN EVOLUTIONIST AND DEVELOPMENTAL APPROACH

Humankind has evolved culturally with the construction of techniques and technologies. From the earliest hunting and gathering, some very simple but highly "intelligent" devices were invented based on an "all or none" trigger that elicits an abrupt change in the state of a particular device. For instance, the traditional snares and traps of the Bushmen are made by "a rope which is spring-loaded by a springy sapling, with a noose and trigger on the ground. When the trigger is released the sapling springs back to tighten the noose" (Liebenberg 1990, p. 59). The action of the trigger produces a change of state in the system, and the animal is caught in the trap. This is, I believe, one of the earliest examples of a "click machine." The click option was "in the mind" of the inventor. The expert hunter can predict the behavior of the animal: following the animal's trails, he observes the most minute details; he imagines the decisions the prey will make under certain circumstances; and he knows the possible options it will consider. We can infer he has in mind, at least, the structure represented by the unary option $(A \vee \sim A)$. We can also presume that our prehistoric ancestors constructed similar traps and triggers for hunting. In fact, they depicted many spoors in great detail in their caverns, which is a sign of their concern with tracking. We can also infer that they had the same propositional structure in mind.

An interesting recent analogy from the traps to the computer merits some consideration. Louis Liebenberg, a South African expert in the way Bushmen track wildlife in the Kalahari, has recently applied a computerized system called CyberTracker to help the trackers identify the animals and their habits, a record that can be of enormous value in the preservation and control of many endangered species. A collection of more than forty spoors of animals is represented on the small screen of a handheld computer connected to a global positioning system (GPS). When the tracker identifies a spoor, he checks the corresponding icon on the computer and makes a click on that particular picture. The CyberTracker instantaneously registers the place and time of the finding; then the tracker can scroll through the displays and record a set of activities, like drinking, feeding, running, fighting, mating, and sleeping, for the animals he sees in the region. This information is transferred to a database, which will help to make a detailed map of the wildlife. What I find particularly interesting is that although most trackers are illiterate, they have learned to use this digital device perfectly well in a few sessions of practice in the field. In other words, without any reading or writing skills, they have shown sufficient "digital skills" to make the wildlife scientific project work. This is a very clear example of the universality of the click option as an elementary component of a digital skill, certainly a much simpler and more general skill than reading or writing. However, in this case, the Bushmen's digital skill also had a very important "symbolic component"—the icons, the schematic pictures, on the computer display. Only an expert tracker could identify a spoor and make good use of the digital device.

Digital skills are found also in infants. Jerome Bruner has described with great wit how he discovered with Ilze Kalnins in the 1970s a way to assess visual skills in babies only six weeks old (Bruner 1983). Bruner and Kalnins presented projected slides to a baby who comfortably watched the pictures in the arms of her mother. As they did so, they found that when the image was blurred the baby immediately switched her gaze away from the screen. This behavior was so systematic that they decided to design a simple experiment. The child was given a pacifier, and when she sucked on it, an electronic device connected to the projector sent the image into focus. When the image was out of focus the baby kept her sight away from the screen for a couple of seconds, and then she started to suck. When the image came into focus she returned to watch the screen. After several positive efforts the experimenters switched to the reverse setting: this time sucking brought the picture out of focus. In this case the baby would watch the screen until the picture was completely blurred and then she would avert her gaze. The most remarkable finding was that the very young infant could combine the two skills, sucking and watching, in a very consistent manner. Sucking is an innate reflex in all mammals, but as the authors could prove, this old reflex can give support to a very delicate modulation of skills. For Bruner the essence of all intelligent activity is the capacity to combine pre-established routines with increasingly more powerful skills. The passage from a routine to a skill is certainly a very tricky one, and we can interpret this experiment as a good demonstration of the unfolding of an elementary digital skill. In fact, the option controlled by the baby is clearly of the unary type $(A \lor \sim A)$: "suck for focus/not suck" in the first setting and $(\sim A \lor A)$: "not suck for focus/suck" in the second. With a simple click the computer has expanded the use of on/off switches for assessing different perceptual, motor, and cognitive skills of infants.

The power to control the environment via a simple switch has been employed also with great success in the training of severely disabled children who cannot speak or otherwise communicate. Many of the so-called "augmentative" digital devices are based on the capacity to make a click; for example, to click on a picture that is related to food when the subject is hungry or to click to produce a sound of alert when he or she is in pain or need. It is indeed amazing how many things the mouth, the forehead, or a limb can control with a switch. This capacity seems universal and culture independent: diverse disabled children can learn the same elementary digital skills. We also have substantial evidence that the brain can develop even complex digital skills (programming, e-mail, Web navigation, etc.) in spite of gross cortical damage. Moreover, a very disabled brain can perfectly support the networking of digital skills.

For example, in some cases of intractable epilepsy a whole hemisphere of the brain, left or right, is removed in order to stop the devastating seizures. The success of this drastic surgery has given hope to those hemispherectomized children and adolescents of living a worthy and productive life. In particular, they go to school and some are able to enter college. In these cases the acquisition of digital skills greatly empowers them in reading, writing, drawing, calculating, and communicating, and the computer becomes a powerful educational tool for their half brain (Battro 2000).

A remarkable discovery is that the "minimal" neuronal architecture required for a click option is not unique to the human species. Many species of birds and mammals have been trained to "make a click" in response to a stimulus, to explore a particular environment, to search for food, and so forth. Indeed, a significant part of the experimental studies with animals has been done with the help of a trigger—buttons to hit with a finger, levers to move with a paw, or switches to peck with a beak. An important general theory of behavior was developed in the first half of the twentieth century using these kinds of devices as the basic tools for experiment and control (Skinner 1938). But today the digital era has opened up a new world to zoologists, ethologists, and animal psychologists that leads well beyond the simple instrumental conditioning of the behaviorists. Many scientists are trying now to study how the animal interacts and communicates via the Web! A bird, for example, can display amazingly complex behavior with the help of a simple trigger. And if the switch is connected to the Web, many unexpected things can happen.

The remarkable work of Irene Pepperberg with African gray parrots is a clear model of this new kind of "click power" in animal experimentation (Pepperberg 2000). Pepperberg and her collaborators have started a systematic study of the ways parrots communicate using digital devices on the Web. The so-called "InterPet Explorer" allows the parrot to navigate a set of sites, including pictures, music, and wildlife videos. They built the bird a navigational system, a customized mouse made of a flat piece of plastic with a hole in which to insert its beak. This is of course a new "digital" function—forced by human culture into the bird's environment and superposed onto the natural "analog" functions that are the product of biological evolution (for instance, making a nest with its beak out of the most diverse materials). Recent research shows that some crows can even make a hook with their beaks by bending a wire in order to catch a piece of food hidden inside a container (Weir, Chapell, and Kaselnik 2002). The fact that a bird can handle both analog and digital tasks with ease reflects the flexibility of its brain and supports the argument that both fundamental skills are embodied in the nervous systems of many species. The case of dolphins is also well known. A group of scientists working with Earth Trust Project Delphis at Sea Life Park Hawaii, for example, have developed a system that allows the dolphins to interact with the experimenter via an underwater touch-screen connected to a computer (Marten 2001). The animals click with their rostrums (noses) to select several options on the screen, which shows pictures of objects. Monkeys and primates are also a good case for the study of digital skills.

POINT/DRAG AND CLICK

One of the greatest inventions of the digital era is the mouse, a device that has analog and digital components in the same piece of equipment. We move the mouse in order to point at something or drag something to a different place (analog), and we click when we have made a decision at that point (digital). The mouse was patented by Douglas Engelbart as early as 1963, and I think the reason for the enormous success of the mouse is precisely the fact that, being a dual interface (analog-digital), it allows the interaction of two fundamental, and different, skills that as a result of long evolution are deeply embodied in our brains.

Computers display a palette of icons, buttons, and symbols that can be activated by a simple click, like the triggers of the Bushman's trap. Sometimes it is not even necessary to move a finger to push a button on the computer or to click on the mouse; with the proper interface, any voluntary movement can release a chain of actions. For example, some disabled persons can use a computer by voice commands alone. I helped a quadriplegic architect draw complex layouts of buildings using a voice-recognition device (Battro 1991). In doing so, his brain underwent a "cortical shift" from the motor areas that control fingers and hands to the Broca area, which controls speech, in order to draw with his voice. Speech is discrete, formed by units: a sentence is composed of words; words are composed of syllables and phonemes. In a sense the architect's brain changed from the analog mode of drawing by hand to the digital or discrete mode of "speaking" to the computer—a remarkable example of the functional plasticity of the nervous system.

Jean-Dominique Bauby—who suffered the devastating "locked-in syndrome," which inhibits any movement, including speech, and transforms the individual, who remains conscious in an inert body—provides us a most extreme example. The only voluntary motor action left to him was blinking his left eye, but this was enough to signal an assistant that a letter should be printed. At the end of many sessions and thousands of clicks he succeeded in writing a book, *The Diving Bell and the Butterfly,* one of the most dramatic testimonies of human endurance I have ever read (Bauby 1997). Of course a proper computer interface could have made Bauby's task much less strenuous, but the essential part is the "option," the covert decision, not the overt behavior or the "click" per se, and the mechanism that produces the intended outcome.

Furthermore, contemporary neuroinformatics is searching for a direct control of the computer by the brain. Recently P. R. Kennedy and colleagues (2000) have implanted special electrodes in the cortex of three patients with cases of locked-in syndrome comparable to Bauby's. A brain-computer interface permits the patient to move a cursor on a computer monitor when he or she is "thinking" of driving the cursor to a target. The increase of the firing rate of the implanted neurons moves the cursor from left to right on the screen, and the speed of the movement is proportional to the neurons' rate of firing. To "mentally control" this displacement (to point the cursor) the patient must develop a specific analog skill to reach the different icons that produce a synthetic speech output or to point to a target letter to be printed. A different pulse train from the cortex, which also provides a distinctive auditory feedback to the patient, triggers the click (digital) part of the option. For some of the tasks, it took three months of exhausting trials to reach significant success, but the way is now open to test other technical improvements. The authors intend now to provide patients with access to some environmental controllers and to the Internet (see also Taylor, Helms Tillery, and Schwartz 2002; Koning and Verschure 2002).

THE COMPUTER, A TOOL FOR THE BRAIN

In a profound and noble sense, the computer used as a tool for the brain, as a *functional prosthesis* or extension of the brain, is also an enormous advantage for the process of globalization and education (Battro 2002a). In particular, it must be stressed that from its very beginning the digital era has been, by default, "open to all," and digital technology does not discriminate between the talented and the handicapped. This is a formidable advantage over many other technologies that have excluded persons with disabilities. The familiar telephone and radio have discriminated against deaf persons, for example. A century later only when the modem was hooked up to the telephone line could deaf people profit from the communication system using a computer to send written messages around the globe—an interesting historical reversal indeed, because—paradoxically—Alexander Graham Bell invented the telephone while trying to improve the way to communicate with the deaf. In the same way, radio packet technology, which links a computer to a radio transmitter, allowed hearing disabled persons to become radio amateurs, an activity forbidden to them only two decades before (Battro and Denham 1989). An important benefit of radio packet technology is that access to the (low-orbiting) radio satellite is free and can be used with the Internet in remote and impoverished places without telephones. Following this line of thought, we can imagine a future with no communication costs for educational purposes.

We must recognize how dramatically a deaf person is bounded to local contacts only: lip reading and sign language use a very restricted frontal space—in contrast to a hearing person, who lives in a sphere of sounds and voices and can communicate with a larger audience at a distance. The digital technologies have radically changed this situation. On one hand, the hearing disabled can reach the whole world, making global contacts in the same way a hearing person does and using exactly the same tool: the Web. This is one of the most unexpected results of globalization, and a very humane one, a hope for other humanitarian improvements to come. On the other hand, the first successful neuroimplant of modern medicine, the cochlear implant, a digital prosthesis connected to the auditory nerve, has changed the life of thousands of hearing disabled children (Giraud, Price, Graham, and Frackowiack 2001).

There are many other examples of new digital technology helping learning disabled children. The idea of a "universal design" for software accessible to a diversity of disabled persons, promoted by the Center for Applied Special Technology (CAST) (Rose and Meyer, 2002), among others, is gaining momentum in education, a clear example of a humane use of digital power. Use of a word processor can significantly enhance the reading and writing skills of a dyslexic person because of the many click options the computer has to check spelling, hear a word pronounced, use a dictionary, and so forth.

Similar progress is being made for visually disabled persons. Computers can generate artificial, synthetic speech from digitized text with increasing sensitivity to syntax and context and without the flat robotic voice produced by the first equipment for the blind. This technology will continue to improve. It is important to note that some of the devices invented for the blind are now used with great success with children who have reading disabilities. As David Rose and Ann Meyer (2000) put it, "the future is in the margins"; very often the disabled child leads the technological and pedagogical digital changes that benefit many nondisabled kids.

THE EDUCATIONAL IMPACT OF DIGITAL TECHNOLOGIES

Development of new information and communication technologies, particularly the Internet, is one of the essential components of globalization (see Jenkins, this volume), as both an instrument and a motor of change. The impact of this technological development is profound in education, changing the lives of families, teachers, and students in many ways. The most radical transformation is produced when these technologies reach the world's remote and poor places. As Nicholas Negroponte (1997) has pointed out, children empowered by digital technology can become agents of change. Some remarkable examples of this come from a recent MIT (Massachusetts Institute of Technology) initiative with computers and communication devices to assist the education of children in poor communities in Cambodia, India, and other parts of the developing world. I have also done similar work with disadvantaged communities in South America, in particular in Argentina and Brazil. It is much easier to teach in a favela with the help of a computer, and the new task is more engaging for the underprivileged child. Young Native Americans of the Andes have also shown remarkable ability to use these instruments, and I can testify that some of them were using computers in their poor and isolated communities well before the central administration in their country adopted the computer for use in urban public schools. The variety of examples around the world is overwhelming, and this spontaneous diversity is more telling than many centralized projects in education.

Of course, as Sherry Turkle (this volume) has argued, because no technology is value free or neutral, we should beware the negative consequences that may contaminate our new ways of communicating and interacting. The teacher and the family are asked to play new, important, and difficult roles in this digital world, where fancy and reality can be confused with or superimposed on each other in strange ways. We will need a surplus of humanity to deal with the artificial in our lives. But I still maintain, based on my experience as a teacher and on the observations of many others, that the primary message we communicate through the Web is love, in spite of the many who use it to stimulate hate and violence and even produce terrorist acts. The educator's task is to foster the good work in us.

DO WE SPEAK DIGITALESE?

Watching a group of people working on a computer—employees in a bank, students in a library, architects in an office—we notice the silent work of the fingers and the amazing results on screen and paper. In each case the user seems to be "talking" to the computer. And most interesting is that the computer user can "understand" this language even if he or she cannot read or interpret the symbols on the screen. I define digitalese as the way humans (and also some animals) interact with a computer via a network of click options. Not to be mistaken for the "digital codes," the internal binary language of the computer, digitalese is a specific human-machine relationship. In a sense we "speak" to this piece of equipment. Digitalese is a universal language with a very simple syntax, the Boolean network of click options. In the world of education, elementary education in particular, this fact is quite significant. Using the syntax of click options, a child may use a computer with nearly the same ease, whatever the task, the brand of hardware or software, or the geographic or cultural setting.

We can also identify in this new language the classic triad of signs—icon, index, and symbol—described by Charles Sanders Peirce (1991). In particular, we find a new *sign/link* that exists only in a digital environment and has remarkable pragmatic consequences. The digital links open a multiplicity of possibilities due to the exponential growth of the Boolean network of click options. When we click on a sign/link on our computer we transform our intentions into actions. We could say that the sign/link unit is the modern equivalent of the *lektón* of the Stoics, something that stays between the concept and the action. We can also find a variety of *digital heuristics*—different paths through virtual space—during a search on the Web.

And what is essential to the process of globalization is that today's digital culture has become the common ground that enables us to speak digitalese as the lingua franca across all frontiers. But the fact that English is still the dominant language in the computer culture around the world may be detrimental to local languages, some with a very rich cultural tradition. No one can predict the course of events, but I see no causal relation between English and digitalese. The first is about humans, the latter about artifacts, computers. Are we bilingual in this new sense? Certainly we speak in one way to our human fellows, in another way to our digital computers. What kind of "code-switching" is a child making when she switches from talking to her brother to talking to her computer? The recent work of Hauser, Chomsky, and Fitch (2002) presents *recursion*, the "capacity of discrete infinity," as the core of human language and as uniquely human. It seems to me that digitalese is also a language, in these authors' strict sense, because of its simple syntax empowered by a never ending exponential growth. Digitalese is not only a new language but also certainly a new *mode* of communication and should be represented in the brain as such. We know that sign language, for instance, is organized in the brain in a way similar to that of spoken language (Hickok, Beluggi, and Klima 2002; Newman, Bavelier, Corina, Jezzard, and Neville 2002), but we have not discovered how digitalese is represented in our cortex. Perhaps we are becoming bilingual and bimodal, using both the universal digitalese of the globalized world and the native language of our local culture. Education might become the bridge between the two environments.

Given all the positive outcomes of the computer in education and the universality of the new language and modality we call digitalese, that the computer is not available to everyone nowadays is an injustice. The existing "digital gap," however, is extrinsic to the technology (related to price, availability, and connectivity). Much controversy surrounds this topic: some maintain that the digital gap will continue to increase between the haves and the have-nots, while others expect that the technology will evolve in such a manner that the gap will be considerably reduced in the next few decades and will produce a qualitative change in poor communities, opening new paths to development. With David Bloom (this volume) I share this optimistic view of the new ways digital technology can boost both the quantity and the quality of education. Computers can evolve as calculators did, from expensive and cumbersome machines to handy and low-cost tools (now marketed as disposable). With satellite and cable communication, a similar revolution can also be expected, one that will reinforce the globalization process in ways we cannot imagine. The impact of a very low–cost connectivity on education will be enormous.

UNFOLDING NEW SKILLS

Globalization ushers in a new era in which human interaction across many borders (educational, political, scientific, artistic, economic, religious, etc.) shapes a new human environment. Digital skills are now embedded in many cultures at many levels. In some countries children start to develop those skills at home, before going to school, before learning to read or write. Both formal education and social and professional demands increasingly stress the need to develop digital skills.

From the standpoint of developmental psychology it is also very interesting to follow the dynamics of those digital skills, as Yan and Fischer (2002) have done in their study of adults confronted with new software. Six students with different expertise in using a computer were tested with a software program commonly used for statistical analysis. Each student was coached by one of the experimenters, who answered questions but never provided systematic instruction. This social interaction served as a scaffold for better performance, those who were less expert needing more scaffolding. The authors observed that each person's performance varied with significant fluctuations during the learning process and followed a distinct path of development. Most interesting, it seems that all six participants showed a transitional pattern with ups and downs—repeated building up and collapse of the performance (scalloping)—before reaching some expertise in the new task. Thus the development of a specific digital skill is a complex, oscillatory, dynamic process, not a simple or linear one. This is important to know in order to provide the right digital education to millions.

In this chapter I sketch some neurocognitive foundations of the digital skills that can be important in education. I analyze at least two basic processes: the logical-mathematical network derived from the elementary click option, and the digital language called digitalese that we use in our interaction with the computer. We can summarize our findings following Howard Gardner's criteria (1999) for multiple intelligences: Focal lesions in the brain (as through acalculia and/or aphasia) might damage an individual's logical-mathematical and/or linguistic skills, but in several patients suffering these lesions, digital skills may remain intact and can even increase with computer practice. Hemispherectomized children show, for instance, increasing digital skills with training. We have not detected, however, any specific lesion that impairs only those digital skills and not other abilities, but this case cannot be excluded a priori. Evolutionary and developmental data on digital skills are evident in animals, infants, and illiterate adults. The core operations are at least two: the click option and what we might call the digital heuristics of digitalese, which has its own codes and notations, in particular the sign/link feature. Every aspect of the digital culture has a specific "end-state" performance, which is the realm of the expert. An extreme case of the digital and discrete perspective (as distinguished from the analog and continuous) is the bold statement made by physicist Stephen Wolfram (2002), a champion of cellular automata: "At the fundamental level, absolutely every aspect of the universe will in the end turn out to be discrete" (p. 730). But it seems difficult to exclude or dismiss the analog component in our lives, minds, and brains. Exceptional digital talents are more common today than some decades ago, when computers were accessible only to scientists. Some digital prodigies are among the most successful and wealthy individuals of our society. But it is more difficult to identify a specific "digital disability." A candidate can be found, perhaps, in the wide spectrum of autism. Transfer of digital skills and interference with other skills are also widely detected, especially among children in rich computer environments. We already have significant data (experimental and clinical) to give cross-cultural evidence of the expanding digital skills among children in the globalized world. With this evidence we might expect a very profound change in education in this century, perhaps emerging not as a change of paradigm, a clash of cultures, but as the unfolding of a very powerful intellectual capacity, a digital intelligence that was waiting for the right tools to flourish. These tools are the digital tools of today.

REFERENCES

Battro, A. M., and P. Denham (1989). *Discomunicaciones: Computación para niños sordos*. Buenos Aires: Fundación Navarro Viola, El Ateneo.

Battro, A. M. (1991). Logo, talents et handicaps. In *Logo et apprentissages*. J. L. Gurtner and J. Retschitzki, eds. Neuchâtel, Switzerland: Delachaux et Niestlé.

Battro, A. M. (2000). *Half a brain is enough: The story of Nico*. Cambridge, UK: Cambridge University Press.

Battro, A. M. (2002a). The computer in the school: A tool for the brain. In *The challenges of sciences: Education for the twenty-first century*. The Vatican: Pontifical Academy of Sciences. Scripta Varia, 104.

Battro, A. M. (in collaboration with P. J. Denham) (2002b). *Aprender hoy: Una colección de ideas*. Buenos Aires: Papers Editores.

Bauby, J.-D. (1997). *The diving bell and the butterfly: A memoir of life in death*. New York: Vintage Books.

Bruner, J. (1983). *In search of mind: Essays in autobiography*. New York: Harper & Row.

Fischer, K. W., and T. R. Bidell (1998). Dynamic development of psychological structures in action and thought. In *Handbook of child psychology*: Vol. 4. A. Damon and R. M. Lerner, eds. New York: Wiley.

Gardner, H. (1999). *Intelligence reframed: Multiple intelligences for the 21st century*. New York: Basic Books.

Giraud, A. L., C. J. Price, J. M. Graham, and R. S. J. Frackowiack (2001). Functional plasticity of language-related brain areas after cochlear implantation. *Brain* 124(7): 1307–1316.

Gruber, H. E., and J. J. Voneche (1977). *The essential Piaget: An interpretative reference and guide.* New York: Basic Books.

Hauser, M. D., N. Chomsky, and W. T. Fitch (2002). The faculty of language: what is it, who has it, and how did it evolve. *Science* 289: 1569–1579.

Hickok, G., U. Beluggi, and E. S. Klima (2002). Sign language in the brain. In *The hidden mind. Scientific American,* special edition, 12 (1): 46–53.

Huttenlocher, P. R. (2002). *Neural plasticity: The effects of environment on the development of the cerebral cortex.* Cambridge, MA: Harvard University Press.

Kennedy, P. R., R. A. E. Bakay, M. M. More, K. Adams, and J. Goldwaithe (2000). Direct control of a computer from the human central nervous system. *IEEE Transactions on Rehabilitating Engineering* 8: 198–202.

Koning, P., and F. M. Verschure (2002). Neurons in action. *Science* 296: 1817–1818.

Liebenberg, L. (1990). *The art of tracking: The origin of science.* Cape Town: David Philip. http://www.cybertrackerworld.com/.

McCulloch, W. (1965). Embodiments of mind. Cambridge, MA: MIT Press.

Marten, K. (2002). Earth Trust Project Delphis. http://www.apple.com/scitech/stories/delphis/.

Negroponte, N. (1997). *Being digital.* New York: Knopf. http://dn.media.mit.edu/.

Newman, A. J., D. Bavelier, D. Corina, P. Jezzard, and H. J. Neville (2002). A critical period for right hemisphere recruitment in American Sign Language processing. *Nature Neuroscience* 5(1): 76–80.

Peirce, C. S. (1991). *Peirce on signs: Writings on semiotics.* J. Hoopes, ed. Chapel Hill: University of North Carolina Press.

Pepperberg, I. (2000). *The Alex studies.* Cambridge, MA: Harvard University Press. http://web.mit.edu/giving/spectrum/winter01/smart-talk.html.

Piaget, J. (1949). *Traité de logique. Essai de logistique opératoire.* Paris: Colin.

Piaget, J. (1952). *Essai sur les transformtions des opérations logiques: Les 256 opérations ternaires de la logique bivalente des propositions.* Paris: Presses Universitaires de France.

Posner, M. I., and M. E. Raichle (1994). *Images of mind.* New York: Scientific American Library.

Rose, D. H., and A. Meyer (2000). The future is in the margins. Wakefield, MA: Center for Applied Special Technology (CAST). http://www.cast.org/udl/index.cfm/I=542.

Rose, D. H., and A. Meyer (2002). *Teaching every student in the digital age: Universal design for learning.* Wakefield, MA: Center for Applied Special Technology (CAST). http://www.cast.org/teachingeverystudent/ideas/tes/.

Skinner, B. F. (1938). *The behavior of organisms: An experimental analysis.* New York: Appleton.

Spelke, E. S. (2002). Developmental neuroimaging: a developmental psychologist looks ahead. *Developmental Science* 5(3): 392–439.

Taylor, D. M., S. I. Helms Tillery, and A. B. Schwartz (2002). Direct control of 3D neuroprosthetic devices. *Science* 296: 1829–1832.

Weir, A. A. S., J. Chapell, and A. Kaselnik (2002). Shaping of hooks in New Caledonian crows. *Science* 297: 981. http://users.ox.ac.uk/~kgroup/tools/tools_main.html.

Wolfram, S. (2002). *A new kind of science.* Champaign, IL: Wolfram Media, Inc. www.wolframscience.com/contact.

Yan, Z., and K. W. Fischer (2002). Always under construction: Dynamic variations in adult cognitive construction. *Human Development* 45: 141–160.

Sherry Turkle

THE FELLOWSHIP
OF THE MICROCHIP

Global Technologies as Evocative Objects

As Winston Churchill (1943) put it, "We shape our buildings and after-
wards, our buildings shape us." Similarly, we shape our technologies
and our technologies shape our habits of mind. This is certainly true of
globally shared information technology. Computational technology
carries not only new instrumental possibilities, the power to get things
done, but also powerful ideas that contribute to personal, social, and
political sensibilities. In Kansas City or New Delhi, when students use
PowerPoint software to present their school reports, they are learning
more than the content of their presentations. They are learning a way
to organize experience. They are learning a set of expectations about
what it means to know and understand. What this generation of
schoolchildren, K–12, shares globally is mediated locally, but exposure
to the evocative power of digital technology—the way it acts on cognition and affect—is one of the generation's defining traits.

COMPUTATIONAL TECHNOLOGY'S
COMPLEX EFFECTS ON THOUGHT

The routines of daily life project computer users into a wide variety of
rich and psychologically evocative computational landscapes. Even in
applications as "simple" as chat rooms or instant messaging, users are

able to experiment with presenting themselves with different names or "handles." They can present themselves as being an age and having a gender other than their own. The shy can present themselves as outgoing; the plain can describe themselves as flamboyant. In more elaborate virtual worlds, such as online multiplayer games, users may assume multiple identities and take roles in multiple familial and social relationships. Once users are citizens of cyberspace, the medium affords a context for complex and even contradictory cognitive and emotional effects. For example, *on the Internet people may become fluent with the manipulation of personae but, in the process, may become less comfortable with their sense of having an authentic self.*

This is particularly striking in the case of adolescents for whom the identity-play characteristic of cyberspace may provide what Erik Erikson (1963) called a "psychosocial moratorium," a central element in how Erikson thought about identity development. It is not surprising that becoming increasingly facile with "cycling through" virtual personae (Turkle 1995) can leave some adolescents both gratified and ungrounded. The same children who write multiple narratives for screen avatars can be ignorant of the simplest strategies for sharing their "real" feelings with other people. Lasch (1979) has suggested that a characteristic malaise of our time is loneliness yet fear of intimacy. The computer is a medium through which one can be a loner yet never be alone. One can find companionship without the demands of friendship. Some of the latest clinical reports (Goldberg 2003) suggest the outlines of a modern character type, an expert dissociator, who is attracted to "life on the screen" and whose functioning is enabled by it. These people combine an ability to engage with ideas and other people at the perceptual level with profound emotional detachment. The computer environment becomes part of a system that enables them to "shift from one state of consciousness to another in order to avoid psychic pain" (Goldberg 2003, p. 7). Again, we have an environment that privileges the manipulation of personae over the knowledge of self.

Similarly, the opacity of simulation software, much touted as making computers user-friendly, may facilitate identity play in online gaming, but its correlate is that computer users often don't understand the rules that underlie their games. This lack of "system understanding" can lead to passivity and feelings of disempowerment, even for so-called "power users." When computer games first came on the scene in the late 1970s and early 1980s, a preteen or teenager's first reaction when introduced to a new game was often, "How can I build it, change it?" And it was quite common for relative novices to get "inside" a new game program and change it (i.e., personalize it) in significant ways. Now, game programs offer opportunities to play with complex narratives and magnificent special effects, but technically, they are closed boxes, too complex to allow for any tinkering with the game itself. Thus on one hand, there is an explosion of narrative; on the other hand, the underlying rules are set in advance and hidden in a place where one cannot see or touch them.

Educators and policy makers need to understand these contradictions as both empowering and limiting the current generation as it prepares for the responsibilities of global citizenship. Yet most often, when educators look at information technology, they tend to focus on rather narrow technical and pedagogical issues. In general, computers are brought into schools because the technology is marketed with the promise of delivering desired content more effectively. But students get far more than content in the transaction; computational technologies model styles of thought. The notion that computers model thought is an idea most often associated with educators who in the 1970s and 1980s wanted to make programming a regular part of every child's education. They argued that computers would carry ideas, and this being the case, they might as well be the strong intellectual ideas associated with programming languages. It is somewhat ironic that in most schools today, the ideas being carried by computation are more likely to be those embedded in productivity software.

FROM POWERFUL IDEAS TO POWERPOINT

In the 1980s, as personal computers moved into schools, there was strong disagreement about what constituted computer literacy. I have noted that for many advocates of making programming central to the curriculum, the case did not rest on the usefulness of programming. Seymour Papert, one of the inventors of the Logo computer language, saw the computer as a carrier of culture, and programming as an element of a new linguistic fluency (Papert 1980). For Papert, programming encouraged children to think like mathematicians, epistemologists, and psychologists because it raised questions about procedural thinking and knowledge structures, as well as encouraging reflection on one's own style of learning. In this cultural and developmental view of programming languages—one that I investigated in my work as a clinician and ethnographer (Turkle 1984)—programming carried "powerful ideas" that could change children's ways of thinking, including their ways of thinking about themselves.

The early computers-in-schools movement had a certain political valence as well. The first school computing facilities were staffed by the members of personal computer and "hobbyist" computer clubs across the country. Many members of those clubs shared a belief that access to the "innards" of the computer was a form of political empowerment (Turkle 1982). Universal access to programming skills seemed like a way to attack the digital divide in terms not just of who owned or used computers but also of who knew how to *control* them. For some people, understanding how a computer worked supported the belief that you could understand how other things worked as well—in both the social and the technical world. The transparent understanding of a computer could become a metaphor for access to power.

The history of this struggle as it played out in schools in the United States and Western Europe through the 1980s reads as something of a cautionary tale. In it strong opponents take diametrically opposed positions. A first group advocates using information technology to enhance educational content in subject areas. From their point of view, the technology should be "invisible." A second group argues for making programming skills the centerpiece of computer literacy because of the powerful ideas they carry. In its view, specific subject content (for example, English grammar or history lessons) is not the centerpiece of how computers should enter educational settings. By the year 2000, the second group seemed to have decisively lost the battle. Most children do not learn to program in school. Computers no longer come with their programming languages "in the box." But the first group, for whom content was key, has not really won either. All around the world children spend precious "media literacy" time learning to use the productivity tools of Microsoft Office. And ironically, as I have noted, those who argued for the evocative power of computational media to carry ideas have been proved right. Technology is not invisible; it is an actor, carrying embedded ideas. But the ideas that children are learning are the ones embedded in online gaming, search engines, and productivity software such as word processing, spreadsheets, and presentation tools. They are definitely not the ideas that the epistemologists of the Logo movement had in mind, but they do constitute a particular aesthetic in educational computing in which *presentation and simulation are seen as their own powerful ideas.*

PRESENTATION AS ITS OWN POWERFUL IDEA

When third-graders present school reports as PowerPoint slide shows, they are learning more than the content of any specific set of slides. The software carries its own particular way of thinking. PowerPoint encourages presentation, not conversation. It does not encourage students to make an argument. It encourages them to make a point. A good slide show, with its swooshing sounds, animated icons, and flashing text, closes down debate rather than opening it up, because it conveys absolute authority. Teachers now regularly take books off reading lists if those books "don't give good PowerPoint." Clear exposition has long been seen as dependent on clear outlining, but the global reach of presentation software has fetishized the outline. Ambiguity can get in the way.

In the early 1990s, I shared one, somewhat utopian, vision of global computation that described it as enabling multiple styles of thought (Turkle, 1984; Turkle and Papert 1990), thus consistent with the spirit of Gardner's work (1983, 1993) on multiple intelligences. I observed that when children learned to program, they were able to make the computer their own in their own way. Some programmed in a top-down, hierarchical, "planner's" style. Others worked like "tinkerers" in a bottom-up, more experimental manner. The technology could carry "epistemological pluralism." I saw the potential for cultural as well as individual differences to assert themselves. But the ubiquity of a software package (or an operating system) may effectively leave the user with only one way to do things.

PowerPoint embodies a notion of "bulleting" as clear thinking (Tufte 2003). This notion, clearly a product of the cultural assumptions of the Western corporate boardroom, is open to challenge by other traditions and other values. Here, I do not wish to question PowerPoint's core assumption but simply to point out how it exemplifies the power of software to carry culture and intellectual values. A generation of children is coming into maturity who are united by the phenomenology of media even as they are divided by the role that media will play in their lives. Depending on children's race, class, and position in global culture, the same experiences with information technology serve some as diversion, even as distraction, and serve others as training for confident use of the tools of power. The digital divide does not simply separate those who have access to computation from those who don't. Rather, even if the very important issues of access could be resolved, there is still a divide between the large mass of users and those who are empowered by computation to do more than play games. Making the leap depends on having food, clothing, and access to educational and social resources that are not found in cyberspace.

Acknowledging the global scale of this second, "empowerment" divide does not make one necessarily hostile to using information technology in educational settings. However, educational policy needs to take into account both the phenomenology of the digital experience and economic and political realities. When one or the other is denied, I am tempted to blame the seductions of simulation. Perhaps the technology is so compelling that it seduces those who work with it into thinking that they can avoid harsh climates in both the psychological and the social domains.

SIMULATION AS ITS OWN POWERFUL IDEA

Our expectations of screen simulations begin with simplicity of use—the idea that you don't have to know how a computer works in order to interact with what is happening on the surface of the screen. In the 1980s, most computer users who spoke of "transparency" were referring to a quality analogous to one found in traditional machines, their ability to "open the hood" and poke around. But when, in the mid-1980s, users of the Macintosh computer began to talk about "transparency," they meant representing their documents and programs with attractive and easy-to-interpret icons. They were referring to an ability to make things work without needing to go below the screen surface. This was, somewhat paradoxically, a kind of transparency enabled by the screen's opacity. Today, the word *transparency* has taken on its Macintosh meaning in both computer talk and colloquial language. In a culture of simulation, when people say that something is transparent, they mean that they can see how to make it work, not that they know how it works. In other words, transparency means epistemic opacity.

Some argue that this new epistemic opacity is empowering. "Anyone" can use the most sophisticated technological tools. But our tools may be teaching us that the world is beyond our understanding. In day-to-day experience, epistemic opacity can translate into passivity, a daily fear of the fragility of technology. For example, in the day-to-day, we learn that technology is dependent on a chip and when it breaks it cannot be fixed but needs to be replaced via global trade relationships. In other words, every opaque technology carries the message that we are interdependent, vulnerable, at "risk" (Beck 1992). And every opaque technology may carry the message that deep understanding may not be worth the trouble.

"Your orgot is being eaten up," flashes the message on the screen (Turkle 1995, pp. 69–70). It is a rainy Sunday afternoon and I am with Tim, thirteen. We are playing SimLife, Tim's favorite computer game, which sets its users the task of creating a functioning ecosystem. "What's an orgot?" I ask Tim. He doesn't know. "I just ignore that," he says confidently. "You don't need to know that kind of stuff to play." I suppose I look unhappy, haunted by a lifetime habit of not proceeding to step two before I understand step one, because Tim tries to appease me by coming up with a working definition of orgot. "I think it is sort of like an organism. I never read that, but just from playing, I would say that's what it is."

The orgot issue will not die. A few minutes later the game informs us: "Your fig orgot moved to another species." I say nothing, but Tim reads my mind and shows compassion: "Don't let it bother you if you don't understand. I just say to myself that I probably won't be able to understand the whole game any time soon. So I just play." I begin to look through dictionaries but find no listing for *orgot*; finally I find a reference to it embedded in the game itself, in a file called READ ME. The text apologizes for the fact that orgot has been given several, in some ways contradictory, meanings in this version of SimLife, but one of them is close to "organism." Tim was right—enough.

Tim's approach to SimLife is highly functional. He says he learned his style of play from video games: "Even though SimLife's not a videogame, you can play it like one." By this he means that in SimLife, like video games, one learns from the process of play. You do not first read a rule book or get your terms straight. Without understanding the rules that underlie the game's behavior, Tim is able to act on an intuitive sense of what will work. As Tim is populating his universe in a biology laboratory scenario, putting in fifty each of his favorite creatures (trilobytes and sea urchins) but only twenty sharks, I listen to him thinking aloud about that decision: "I don't want fifty of *those*; I don't want to ruin this." Twenty is less than fifty, and time will tell if it is less by the right amount. "My trilobytes went extinct," Tim says. "They must have run out of algae. I didn't give them algae. I forgot. I think I'll do that now." Tim can keep playing even when he has no very clear idea what is driving events. While I was fruitlessly looking up *orgot*, Tim got deep into an age-of-the-dinosaurs scenario in SimLife. On the positive side, a player like Tim is learning to think about complex phenomena as dynamic, evolving systems. From one point of view, he has made far better use of his time than I have.

And yet Tim's video game habits of mind also raise larger questions. When his sea urchins become extinct, I ask him why.

> *Tim:* I don't know, it's just something that happens.
>
> *ST:* Do you know how to find out why it happened?
>
> *Tim:* No.
>
> *ST:* Do you mind that you can't tell why?
>
> *Tim:* No. I don't let things like that bother me. It's not what's important (Turkle 1995, p. 69).

Fifty years ago, a child's world was full of things that could be understood in simple, mechanical ways. A bicycle could be understood in terms of its pedals and gears, a wind-up car in terms of its clockwork springs. The people who built or bought the first generation of personal computers understood them down to the bits and bytes. The operating systems that followed were far more complex but invited that "old-time" reductive understanding. Today, computer users such as Tim can completely ignore such understandings. Tim can stay on the surface, taking things at (inter)face value.

Simulations help users think about complex phenomena as dynamic, evolving systems. But they also get people accustomed to manipulating a system whose core assumptions they may not understand and which may or may not be "true." This is the case in a game like SimLife, and it is true in the simulation worlds used in science, engineering, and design.

SIMULATION AND ITS DISCONTENTS

Engineers, scientists, and architects who have moved from working with pencils and physical models to using computer-aided visualization and design tools describe how their new tools offer a new sense of power—in particular, a new ability to manipulate and experiment with shape and form and materials (Turkle 1995; Turkle, Dumit, Gusterson, Mindel, and Silbey 2002). But as in the case of children playing with simulation games, they also describe losses as they moved from physical to virtual worlds. One architect explained how his students lost contact with the physical site of a building project once it had been transformed into "contour lines" on a screen:

> Students can look at the screen and work at it for a while without learn-ing the topography of a site, without really getting it in their head as clearly as they would if they knew it in other ways, through traditional drawing for example. . . . When you draw a site, when you put in the contour lines and the trees, it becomes ingrained in your mind. You come to know the site in a way that is not possible with the computer. (Turkle 1995, p. 64)

Another architect noted an increased sense of design mastery but a loss of attachment to his work: "You love things that are your own marks. In some primitive way, marks are marks. . . . I can lose this piece of paper in the street and if [a day later] I walk on the street and see it, I'll know that I drew it. With a drawing that I do on the computer . . . I might not even know that it's mine" (Turkle 1995, p. 64).

A similarly ambivalent situation exists in the field of chemistry. There, I interviewed students who can play with simulated molecules on the screen in ways that were never possible with balls and sticks of physical models. The virtual models can be stacked and rotated and twisted in three dimensions. Some students described how their new ability to manipulate and visualize data quickly made working with computer-mediated molecules feel more like a "hands-on experience" than working with "wet ones." Some felt closer to chemistry because it was now opened up to visual intuition. One student described how using a program that simulated molecular structures on a screen gave her "the understanding that comes when you see things actually happen. . . . [It was] like seeing the molecule moving" (Turkle 1995, pp. 64–65). Yet others described the same program as taking the physicality, the reality, the joy, out of "bench chemistry." One put it this way: "A monkey could do this."

Physicists were similarly divided in their judgments about the effects of simulation on their science. In a study of MIT physicists, they granted that only computer simulations could provide visual intuitions about quantum physics or what it would look like to travel down a road at nearly the speed of light (Turkle 1995, p. 66). But the computer was deemed "bad" when it interfered with the most direct possible experience that one could have of the knowable world. Physicists spoke reverently of "learning Newton's laws by playing baseball" (p. 65) and were open about describing simulation as the "enemy of good science." For example, one said, "I like physical objects that I touch, smell, bite into. The idea of making a simulation . . . excuse me, but that's like masturbation" (p. 66). One physicist talked about how simulation was changing how his students thought:

> My students know more and more about computer reality, but less and less about the real world. And they no longer even really know about computer reality, because the simulations have become so complex that people don't build them any more. They just buy them and can't get

beneath the surface. If the assumptions behind some simulation were flawed, my students wouldn't even know where or how to look for the problem. So I'm afraid that where we are going here is towards Physics: The Movie. (Turkle 1995, p. 66)

I was reminded of this comment about *"Physics: The Movie"* when I took my seven-year-old daughter to Italy and she commented when staring into the Mediterranean, "Look Mommy, a jellyfish! It looks so realistic!" A screen simulation of a fish tank had become her modeling tool for jellyfishness, as it is for children all over the world who have never seen a jellyfish but who have played with simulations of ocean life. Like Baudrillard contemplating Disneyland's Mainstreet, I had come to a crisis of the gold standard (Baudrillard 1983).

Simulations enable us to abdicate authority to the programmer; they give us permission to accept the opacity of the model that plays itself out on our screens. But this is a contested terrain; there can be an active as well as a passive response to the seduction of simulation. Simulation games are not just objects for thinking about the real world; we can also use them as objects of resistance: they can provoke us to reflect on how the real world has itself become a simulation game (Starr 1994).

SIMULATION, RESISTANCE, AND READERSHIP SKILLS

One can accept simulations on their own terms, the stance that Tim encouraged me to take. This might be called simulation resignation. Or one can take the cultural pervasiveness of simulation as a challenge to develop a new social criticism. This new criticism would discriminate among simulations. It would take as its goal the development of simulations that help users understand and challenge the model's built-in assumptions.

I think of this new criticism as the basis for a new class of skills: *readership skills for the culture of simulation.* Developing them is a challenge to global educators. On one level, high school sophomores playing SimCity for two hours may learn more about city planning than they would pick up from a textbook; but on another level, they may not know how to think about what they are doing. When I interview a tenth-grader named Marcia about SimCity, she boasts of her prowess and reels off her "Top ten most useful rules of Sim." Among these, number six grabs my attention: "Raising taxes always leads to riots."

Marcia seems to have no language for discriminating between this rule of the game and the rules that operate in a "real" city. She has never programmed a computer. She has never constructed a simulation. She has no language for asking how one might write the game so that increased taxes led to increased productivity and social harmony. And she certainly does not see herself as someone who could change the rules. Like Tim confronted with the orgot, she does not know how to "read" a simulation. Marcia is like someone who can pronounce the words in a book but doesn't understand what they mean. She does not know how to measure, criticize, or judge what she is learning. What does Marcia need to know about her technology? Marcia may not need to see the registers on her computer or the changing charges on a computer chip, but she needs to see *something*. She needs to be working with simulations that teach her about the nature of simulation itself, that teach her enough about how to build her own that she can become a literate "reader" of the new medium.

Increasingly, understanding the assumptions that underlie simulation is a key element of political power. People who understand the distortions imposed by simulations are in a position to call for more direct economic and political feedback, new kinds of representation, and more channels of information. They may demand greater transparency in their simulations, may insist that the games we play (particularly the ones we use to make real-life decisions) make their underlying models more accessible.

We come to written text with centuries-long habits of readership. At the very least, we have learned to begin with the journalist's traditional questions: who, what, when, where, why, and how. Who wrote these words, what is their message, why were they written, how are they situated in time and place, politically, economically, and socially? In my view, a central goal of global media literacy should be to teach students to interrogate simulations in much the same spirit. The specific questions may be different but the intent is the same: to develop habits of readership appropriate to being informed and critical citizens in a culture of simulation.

CODA: GLOBAL COMPLEXITIES AND
THE MYTH OF TECHNOLOGICAL CLARITIES

Hopes and fears for global technology have become a contested terrain on which different "camps" argue different effects. This essay has stressed the ambiguities and contradictions that computational technologies engender in human thought and affect, because I believe that the important work in this domain needs to be done in this "gray zone" rather than in the more simplistic "computers are all good or all bad" style of analysis that has been endemic in discussions of the Internet and global culture. Global technology is a terrain on which ideological battles are played; chief among these are differences of opinion about the role technology can play in driving social change. Yet global technology is a terrain to which old ideological battles are drawn.

At the MIT Media Lab, for example, members of the research consortium "Digital Nations" have argued that computational media might enable Third World countries to leapfrog industrial countries to a favored postindustrial position, that the Internet provides global exposure to scientific ways of thinking that will enable a similar leap from illiteracy to scientific sophistication, and that solar-powered digital networks will strengthen local community ties in Third World societies.

There are however, complicating realities that challenge any such simple visions. A Digital Nations project in Delhi, India, that introduced impoverished Indian children to scientific instrumentation in the hope of opening their minds to the scientific method is a good example of how complexity can subvert the best of intentions. The project was part of the Computer Clubhouse project, directed by Mitchel Resnick and sponsored by Intel Corporation. The Indian students took over a dilapidated storefront as a meeting place. A thirteen-year-old boy at the clubhouse looked at local water under a microscope connected to a computer and was concerned by all the impurities he saw. So he and his friends investigated the way water was stored and treated in different homes in their neighborhood. The thirteen-year-old found that boiling water before drinking could be helpful, and he convinced his parents to boil the water at home. He became something of a hero at the clubhouse. His friends and teachers took a picture of him at his home, with his microscope, the bad water, and the helpful kerosene stove. But because the other families of Clubhouse children had no money for fuel, the water at their homes went untreated. The computers, digital microscopes, and MIT expertise were irrelevant. Some of the children felt ashamed. In the utopian narrative, scientific discovery is followed by technological action. There is little room for human beings who did not have the wherewithal to get the job done.

I teach a graduate seminar with Professor Resnick in which I was told this story surrounded by about twenty technologically savvy MIT students from all over the world. These are, arguably, the students who will design and deploy the global technologies of the future. They found the story sad, unfortunate, containing some private pathos; but there was little conversation about its political dimension. One student suggested that Intel should supply a "slush fund" for Computer Clubhouse students who might need monies for special support, turning a problem about profound and systemic poverty into an actionable item for a clubhouse financial aid program. The global contradictions we face are great: we can give Indian families information technology, but we cannot give them clean drinking water. Such contradictions are so frustrating that we are tempted to use defense mechanisms, such as denial or turning to good work we can do closer to home. Beyond this, the mindset of the MIT audience, its commitment to technological optimism, kept them fixed on the possibility of a technological fix for what they framed as a technological problem (bad water). But the children's problem of finding fuel for their families was not simply "technological." And its solution will require the mobilization of not only technical resources but social, political, and economic ones as well.

This essay has focused on the experience of using technology and has taken the artifact as an actor that imposes its personality in interchanges with the user. But the optimism of my MIT students—so taken with the idea of a technological fix for complex global problems, including those in education—brings me to the hearts and minds of those who actually design the technology, who stand behind its aesthetics. Their power to shape future sensibilities is enormous; my concern is that their psychological styles, both affective and cognitive, will be embodied in the next generation of artifacts. To put it too simply, they are comforted by defense mechanisms associated with mastery and excited by aesthetic values that demand a level of clarity that rules out the complexities of contemporary global cultures.

The pioneers of computing, and those who referred to themselves as computer "hackers" (before this term connoted criminality), had a style of computer mastery that played with risk, with virtuosity—flying by the seat of their pants. If they were "addicted" to computing, it was as a medium for playing with the issue of control. And playing with control meant constantly walking that narrow line between having it and losing it. MIT hackers called this "sport death." One described it by saying, "The essence of sport death is to see how far you can push things, to see how much you can get away with." Programming evoked the thrill of walking on the edge of a cliff, of being able "to hold the system in your head for that half second, and hope you can save it, but knowing that it might all crash." It has been called the psychology of "scary/safe." Life is danger and triumph, screen to screen.

The computer and its simulated worlds can provide defenses for our anxieties. A first line of defense can be to deny vulnerability. It is reassuring to have a medium that offers reassurance through a promise of total mastery. It is reassuring to play in safe microworlds where the rules are clear. On the global scene, computer gaming, computer programming, and virtual realities share a great deal with the rule-driven and bounded world of Tolkien's *Lord of the Rings*. The commonalities were not lost on the earliest generations of computer enthusiasts. In the early 1970s, the computer scientists at Stanford University's Artificial Intelligence Laboratory were so enamored of *The Lord of the Rings* that they built three elfin fonts for the Stanford printers. Two of the researchers wrote a Tolkienesque, single-player quest game that became known as Adventure as it spread worldwide via the nascent Internet. The personal computer movement of the 1970s and early 1980s was deeply immersed in Tolkien and translated his fantasy worlds into hugely popular (and enduring) role-playing games such as Dungeons and Dragons.

What the magic of Tolkien shares with computer code is that each offers fantasy objects that one can control and the opportunity to assert and reassert mastery. Each episode of the Tolkien narrative presents a danger; each has a resolution in mastery before another danger appears. Just as in a program, the reader goes from one block of intransigent code to another. The analogy to programming intrigued an early generation of hackers: the analogy to computer games is more broadly apparent today. Each screen, each level of a computer game poses danger; each screen is mastered in its turn, whereupon one moves to the next screen and return to danger once more. Life is exhausting, but the repetition of microworld triumphs is reassuring. In the fellowship of the microchip, you may crash but ultimately you win.

We used to call hackers "computer people." No more. In a certain sense, if we take the computer to be a carrier of a way of knowing, of a way of seeing the world and what is important, we are all computer people now. Our global immersion in code bears more than a family resemblance to our global immersion in games and fantasy. Computer programs and Middle Earth are compelling on a global scale. They are complex, multilayered, and self-referential. However, we have come to a moment in history when playing in closed systems of our own devising reinforces dangerous habits of mind. When we think about Tolkien and about computing, we are not thinking about ambivalence. We are not thinking about battles that don't end in infinite justice. But the simple clarities of our globalized computer worlds depend on their virtuality. The real world is messy and painted in shades of gray. In that world we need to be comfortable with ambivalence and contradiction. We need to be able to put ourselves in the place of others in order to understand their motivations. Above all, we need to resist binary formulations. For these things we can't look to computation any more than we can look to Middle Earth.

NOTE

This material is based in part on work supported by the National Science Foundation under grant no. 0220347. Any opinions, findings, and conclusions or recommendations expressed in this material are those of the author and do not necessarily reflect the views of the National Science Foundation.

REFERENCES

Baudrillard, J. (1983). *Simulations*. Translated by Paul Foss, Paul Patton, and Philip Beitchman. New York: Semiotext(e), Inc.

Beck, U. (1992) *Risk society: Towards a new modernity.* Newbury Park, CA: Sage Publications.

Churchill, W. (1943). 28 October 1943 speech to the House of Commons (meeting in the House of Lords). http://www.winstonchurchill.org /quotes.htm

Erikson, E. (1963). *Childhood and society.* 2nd rev. ed. New York: W. W. Norton.

Gardner, H. (1983). *Frames of mind: The theory of multiple intelligences.* New York: Basic Books.

Gardner, H. (1993). *Multiple intelligences: The theory in practice.* New York: Basic Books.

Goldberg, P. (2003). Discussion of Sherry Turkle's "Whither psychoanalysis in computer culture?" Techno-analysis Conference, Berkeley, October 4.

Lasch, C. (1979). *The culture of narcissism: American life in an age of diminishing expectations.* New York: Warner.

Papert, S. (1980). *Mindstorms.* New York: Basic Books.

Starr, P. (1994). Seductions of Sim: Policy as a simulation game. *The American Prospect* 17: 19–29.

Tufte, E. R. (2003). *The cognitive style of PowerPoint.* Cheshire, CT: Graphics Press.

Turkle, S. (1982). The subjective computer: A study in the psychology of personal computation. *Social Studies of Science* 12(2): 173–205.

Turkle, S. (1984). *The second self: Computers and the human spirit.* New York: Simon & Schuster.

Turkle, S. (1995). *Life on the screen: Identity in the age of the Internet.* New York: Simon & Schuster.

Turkle, S. (forthcoming). Whither psychoanalysis in computer culture. *Psychoanalytic Psychology.*

Turkle, S., and S. Papert (1990). Epistemological pluralism: Styles and voices within the computer culture. *Signs: Journal of Women in Culture and Society* 16(1): 128–157.

Turkle, S., J. Dumit, H. Gusterson, D. Mindel, and S. Silbey (2002). *Information technologies and professional identity: A comparative study of the effects of virtuality.* NSF grant no. 0220347.

SIX

POP COSMOPOLITANISM

Mapping Cultural Flows
in an Age of Media Convergence

If there is a global village, it speaks American. It wears
jeans, drinks Coke, eats at the golden arches, walks on
swooshed shoes, plays electric guitars, recognizes Mickey
Mouse, James Dean, E.T., Bart Simpson, R2-D2, and
Pamela Anderson.

Gitlin 2001

The twain of East and West have not only met—they've
mingled, mated, and produced myriad offspring, inhabitants of one world, without borders or boundaries,
but with plenty of style, hype, and attitude. In Beijing,
they're wearing Levis and drinking Coke; in New York,
they're sipping tea in Anna Sui. While Pizzicato Five is
spinning heads in the U.S., Metallica is banging them
in Japan.

Yang, Gan, Hong, and the staff of A. Magazine 1997

BERT AND BIN LADEN:
RETHINKING CULTURAL IMPERIALISM

The story made its rounds in the fall of 2001: a Filipino high school
student created a Photoshop collage of *Sesame Street*'s Bert interacting
with terrorist leader Osama bin Laden as part of a series of "Bert
Is Evil" images the student posted on his home page. Other images
depicted Bert as a Ku Klux Klansman or as having sex with Pamela

Anderson. In the wake of September 11, a Pakistan-based publisher scanned the Web for bin Laden images that could be printed on anti-American signs, posters, and T-shirts. CNN reporters recorded the unlikely image of a mob of angry Pakistanis marching through the streets waving signs depicting Bert and Bin Laden. American public television executives spotted the CNN footage and threatened to take legal action: "The people responsible for this should be ashamed of themselves." Coming full circle, other *Sesame Street* spoofs began to surface on the Web, linking various characters with the terrorists.[1]

This story illustrates several themes that are central to my argument. First, it suggests the rapid flow of images across national borders in an age of media convergence, a flow facilitated both by commercial strategies (such as the localization and global distribution of *Sesame Street* and CNN) and by grassroots tactics (such as the use of Photoshop to appropriate and manipulate these images and of the Web to distribute them). Second, it suggests that those media flows are apt to be multidirectional, creating temporary portals or "contact zones" between geographically dispersed cultures (here, Pakistan and the Philippines). Third, it suggests the unpredictable and contradictory meanings that get ascribed to those images as they are decontextualized and recontextualized at the sites of consumption. Finally, the story suggests the increased centrality of teens and youth to the global circulation of media in an era when a teen's Web site can become the center of an international controversy.

I have spent my career studying American popular culture, adopting an approach based on older notions of national specificity. In recent years, however, it has become increasingly difficult to study what's happening to American popular culture without understanding its global context. I mean this not simply in the predictable sense that American pop culture dominates (and is being shaped for) worldwide markets but also in the sense that a growing proportion of the popular culture that Americans consume comes from elsewhere, especially Asia. This essay represents a first stab at explaining how and why Asian popular culture is shaping American entertainment.

The analysis must start with the concept of media convergence. Most industry discourse about convergence begins and ends with what I call the black box fallacy: sooner or later all media is going to be flowing through a single black box in our living rooms, and all we have to do is figure out which black box it will be. Media convergence is not an endpoint; rather, it is an ongoing process occurring at various intersections among media technologies, industries, content, and audiences. Thanks to the proliferation of channels and the increasingly ubiquitous nature of computing and telecommunications, we are entering an era when media will be everywhere and we will use all kinds of media in relation to each other. We will develop new skills for managing that information, new structures for transmitting information across channels, new creative genres that exploit the potentials of those emerging information structures, and new modes of education to help students understand their impact on their world. Media convergence is more than simply the digital revolution; it involves the introduction of a much broader array of new media technologies that enable consumers to archive, annotate, transform, and recirculate media content. Media convergence is more than simply a technological shift; it alters the relationship among existing technologies, industries, markets, genres, and audiences. This initial wave of media changes exerts a destabilizing influence, resulting in a series of lurches between exhilaration and panic. Yet media convergence is also sparking creative innovation in almost every sector of popular culture; our present media environment is marked by a proliferation of differences, by what Grant McCracken calls "plenitude" (see McCracken 2003).

In a forthcoming book I will describe and document the social, cultural, political, legal, and economic ramifications of media convergence (Jenkins 2003). In this essay I focus on the interplay between

> *Corporate convergence*—the concentration of media ownership in the hands of a diminishing number of multinational conglomerates that thus have a vested interest in insuring the flow of media content across different platforms and national borders

and

> *Grassroots convergence*—the increasingly central roles that digitally empowered consumers play in shaping the production, distribution, and reception of media content.

These two forces—the top-down push of corporate convergence, the bottom-up pull of grassroots convergence—intersect to produce what might be called global convergence, the multidirectional flow of cultural goods around the world. Ulf Hannerz is describing global convergence when he writes: "[World culture] is marked by an organization of diversity rather than by a replication of uniformity. . . . The world has become one network of social relationships and between its different regions there is a flow of meanings as well as of people and goods" (Hannerz 1990, p. 237).

Global convergence is giving rise to a new pop cosmopolitanism.[2] Cosmopolitans embrace cultural difference, seeking to escape the gravitational pull of their local communities in order to enter a broader sphere of cultural experience. The first cosmopolitans thought beyond the borders of their village; the modern cosmopolitans think globally. We tend to apply the term to those who develop a taste for international food, dance, music, art, or literature—in short, those who have achieved distinction through their discriminating tastes for classical or high culture. Here, I will be using the term *pop cosmopolitanism* to refer to the ways that the transcultural flows of popular culture inspire new forms of global consciousness and cultural competency. Much as teens in the developing world use American popular culture to express generational differences or to articulate fantasies of social, political, and cultural transformation, younger Americans are distinguishing themselves from their parents' culture through their consumption of Japanese anime and manga, Bollywood films and bhangra, and Hong Kong action movies. This pop cosmopolitanism may not yet constitute a political consciousness of America's place in the world (and in its worse forms, may simply amount to a reformation of orientalism), but it opens consumers to alternative cultural perspectives and the possibility of feeling what Matt Hills calls "semiotic solidarity" with others worldwide who share their tastes and interests (Hills 2002).

James L. Watson (this volume) argues that the introduction of digital technologies will "accelerate" the "standardization of everyday life."[3] I disagree. Certainly, networked computing will accelerate and intensify the worldwide flow of cultural goods, but precisely because networked computing is multidirectional and lowers transaction costs, it will insure that more non-Western goods make it into the West. Moreover, tapping into the Internet will enable consumers to trace those goods back to their source, to learn more about their originating culture, and to form relationships with their original producers and consumers. Pop cosmopolitanism cannot be reduced to either the technological utopianism embodied by Marshall McLuhan's "global village" (with its promises of media transcending the nation-state and democratizing cultural access) or the ideological anxieties expressed in the concept of media imperialism (with its threat of cultural homogenization and of "the West suppressing the Rest," as Ramaswami Harindranath describes it [see Harindranath 2003, p. 156]).

The media imperialism argument blurs the distinction between at least four forms of power—economic (the ability to produce and distribute cultural goods), cultural (the ability to produce and circulate forms and meanings), political (the ability to impose ideologies), and psychological (the ability to shape desire, fantasy, and identity). Within this formulation, Western economic dominance of global entertainment both expresses and extends America's status as a superpower; the flow of cultural goods shapes the beliefs and the fantasies of worldwide consumers, reshaping local cultures in accordance with American economic and political interests. The classic media imperialism argument ascribed almost no agency to the receiving culture and saw little reason to investigate actual cultural effects; the flow of goods was sufficient to demonstrate the destruction of cultures.[4] Ethnographers have found that the same media content may be read in radically different ways in different regional or national contexts, with consumers reading it against the backdrop of more familiar genres and through the grid of familiar values. Even within the same context, specific populations (especially the young) may be particularly drawn toward foreign media content while others may express moral and political outrage. Most will negotiate with this imported culture in ways that reflect the local interests of media consumers rather than the global interests of media producers.

To be sure, there is probably no place on the planet where one can escape the shadow of Mickey Mouse. Entertainment is America's largest category of exports. The Global Disney Audiences Project, for example, deployed an international team of scholars to investigate the worldwide circulation of Disney goods. They found that in eleven of eighteen countries studied, 100 percent of all respondents had watched a Disney movie, and many of them had bought a broad range of other ancillary products (Wasko, Phillips, and Meehan 2001). But while still strong, the hold of American-produced television series on the global market has slipped in recent years (Foroohar 2002; Klein 2002). Local television production has rebounded, and domestic content dominates the prime evening viewing hours, with American content used as filler in the late-night or afternoon slots. Hollywood faces increased competition from other film-producing nations—including Japan, India, and China—that are playing ever more visible roles within regional, if not yet fully global, markets. Major media companies, such as Bertelsmann, Sony, and Universal Vivendi, contract talent worldwide, catering to the tastes of local markets rather than pursuing nationalistic interests; their economic structure encourages them not only to serve as intermediaries between different Asian markets but also to bring Asian content into Western countries. Many American children are more familiar with the characters of Pokemon than they are with those from the Brothers Grimm or Hans Christian Andersen, and a growing portion of American youth are dancing to Asian beats. With the rise of broadband communications, foreign media producers will distribute media content directly to American consumers without having to pass by U.S. gatekeepers or rely on multinational distributors. At the same time, grassroots intermediaries will play an increasingly central role in shaping the flow of cultural goods into local markets.

Adopting a position that if you can't beat them, merge with them, the American entertainment industry has become more aggressive in recruiting or collaborating with Asian talent. Sony, Disney, Fox, and Warner Brothers have all opened companies to produce films—aimed both at their domestic markets and at global export—in Chinese, German, Italian, Japanese, and other languages. American television and film increasingly remake successful products from other markets, ranging from *Survivor* and *Big Brother,* which are remakes of successful Dutch series, to *The Ring,* a remake of a Japanese cult horror movie, and *Vanilla Sky,* a remake of a Spanish science fiction film. Many of the cartoons shown on American television are actually made in Asia (increasingly in Korea), often with only limited supervision by Western companies.

Some have argued that Hollywood entertainment has always been global entertainment. Whereas many national cinemas respond to a relatively homogenous local market, Hollywood has had to factor in the tastes of a multicultural society. Richard Pells writes: "The United States has been a recipient as much as an exporter of global culture. . . . American culture has spread throughout the world because it has incorporated foreign styles and ideas. What Americans have done more brilliantly than their competitors overseas is repackage the cultural products we received from abroad and then retransmit them to the rest of the planet" (Pells 2002; also see Olson 1999). Pells sees this as an ongoing development that has shaped the evolution of American pop culture, not simply a cosmetic shift in response to recent economic trends or cultural developments.

These shifts complicate any simple mapping of the relationship among economic, political, and cultural power. We still must struggle with issues of domination and with the gap between media have and have-not nations, but we do so within a much more complicated landscape. As Arjun Appadurai has famously asserted, "for the people of Irian Jaya, Indonesianization may be more worrisome than Americanization, as Japanization may be for Koreans, Indianization for Sri Lankans, Vietnamization for Cambodians, and Russianization for the people of Soviet Armenia and the Baltic Republics" (Appadurai 1996, p. 32). The result is not so much a global culture that eradicates local differences as a culture that continually produces local differences in order to gain a competitive advantage within the global marketplace. Appadurai writes, "Electronic mediation and mass migration . . . seem to impel (and sometimes compel) the work of the imagination. Together, they create specific irregularities because both viewers and images are in simultaneous circulation. Neither images nor viewers fit into circuits or audiences that are easily bound within local, national, or regional spaces" (Appadurai 1996, p. 4).

POKEMON AND THE IRON CHEF:
STRATEGIES OF CORPORATE CONVERGENCE

The flow of Asian goods into Western markets has been shaped through the interaction of three distinct kinds of economic interests: (1) national or regional media producers who see the global circulation of their products not simply as expanding their revenue stream but also as enhancing national pride; (2) multinational conglomerates that no longer define their production or distribution decisions in national terms but seek to identify potentially valuable content and push it into as many markets as possible; and (3) niche distributors who search for distinctive content as a means of attracting upscale consumers and differentiating themselves from stuff already on the market. For example, in the case of world music, international media companies, such as Sony, identify international artists and market them aggressively in their local or regional markets. As those artists are brought westward, the companies make a commercial decision whether they think the musicians will open mainstream, in which case the companies retain distribution rights within the United States, or niche, in which case they subcontract with a boutique label or third-party distributor (Levin 2002).

In a compelling analysis of the impact of Japanese transnationalism on popular culture, Koichi Iwabuchi draws a distinction between the circulation of cultural goods, that are essentially "odorless," bearing few traces of their cultural origins, and those that are embraced for their culturally distinctive "fragrance" (Iwabuchi 2002). In some cases, mostly where these goods are targeting niche or cult audiences, these goods are strongly marked as coming from some exotic elsewhere; in other cases, especially where they are targeted to the mainstream, their national origins are masked and the content retrofitted to American tastes.

As Iwabuchi has documented, Japanese media industries sought ways to open Western markets to their "soft goods," or cultural imports, based on the overseas success of their hardware and consumer electronics. Seeking global distribution for locally produced content, Japanese corporations such as Sony, Sumitomo, Itochu, and Matsushita bought into the American entertainment industry. They saw children's media as sweet spots in Western societies. Much as Hollywood's ability to compete in international markets rests on its ability to recoup most of its production costs from domestic grosses, the success of Japanese-made comics and animation meant that these goods could enjoy competitive prices as they entered Western markets. In Japan, manga constituted 40 percent of all books and magazines published, and more than half of all movie tickets sold were to animated films (Ahn 2001).

More than two hundred animation programs were aired each week on Japanese television, and about seventeen hundred animated films (short or feature length) were produced for theatrical distribution each year. Japanese media producers had created a complex set of tie-ins among comics, animated films and television series, and toys, which allowed them to capitalize quickly on successful content and bring it to the largest possible audience. They hoped to export this entire apparatus—the programs, the comics, and the toys—to the West. In the domestic market, anime and manga appealed to a broad cross-section of the public, but as they targeted the West, Japanese media companies targeted children as the primary consumers of their first imports. As this generation matured, the companies anticipated that they would embrace a broader range of Japanese-made media.

Illustrating the deodorization process, Anne Allison shows how the TV series *Mighty Morphin Power Rangers* was stripped of any specific connotations of Asianness and remade for distribution in the West, not simply through dubbing the dialogue but by recasting the characters with multiracial American actors and reshooting some of the footage in Southern California (Allison 2000). She contrasts the *Power Rangers'* success with the relative failure of *Sailor Moon,* whose producers made fewer efforts to retool it for American tastes and which remained less clearly compatible with American genre conventions. While the success of these exports can be ascribed to their "freshness" and distinctiveness, that difference was understood more in terms of genre innovation than of their Japanese origins. *Pokemon* was more open about its Japanese roots yet still underwent modifications, such as changing dumplings into doughnuts, to make it more accessible to the U.S. market (Allison 2002). (Of course, Scholastic rewrote the *Harry Potter* books to change British expressions it thought would be lost on American children.) By contrast, Allison argues, American cultural exports typically retain recognizable ties to the United States, a claim supported by the findings of the Global Disney Audiences Project, which found that the majority of consumers in a worldwide survey saw Disney as distinctly American or Western in its cultural values and orientation (Wasko et al. 2001).

Allison overlooks, however, the degree to which the national origins of children's programs are being blurred worldwide: children's programs are more apt to be dubbed in local languages even in countries where subtitling is the norm for adult fare, and many forms of localization occur in American children's programming as it enters those markets. *Sesame Street* is an obvious example. Consumers worldwide know *Sesame Street* but don't recognize Bert or Big Bird because the muppets are redesigned for local tastes. The American-based Children's Television Workshop works closely with local media companies to generate new content appropriate to local cultures and languages while setting content and technical standards that must be met by any *Sesame Street* franchise (Hendershott 1998). The difference between the remaking of *Mighty Morphin Power Rangers* for the American market and the remaking of *Sesame Street* for the Japanese market may be less clear-cut than Allison proposes, having to do with the degree of control the producing country exercises and the degree to which local audiences are aware of the transformations that have occurred. Allison herself suggests that Japanese-produced animation has emerged as a taste category even among relatively young consumers who comment on anime's coolness and cuteness.

For an example of how "fragrance" may enhance commercial prospects, consider the cult success of *Iron Chef*. Produced by Fuji International Television, the series entered North America through Asian-language television stations in the mid-1990s, where it developed a cult following among channel-surfing pop cosmopolitans (Hoketsu 2001). The Food Network brought the series to an even broader audience. On one hand, much of its appeal comes from its clever appropriations from Asian martial arts traditions. The Chairman, played by Kaga Takeshi, lives in a castle and rules over an army of "Iron Chefs." American fans express a fascination with the ornate decor and costumes, the pomp and circumstance surrounding the cooking competitions, the mystique of clan loyalties, and the preparation of foods with exotic and unfamiliar ingredients. While the series was dubbed for its Food Network broadcast, the mysterious Chairman speaks Japanese with English subtitles. Opening segments situate the chosen ingredients within Japanese history and culture. On the other hand, the show frequently pits Japanese cooks against representatives of other world cuisine, with recurring characters embodying Chinese, French, and Italian traditions. Each week, the rival chefs have to prepare a broad range of dishes based on an assigned ingredient, sometimes distinctly Japanese, sometimes foreign; the cooking battles are often a struggle between chefs committed to a traditional Japanese approach and those who assimilate and transform Western approaches. *Iron Chef* balances two distinct kinds of audience interests: on one hand, the high camp surrounding its martial arts theatricality and, on the other, a growing public fascination with international cuisine at a time when once exotic ingredients are more widely available in Western grocery stores (James 1996). Confident that it understood its appeal, United Paramount Network (UPN) sought to remake the program for an American audience, recasting William Shatner as the illusive Chairman, employing U.S.-based chefs, and displacing its martial arts borrowings with references to professional wrestling. UPN entertainment division head Tom Noonan explained, "Candidly, this show isn't about Wasabi or pudding or sushi. It's about the Iron Chefs that compete against each other in this sort of intense, very theatrical, over-the-top, gladiator-like style" (Kaplan 2001). The series was widely seen as a failure to successfully Americanize Asian content. As the *San Jose Mercury News* explained, "something's lost during the translation" (McCollum 2001).[5]

At the moment, Japanese style is marketed as a distinctive fragrance to niche or cult audiences and deodorized for broader publics, but this distinction is starting to break down as American consumers develop a preference for those qualities they associate with Japanese cultural productions. Much of this process of recontextualizing Japanese content is currently occurring at the grass roots.

THE DESI AND THE OTAKU:
TACTICS OF GRASSROOTS CONVERGENCE

Cosmopolitans and locals, Hannerz notes, have a common interest in preserving cultural differences in the face of pressures toward homogeneity. The locals care little about diversity per se but want to hold onto their own traditions. The cosmopolitans recognize that they will not get the diversity they crave "unless other people are allowed to carve out special niches for their cultures and keep them" (Hannerz 1990, p. 250). Grassroots convergence serves the needs of both cosmopolitans and locals. A global communication network allows members of diasporic communities to maintain strong ties with their motherlands, insuring access to materials and information important to their cultural traditions and preserving social connections with those they left behind (Punathambekar 2003). Cosmopolitans use networked communication to scan the planet in search of diversity and communicate with others of their kind around the world.

This section documents the role of grassroots intermediaries in shaping the flow of Asian cultural goods into Western markets. Specifically, I consider two kinds of cultural communities: the South Asian diasporic community (the "desis") that prepares the way for Bollywood films and Bhangra music, and western fans (the "otaku") who insure the translation and circulation of Japanese anime and manga. In both cases, grassroots cultural production and distribution demonstrated a demand for Asian content that preceded any systematic attempts to distribute it commercially in the West. Yet we underestimate the impact of these grassroots intermediaries if we see them as markets or even marketers; they also play a central role in shaping the reception of those media products, emphasizing rather than erasing the marks of their national origin and educating others about the cultural traditions they embody.

The westward flow of Indian media content reflects successive generations of South Asian immigration. Immigrant grocery stores became the initial points of distribution for Hindi videos, which enabled a nostalgic reconnection with the world left behind.[6] Bhangra emerged in the club cultures of Europe and North America, building upon regional traditions from India, but expanded to reflect points of contact with reggae, hip-hop, and techno within an increasingly globalized youth culture (Lipsitz 1994; Zuberi 1996). Sunaina Marr Maira writes: "A uniquely Indian American subculture allows second-generation youth to socialize with ethnic peers while reinterpreting Indian musical and dance traditions through the lens of American popular culture" (Maira 2002). Cultural shows on college campuses and festivals in local neighborhoods enabled participants to perform and attendees to reaffirm ethnic identities (Kavoori and Joseph 2002; Shukla 1997). Combining classic dance and current club styles, the cultural shows construct India as both timeless and contemporary, as both a world away and right in one's own backyard, reflecting the conflicted character of diasporic culture. In Boston, Los Angeles, and elsewhere around the country, theaters (still mostly ma-and-pa operations) are opening that exclusively show Hindi-language films. The United States and Britain now account for 55 percent of international Bollywood ticket sales (Bollywood Goes Global 2000).

Pop cosmopolitans are drawn increasingly toward Indian fashion, music, and cinema, surfing the circuits of distribution, which enable first- and second-generation immigrants to maintain ties within the diaspora. Perhaps they stumble into an immigrant grocery store in search of ingredients for a favorite curry and leave with a few videos. Perhaps they catch some Bhangra at a local club. Perhaps an Indian-born friend invites them to one of the culture shows. Perhaps they happen onto a Bollywood Web site or flip across an Indian-language cable station.

In this context, it is hardly surprising that Indian styles are increasingly appropriated by Western performers, such as Madonna's use of henna and Indian religious iconography in her "Ray of Light" tour or Baz Luhrman's imitation of a Bollywood aesthetic in *Moulin Rouge*. These Western appropriations have further increased American awareness of the richness and vitality of Indian popular culture, as is suggested by the surprising box office success of Mira Nair's film *Monsoon Wedding*. Based on that success, Nair was commissioned to develop a sitcom focused on an Indian American family that will air on ABC and to adapt her film into a Broadway musical that will open in 2004 (Fleming 2002; Lahr 2002; Littleton 2002). Seeking to tap British interest in all things Bollywood, Andrew Lloyd Webber commissioned *Bombay Dreams,* an original stage musical with an all-Asian cast and music by distinguished Bollywood composer A. R. Rahman (See Bright Launch 2002; Indian Summer 2002). As Webber explained, "there are more people seeing Bollywood musicals on screens on any given night than there are people watching plays in the West End" (Foroohar 2002). American and British film companies are helping to finance the production of Hindi-language films with expectations that they will do well not only in Asia but in the West. Summing up these trends, Indian American filmmaker Kavita Munjai claims, "the young generation is flocking to see Hindi blockbusters. India is the flavour of the day in America now" (Chatterjee 2001).

As Maira notes, the desis display deeply ambivalent feelings to Indo-chic, sometimes proud to see their national culture gain greater visibility, sometimes uncomfortable with the way Western consumers misunderstand or misuse these traditions, and sometimes uncertain whether their own hybrid identities give them any stable position from which to police the authenticity of these new transcultural appropriations. What does it mean that Indo-chic flourishes at a moment when, post–September 11, there is also a rise in "Paki-bashing"? Does the decontextualized consumption of cultural goods necessarily lead to a greater understanding within an ethnically diverse and somewhat segregated society? Does the ability to dance to the Other's music lead to any real appreciation of their social condition or political perspective? Conflicts arise from the fact that the desis and the pop cosmopolitans are consuming at cross-purposes: one group seeking to make peace with its parent culture, even as it carves out a place for itself in the new world; the other seeking to escape the constraints of its local culture and tap into the coolness it now associates with other parts of the world (Gillespie 1995).

The pop cosmopolitan walks a thin line between dilettantism and connoisseurship, between orientalist fantasies and a desire to honestly connect and understand an alien culture, between assertion of mastery and surrender to cultural difference.

These same paradoxes and contradictions surface when we turn our attention to American fans of Japanese anime, the otaku. *Otaku* is a Japanese term used to make fun of fans who have become such obsessive consumers of pop culture that they have lost all touch with the people in their immediate vicinity. American fans have embraced the shameful term, asserting what Matt Hills calls a "semiotic solidarity" with their Japanese counterparts (Hills 2002); constructing their identity as "otaku" allows them to signal their distance from American taste cultures and their mastery over foreign content. While a minority of otaku are Asian or Asian American, the majority have no direct ties to Japan. Sean Leonard, the president of the Anime Society at the Massachusetts Institute of Technology (MIT), is typical of many of his generation whose interest stemmed from their initial exposure to Japanese children's programming:

I first discovered anime around when I was in tenth grade. I started hearing and watching a little *Sailor Moon,* which aired periodically on [the] USA [channel]. What really got me into it, though, was when a Mexican friend of mine lent me the first ten episodes of *Fushigi Yuugi [The Mysterious Play],* fansubbed [subtitled by amateur fans]. It's a really cool shoujo series [aimed at young girls], and it was totally different, and totally more complex, than anything else I had seen before. I resolved that I really liked anime and that I would pursue it. Shortly thereafter, I decided to look at anime from an academic perspective: I wanted to figure out its history, its creators, its principles, and all of that stuff.[7]

Initially, anime, like Bollywood videos, entered the United States through small distributors who targeted Asian immigrants. Fans would venture into ethnic neighborhoods in search of content; in New York and San Francisco they turned to a handful of Japanese bookstores for manga that had not yet been translated or distributed in North America.[8] The Web enabled fans to start their own small-scale (and sometimes pirate) operations to help import, translate, and distribute manga and anime. As Leonard explains, "Fansubbing has been critical to the growth of anime fandom in the West. If it weren't for fans showing this stuff to others in the late seventies, early nineties, there would be no interest in intelligent, 'high-brow' Japanese animation like there is today." On college campuses, student organizations build extensive libraries of both legal and pirated materials and host screenings designed to educate the public about anime artists, styles, and genres. The MIT Anime Society, for example, hosts weekly screenings from a library of more than fifteen hundred films and videos.[9] Since 1994 the club has provided a Web site designed to educate Americans about anime and anime fan culture. Last year it also launched a newsletter with interviews, commentary, and reviews.

Increasingly, larger commercial interests are capitalizing on this growing otaku culture. Disney, for example, has purchased the American rights to the films of Hayao Miyazaki *(Princess Mononoke, Spirited Away),* dubbed them with the voices of American film stars, and insured their distribution across North America. The Cartoon Network features a wide array of anime series as part of its late-night "adult swim" programming. ADV Films, the major importer of anime series for the American market, has announced the launch of a 24 hours

Anime Network (Anime Airwaves 2003, p. 102). Tokyopop, a San Francisco–based company, will publish four hundred volumes of translated manga for American consumption this year. Shueisha, the Japanese comics publisher, launched a monthly English-language version of its successful weekly, *Shonen Jump,* predicting that it would be selling one million copies a month in the American market within the next three years. It is a striking mark of the growing competence and confidence of American manga fans that *Shonen Jump* is being published Japanese style—with text designed to be read from back to front and right to left—rather than flipping the pages (Sakamoto 2003; Sakimaki 2002; Wolk 2001).

Ethnographers who have studied this subculture disagree about the degree to which otaku seek any actual connection with real-world Japan or simply enter into an imaginary world constructed via anime genres. As Susan Napier writes, "the fact that anime is a Japanese . . . product is certainly important but largely because this signifies that anime is a form of media entertainment outside the mainstream, something 'different'" (Napier 2000, p. 242; see also Newitz 1994; Tobin 1998). Napier suggests that fans are attracted to the strange balance of familiar and alien elements in Japanese animation, which openly appropriates and remakes Western genre conventions. Some anime fans do cultivate a more general knowledge of Japanese culture. They meet at sushi restaurants; clubs build partnerships via the Internet with sister organizations in Japan. Members often travel to Japan in search of new material or to experience the fan culture there more directly; some study the Japanese language in order to participate in various translation projects. As American fans go online and establish direct contact with their Japanese counterparts, they create an opening for other kinds of conversation. Discussion lists move fluidly from focus on anime- and manga-specific topics onto larger considerations of Japanese politics and culture. These different degrees of cultural engagement are consistent with what Hannerz has told us about cosmopolitanism more generally: "[In one kind of cosmopolitanism], the individual picks from other cultures only those pieces which suit himself. . . . In another mode, however, the cosmopolitan does not make invidious distinctions among the particular elements of the alien culture in order to admit some of them into his repertoire and refuse others; he does not negotiate with the other culture but accepts it as a package deal" (Hannerz 1990, p. 240). What cosmopolitanism at its best offers us is an escape from parochialism and isolationism, the beginnings of a global perspective, and the awareness of alternative vantage points.

THE MANGAVERSE AND THE ANIMATRIX: FORMS OF CORPORATE HYBRIDITY

American films and television programs become absolutely mainstream as they are introduced into Japan, China, or India. They come with massive marketing campaigns that make it hard for anyone anywhere on the planet to remain unaware that they have Jedi in their midst, for example. Historically, imported media products have been marginalized in the American market. European cinema shows only at art cinema venues; British comedies are packaged for elite public broadcasting audiences; and Asian content gets absorbed into the outer reaches of the cable dial. Foreign media get introduced on the fringes of an expanded menu of options without touching the mainstream. But at least some Asian media are gaining unprecedented visibility and influence. *Pokemon* and *Yu-Gi-Oh* are unavoidable aspects of contemporary children's culture. *Crouching Tiger, Hidden Dragon* played at the multiplexes. And Madonna's borrowings from Bhangra made it into the top forty. As these trends continue, major American media companies seek new models of collaboration with international artists. We might describe these developments as corporate hybridity. Hybridity has often been discussed as a strategy of the dispossessed as they struggle to resist or reshape the flow of Western media into their culture.[10] Here, hybridity can be seen as a corporate strategy, one that comes from a position of strength rather than vulnerability or marginality, one that seeks to control rather than contain transcultural consumption.

Christina Klein has examined the distinctly transnational status of *Crouching Tiger, Hidden Dragon* (Klein 2003). Its director, Ang Lee, was born in Taiwan but educated in the United States; this was the first film Lee produced on Chinese soil. Its financing came from a mixture of Japanese- and American-based media conglomerates. The film was produced and written by Lee's long-term collaborator, the American James Schamus. The cast included performers drawn from across the Chinese diaspora—Zhang Ziyi (mainland China), Zhang Zhen (Taiwan), Chow Yun-Fat (Hong Kong), and Michelle Yeoh (Malaysia). Ang Lee describes *Crouching Tiger* as a "combination platter," stressing its borrowings from multiple cultural traditions. James Schamus agrees: "We ended up making an eastern movie for western audiences and in some ways a more western movie for eastern audiences."[11]

We are apt to see more "combination platter" movies as Hollywood assimilates a generation of Hong Kong directors, technicians, and performers whom it recruited following Chinese reunification. Exploiting political turmoil and economic disarray in Hong Kong, American media companies raided what had emerged as a powerful competitor worldwide. On the surface, this recruitment parallels similar moments in film history when Hollywood sought to buy out competing national cinemas or to imitate styles and genres that had proven successful in the global marketplace. Yet it is one thing to absorb Arnold Schwarzenegger or Mel Gibson, another to absorb Jet Li or Chow Yun-Fat. Their marked ethnic and racial differences could not be easily ignored as Hollywood sought Western vehicles for these Eastern stars. In some cases, the films tap orientalist fantasies, as when Chow Yun-Fat was cast in *Anna and the King* or Michelle Yeoh appeared as a seductive foreign agent in *The World Is Not Enough*. In other cases, the films deal explicitly with themes of cultural relocation and assimilation, as in Jackie Chan's *Shanghai Noon* or *Rumble in the Bronx*. Director John Woo has maintained similar themes and styles but relocated them to Western genres and performers *(Face/Off, Mission: Impossible 2)*. More recently, however, Woo has drawn on his outsider perspective to revisit key moments in American cultural history, exposing the forgotten role played by Navahos in transmitting messages during World War II in *Windtalkers* and turning in his current production to examining the role Chinese coolies played in constructing the transcontinental railroad in *Men of Destiny*.

American media producers are similarly responding to the growing popularity of anime and manga by soliciting Japanese-style content to augment their existing franchises—bringing a distinctly Asian style to bear on characteristically American content. In 2002, for example, Marvel experimented with a new Mangaverse title that reimagined and resituated their stable of superheroes within Japanese genre traditions: Spiderman is a ninja, the members of the Avengers assemble into a massive robot, and the Hulk turns into a giant green monster (Guzman 2002). Initially conceived as a one-shot novelty, the Mangaverse proved so successful that Marvel has launched an entire new production line, Tsunami, which will produce manga-style content for the American and global market, mostly working with Asian or Asian American artists (Tsunami Splash 2003, p. 100). Similarly, Disney's *Kingdom Hearts* emerged from collaboration with the Japanese game company Squaresoft, creators of the successful *Final Fantasy* franchise. The game mixes more than one hundred characters from Disney's animated films with the more anime-style protagonists associated with previous Squaresoft games.[12]

The Matrix is perhaps the most successful and visible example of this absorption of Japanese pop culture influences into the American mainstream. The film's directors, the Wachowski Brothers, hired Japanese manga artists to do the film's storyboards and Hong Kong martial arts choreographer Yuen Wo Ping to stage the action sequences, hoping to produce a live-action counterpart to *Ghost in the Shell* and *Akira*. In anticipation of the release of *The Matrix Reloaded*, Warner Brothers commissioned the Animatrix, a series of short animated prequels created by Yoshiaki Kawajiri, Takeshi Koike, Mahiro Maeda, and a range of other distinguished Asian animators that could be downloaded from the Web.[13]

These examples of corporate hybridity depend on consumers with the kinds of cultural competencies that could only originate in the context of global convergence, requiring not simply knowledge of Asian popular culture but an understanding of its similarities and differences with parallel traditions in the West. These works allow pop cosmopolitans to demonstrate their mastery, counting on them to teach other audience members how to decode these works. At the same time, the Mangaverse and Animatrix provide an opening for fans of more mainstream franchises to savor the "fragrance" of Asian popular culture, potentially expanding the market for cultural imports.

PEDAGOGICAL IMPLICATIONS

Many current efforts toward multicultural education start from assumptions of ethnic purity or cultural authenticity at odds with the current moment of global convergence. Our classrooms are increasingly internationalized, though ties to mother countries break down over multiple generations. Our students come from mixed racial or ethnic families that owe allegiance to multiple cultural traditions; they may have strong identifications with youth subcultures that cut across national and racial borders; they may engage in patterns of intercultural consumption that heightens their awareness of other traditions and practices. Children's media have been central to current corporate strategies of global convergence, whereas youth have played central roles as grassroots intermediaries facilitating the flow of Asian popular culture into the American marketplace. As such, they are already inhabiting a different kind of cultural landscape than their parent's generation, already more aware of Asian perspectives, already occupying a space betwixt and between, loyal to neither one national or ethnic tradition nor another.

Darrell Hamamoto, a professor of Asian American studies, told *USA Today* that this trend toward "Asiaphilia" will do little to alter the stereotyping of Asian Americans: "It's all superficial and there's no depth to it. Beneath this adoration of all things yellow, all things Asian, comes this condescension. In its most benign form, it's patronizing, and in its most severe form, it's a killer" (Barker 2001). He may well be right. There is no guarantee that pop cosmopolitanism will lead to any real understanding between different cultures, since as Hannerz notes, it often involves the selective appropriation and repurposing of other cultural traditions for one's own interests: "Cosmopolitanism often has a narcissistic streak" (Hannerz 1990, p. 240). Yet Hannerz also warns against too easy a dismissal of cosmopolitanism as a kind of dilettantism, suggesting that the "surrender" of oneself to a foreign culture enables fresh perceptions upon which a deeper understanding can be built. While the uneven flow of cultural materials across national borders often produces a distorted understanding of national differences, it also represents a first significant step toward global consciousness.

Pop cosmopolitanism is generating its own intelligentsia, its own critics, historians, translators, and educators. These fans and consumers are also producing their own vernacular theories of globalization, their own understandings of the role Asian content plays in American cultural life, their own explanations for why this material is becoming so accessible to them. Educators need to recognize that these patterns of consumption generate a hunger for knowledge, a point of entry into a larger consideration of cultural geography and political economy. What kinds of educational intervention build upon that hunger and push it toward a greater understanding of America's place in the world? What kinds of pedagogical interventions might displace orientalist stereotypes with a more nuanced account of cultural difference and national specificity?

Shigeru Miyagawa's multimedia project, Star Festival, offers one glimpse of what this kind of intervention might look like. Star Festival offers a virtual environment in which students can explore and learn more about contemporary Japanese culture and society (Karagianis 2001). Based on Miyagawa's own personal history, the project depicts a Japanese American professor's return to the city where he was born and his attempts to resolve internal questions about his cultural identity. The professor has dropped his PDA (personal digital assistant) and the player has recovered it. As players search through the city for its owner, they learn things about the professor's family history and about the cultural traditions that drew him back to Japan. What emerges is a picture not of a pristine Asian culture cut off from Western life but a culture that exists in dialogue with American influences. In one key sequence, we visit a shop that constructs papier-mâché figures used in cultural festivals. Alongside more traditional Japanese icons, we see re-creations of Tarzan, Superman, John Wayne, Rambo, and an array of other Western pop culture figures. Star Festival's curricular guide identifies a range of classroom activities that students at varied grade levels can complete as they work their way through the CD-ROM. Some involve learning about Japanese cultural traditions, such as origami or fish printing. Others involve exploring students' own mixed cultural and racial identities, such as by constructing family trees and documenting their own families' migrations. Miyagawa sees the project as enabling students not simply to learn more about Japan but also to learn more about themselves and to develop a greater respect for the diversity of cultural identities within the current classroom. Miyagawa has said about his own experience returning to Japan after a lifetime spent in America, "It was probably the single, most painful realization of my identity. I had my hopes up to then that returning to Japan would cure all the pain of the past. It was just a further reminder that I was not American, and I was not Japanese. I was neither, and I was both." Miyagawa said that Star Festival helped him to resolve this contradiction in his own thinking and has moved him to try to help students better grasp their own mixed cultural identities: "The big thing I learned is that it's okay to have more than one home. You don't have to choose between two countries. It's not either/or. Finally I realized that home is not a geographic place, but it's a place in your heart and soul" (Karagianis 2001).

Yet pedagogical interventions need not be so elaborate. Teachers can bring examples of Asian pop cultural materials into their classrooms, drawing on the expertise of students to spark debates about what these materials mean and what kinds of cultural changes they represent. For example, I introduced to my MIT students Sheila Chandra's album, *Weaving My Ancestor's Voices*. Chandra, whose mother was Indian and father Irish, has produced a new kind of pop music based on the fusion of elements drawn from Classical Indian and Celtic musical traditions. I played some selections from the album for my students, read her linear note explanation of how she was trying to use music to make sense of her mixed cultural heritage, and asked them what they thought. One Indian-born student with a strong background in classical music objected, "I can't listen to it. It sounds all wrong to me." A second-generation Indian American student retorted, "But the music sounds the way we feel. We feel all wrong." This exchange sparked a larger discussion of how these hybrid forms of music express the conflicts and contradictions of inhabiting a diasporic culture. As the conversation expanded to include students who were not from Asia, further differences in perspective emerged. One second-generation desi had dismissed Bollywood films as "corny" and "amateur" compared to Hollywood blockbusters, while a pop cosmopolitan celebrated their vibrancy and originality. Suddenly, students were debating who has the right to judge the merits of these films and what criteria should be applied. If carefully supervised to insure a climate of mutual respect, such classroom discussions can focus attention on the different investments students make in these imported cultural materials depending on their own personal backgrounds and intellectual interests. Taking this perspective in turn paves the way for a larger consideration of the uneven flow of cultural influences across national borders, of the cultural traditions from which these materials originate, of the different factors that promote or threaten diversity worldwide, and of the larger history of exchanges between East and West that have taken us from the Silk Road to the World Wide Web. The goal should be not to push aside taste for popular culture in favor of preference for a more authentic folk culture or a more refined high culture but rather to help students build upon what they have already learned about cultural difference through their engagement with Asian media imports and to develop a more sophisticated understanding of how these materials reflect the current "garage sale" state of global culture (Rosaldo 1992).

NOTES

1. For the most thorough discussion of the Bert and bin Laden story, see http://www.lindqvist.com/index.php?katID=7&lang=eng&incl=bert.php.

2. For another take on what I am calling pop cosmopolitanism, see Roberts 2000.

3. For another interesting take on the impact of digital media on cultural diversity, see Keniston 1998.

4. For overviews of the debates on media imperialism, see Tomlinson 1991, Howe 1996, Liebes and Katz 1990, and Featherstone 1996.

5. For other negative reactions to the Americanization of the series, see Goodman 2001 and Levy 2001.

6. On the role of ethnic groceries in preserving diasporic traditions, see Nafficy 1992.

7. Sean Leonard, personal correspondence, February 2003.

8. On manga fandom, see Schodt 1996; Kinsella 2000; and Macias and Horn 1999.

9. Sean Leonard, personal correspondence, February 2003.

10. For useful overviews of the literature about hybridity, see Pieterse 1995; Canclini 2001.

11. Ang Lee and James Schamus as quoted in *The Guardian*, November 7, 2000, http://film.guardian.co.uk/interview/interviewpages/0,6737,394698,00 .html. Elsewhere, Schamus explained, "We wanted to make a quintessentially Chinese film that could speak to worldwide audiences in much the same way

that Hollywood makes quintessentially American films that speak to world-wide audiences. The film embraces its international audiences, I hope, with the same amount of generosity that Hollywood films often have toward worldwide audiences. So, rather than making a kind of Hollywood version of a Chinese movies, I think we ended up making a Chinese version of an international blockbuster." A. C. Basoli, "Kung Fu Writing: A Conversation with James Schamus," online at *http://www.moviemaker.com/hop/01/scrn-Schamus.html*.

12. For more information, see http://www.kingdomhearts.com.

13. See http://whatisthematrix.warnerbros.com/rl_cmp/animatrix_trailer_640.html.

REFERENCES

Ahn, J. (2001). *Animated subjects: On the circulation of Japanese animation as global cultural products.* Paper presented at the Globalization, Identity and the Arts Conference, University of Manitoba, Winnipeg.

Allison, A. (2000). A challenge to Hollywood: Japanese character goods hit the U.S. *Japanese Studies* 20(1): 67–88.

Allison, A. (2002). *The cultural politics of Pokemon capitalism.* Paper presented at Media-in-Transition 2: Globalization and Convergence Conference, Massachusetts Institute of Technology, Cambridge, MA.

Anime Airwaves. *Wizard*, March 2003.

Appadurai, A. (1996). *Modernity at large: The cultural dimensions of globalization.* Minneapolis: University of Minnesota Press.

Barker, O. (2001). The Asianization of America but Eastern influences do not mean Asian-Americans are insiders. *USA Today*, March 22.

Bollywood goes global. (2000). *Newsweek International*, February 28.

Bright Launch. *The Hindu*, June 28 2002.

Canclini, N. G. (2001). *Consumers and citizens: Globalization and multicultural conflicts.* Minneapolis: University of Minnesota Press.

Chatterjee, A. (2001). *Leela* is a Hollywood production with the soul of a Hindi film. Rediff.com (January 2). http://www.rediff.com/entertai/2001/jan/021leela.htm.

Featherstone, M. (1996). Localism, globalism and cultural identity. In *Global local: Cultural production and the transnational imaginary.* Rob Wilson and Wimal Dissanayake, eds. Durham: Duke University Press.

Fleming, M. (2002). Monsoon forecast for Broadway. *Variety*, December 15.

Foroohar, R. (2002). Hurray for Globowood: As motion-picture funding, talent and audiences go global, Hollywood is no longer a place, but a state of mind. *Newsweek International*, May 27.

Gillespie, M. (1995). *Television, ethnicity and cultural change.* London: Routledge.

Gitlin, T. (2001). *Media unlimited: How the torrent of images and sounds overwhelms our lives.* New York: Metropolitan.

Goodman, T. (2001). Iron Chef USA is an abomination: UPN remake is an insult to food fans. *San Francisco Chronicle*, November 16.

Guzman, R. A. (2002). Manga revises Marvel heroes. *San Antonio Express-News*, January 23.

Hannerz, U. (1990). Cosmopolitans and locals in world culture. In *Global culture: Nationalism, globalization, and modernity*. M. Featherstone, ed. London: Sage.

Harindranath, R. (2003). Reviving "cultural imperialism": International audiences, global capitalism and the transnational elite. In *Planet TV*. L. Parks and S. Kumar, eds. New York: New York University Press.

Hendershott, H. (1998). *Saturday morning censors*. Durham: Duke University Press.

Hills, M. (2002). Transcultural Otaku: Japanese representations of fandom and representations of Japan in Anime/Manga fan cultures. Paper presented at Media-in-Transition 2: Globalization and Convergence Conference, Massachusetts Institute of Technology, Cambridge, MA.

Hoketsu, K. (2001). *Iron Chef: The official book*. Berkeley, CA: Berkeley Publishing Group.

Howe, D. (1996). Commodities and cultural borders. In *Cross-Cultural Consumption: Global Markets, Local Realities*. London: Routledge.

Indian Summer: Raising the Curtain on Bombay Dreams. *Theatregoer*, June 2002.

Iwabuchi, K. (2002). *Recentering globalization: Popular culture and Japanese transnationalism*. Durham: Duke University Press.

James, A. (1996). Cooking the books: Global or local identities in contemporary British food cultures? In *Cross-cultural consumption: Global markets, local realities*. David Howes, ed. London: Routledge.

Jenkins, H. (2003). *Convergences: Why media change matters*. Manuscript in preparation.

Kaplan, D. (2001). Iron Chef to America. *New York Post*, May 18.

Karagianis, E. (2001) Two worlds touch: Prof.'s CD-ROM helps kids cope with bi-cultural identity. *MIT Spectrum* (spring). http://web.mit.edu/giving/spectrum/spring01/two-worlds-touch.html.

Kavoori. A. P., and C. A. Joseph (2002). Why the dancing diasporic Desi men cross-dressed. *Jump Cut* (45) (fall 2002) http://www.ejumpcut.org/currentissue/kavoori/index.html.

Keniston, K. (1998). *Cultural diversity or global monoculture: The impacts of the information age*. Paper presented at conference on The Global Village, Bangalore, Karnataka, India, http://web.mit.edu/kken/Public/papers1/Cultural%20Diversity.htm.

Kinsella, S. (2002). *Adult Manga: Culture and power in contemporary Japanese society*. Honolulu: University of Hawaii Press.

Klein, C. (2002). The globalization of Hollywood. Paper presented at the Modern Language Association conference, New York, NY.

Klein, C. (2003). Crouching Tiger, Hidden Dragon: *A Transnational Reading*. Manuscript in preparation.

Lahr, J. (2002). Whirlwind: How the filmmaker Mira Nair makes people see the world her way. *The New Yorker*, December 9.

Levin, M. (2002). Independent distributors and specialty labels move product in the U.S. by such international artists as Shakira. Copyright 2002 BPI Communications, Inc. Used with permission from *Billboard,* November 2.

Levy, D. (2001). Iron Chef. *Oakland Press Online Edition,* November 16.

Liebes, T., and E. Katz (1990). *The export of meaning: Cross-cultural readings of* Dallas. Oxford, UK: Oxford University Press.

Littleton, C. (2002). Nair, CWM bring family values to ABC for comedy. *Hollywood Reporter,* December 5.

Lipsitz, G. (1994). *Dangerous crossroads: Popular music, postmodernism, and the politics of place.* London: Verso.

Macias P., and C. G. Horn, eds. (1999). *Japan edge: The insider's guide to Japanese pop subculture.* San Francisco: Cadence Books.

McCracken, G. (2003). *Plenitude* (manuscript in preparation). http://www.cultureby.com/books/plenit/cxc_trilogy_plenitude.html.

Maira, S. M. (2000). Henna and hip hop: The politics of cultural production and the work of cultural studies. *Journal of Asian American Studies* 3(3): 329–369.

Maira, S. M. (2002). *Desis in the house: Indian American youth culture in New York City.* Philadelphia: Temple University Press.

McCollum, C. (2001). "Iron Chef USA: Something's lost during translation. *San Jose Mercury News,* November 16.

Naficy, H. (1992). *The making of exile cultures: Iranian television in Los Angeles.* Minneapolis: University of Minnesota Press.

Napier, S. (2000). *Anime from Akira to Princess Mononoke: Experiencing Japanese animation.* New York: Palgrave.

Newitz, A. (1994). Anime Otaku: Japanese animation fans outside Japan. *Bad Subjects* 13. http://eserver.org/bs/13/Newitz.html.

Olson, S. R. (1999). *Hollywood planet.* New York: Lawrence Erlbaum.

Pells, R. (2002). American culture goes global, or does it? *Chronicle of Higher Education,* April 12. http://chronicle.com/free/v48/i31/31b00701.htm.

Pieterse, J. N. (1995). Globalization as hybridization. In *Global modernities.* M. Featherstone, ed. New York: Sage Foundation.

Punathambekar, A. (2003). *Bollywood bytes: A story of how I found an Online Adda.* Manuscript in preparation.

Roberts, M. (2000). *Notes on the Global Underground: Subcultural Elites, Conspicuous Cosmopolitanism.* Paper presented at the Globalization, Identity and the Arts Conference, University of Manitoba, Winnipeg. http://www.umanitoba.ca/faculties/arts/english/media/workshop/papers/roberts/roberts_paper.pdf.

Rosaldo, R. (1992). *Culture and Truth: The Remaking of Social Analysis.* Boston: Beacon Press.

Sakamoto, M. (2003). Shonen Jump Manga takes giant leap into U.S. market. *Japan Economic Newswire,* January 5.

Sakimaki, S. (2002). Manga mania: Cartoonists eye America. *Washington Post,* September 5.

Schodt, F. (1996). *Dreamland Japan: Writings on modern Manga.* Berkeley, CA: Stone Bridge.

Shukla, S. (1997). Building diaspora and nation: The 1991 cultural festival of India. *Cultural Studies* 11(2): 296–315.

Tobin, J. (1998). An American Otaku or, a boy's virtual life on the Net. In *Digital diversions: Youth culture in the age of multimedia*. J. Sefton-Green, ed. London: University College of London Press.

Tomlinson, J. (1991). *Cultural imperialism*. Baltimore: Johns Hopkins University Press.

Tsunami Splash. *The Wizard*, March 2003.

Wasko, J., M. Phillips, and E. R. Meehan, eds. (2001). *Dazzled by Disney? The global Disney audiences project*. London: Leicester University Press.

Wolk, D. (2001). Manga, Anime invade the U.S.: Japanese comics and animation work together to attract readers. *Publisher's Weekly*, March 12.

Yang, J., and D. Gan, T. Hong, and the staff of *A. Magazine*, eds. (1997). *Eastern Standard Time: A guide to Asian influence on American culture from Astro Boy to Zen Buddhism*. Boston: Houghton Mifflin.

Zuberi, N. (1996). *Sounds English: Transnational Popular Music*. Chicago: University of Chicago Press, 2002.

SEVEN

James L. Watson

GLOBALIZATION IN ASIA

Anthropological Perspectives

INTRODUCTION: IDEOLOGICAL TURMOIL
IN CONTEMPORARY ASIA

This chapter surveys some of the major issues confronting anthropologists who work in the rapidly changing societies of East Asia, Southeast Asia, and South Asia. Since Asian socialisms collapsed in the 1990s, meaningful ideologies and various forms of hybrid capitalisms have come to guide government policies. The Communist Party in China exchanged Karl Marx and Mao Zedong for Adam Smith and Deng Xiaoping. At this writing, Vietnam and North Korea remain staunchly socialist, but like Cuba, these countries play only minor roles in the world economy.

A consumer revolution, led by emerging middle classes, swept through Asia during the 1980s and 1990s. Asia's political elites have not responded well to this challenge, and hence, in many Asian societies the hard realities of political control are in constant tension with the conduct of everyday life. In China, national leaders have embraced an updated version of nationalism as a means to retain power (as a convenient substitute for socialist utopianism). Given the pressures of the world economy, this is not a viable long-term strategy: those who ride the tiger of nationalism rarely survive the experience.

The Chinese government's leaden response to the 2003 outbreak of SARS (severe acute respiratory syndrome) is further evidence that the pressures of globalization will undermine autocratic systems in Asia. The episode demonstrated to the world at large that it is dangerous to allow any political system to avoid the scrutiny of global institutions, such as the World Health Organization (not to mention the Nuclear Regulatory Agency).

Although the arena of international politics and global surveillance is inherently fascinating, this chapter is primarily concerned with the ways in which ordinary people have experienced the processes of globalization. Anthropologists concentrate on the mundane: Does the introduction of American television programs transform life expectations in China? How does the demand for women's labor transform family life in Thailand? What do Hong Kong office workers eat for breakfast? Are young Pakistanis who wear Nike sneakers, drink Coca-Cola, and eat Big Macs agents of culture change? Is Mickey Mouse American, or is he Japanese? Does it matter?

The anthropological lens is a fine-grained one; it focuses on the micro to illustrate the macro. It should not be surprising, therefore, that anthropologists are often critical of grandiose theories that portray globalization as an all-inclusive, all-consuming process of cultural homogenization. It is only fair to acknowledge, however, that there are serious limitations to the anthropological approach. Anthropologists do not (indeed cannot) claim that their case studies are "representative" of social behavior in an entire society. Case studies are based on the personal experience of living in a specific community of people who share common characteristics—defined according to the nature of the study. Today, in contrast to the 1960s and 1970s, the "community" in question is likely to be something other than a rural village: It may be a school, a factory, an urban neighborhood, a nongovernmental organization (NGO), or a McDonald's restaurant (incorporating management, workers, and consumers).

With these considerations in mind, we begin with the general (theories of globalization) and move to the specific (case studies of local responses). The relevance of these discussions to education is discussed in the conclusion.

BACKGROUND: TERMINOLOGY AND
THEORIES OF GLOBALIZATION

Globalism and *globalization* entered everyday English usage in the early 1960s, following the publication of Marshall McLuhan's *Gutenberg Galaxy* (1962). Malcolm Waters, a leading authority on the subject, defines globalization as a "process in which the constraints of geography on social and cultural arrangements recede and [as a consequence] people become increasingly aware that [such constraints] are receding" (1995, p. 3). The term *globalism* is a surprisingly recent creation, appearing for the first time in the 1986 second edition of the *Oxford English Dictionary*. The *OED*'s definition of *globalize* is simple and to the point: "to render global." The earliest attribution for the term *globalization* is a 1962 article in *Spectator* magazine.

In popular usage, *globalization* is linked to the idea that advanced capitalism, aided by digital and electronic technologies, will eventually destroy local traditions and create a homogenized, world culture. Critics of globalization argue that human experience everywhere is becoming essentially the same. Is this a fair characterization of life at the beginning of the twenty-first century?

Homo sapiens is still a far cry from creating a single, overarching cultural system—as envisioned by Isaac Asimov, Marshall McLuhan, and a host of other utopian visionaries of the midtwentieth century. The actual process of globalization has been fitful, chaotic, and slow. Some observers of contemporary politics argue that a rudimentary version of world culture is taking shape among highly educated people, notably those who operate in the rarefied domains of international finance, media, and diplomacy. Hyperelites of this nature constitute what Samuel Huntington (in his *Clash of Civilizations* [1996]) calls a "Davos culture," named after the Swiss town that hosts annual meetings of the World Economic Forum. Whatever their ethnic, religious, or national origin, Davos participants are said to follow a recognizable lifestyle characterized by standardized behavior (social ease, aristocratic manners, and the ability to tell jokes), technological sophistication (knowledge of the latest software, communications systems, and media innovations), advanced understanding of financial markets and currency exchange, postgraduate education in elite institutions, common dress and grooming codes, similar body preoccupations (dietary restraint, vitamin regimes, fitness routines), and a command of American-style English—which they use as a primary medium of communication. Davos people, it is claimed, are instantly recognizable and feel more comfortable in each other's presence than they do among less sophisticated compatriots. The World Economic Forum no longer commands the attention it did in the 1990s, but the term *Davos* has entered world vocabulary as a synonym for late-twentieth-century cosmopolitanism.

Expanding on this idea, the sociologist Peter Berger (1997) argues that the globalization of Euro-American academic agendas and lifestyles has created a worldwide "faculty club culture." Since the 1960s, international funding agencies have supported academic exchanges and postgraduate training for scholars in developing countries, allowing them to build alliances with Western colleagues. The long-term consequence, Berger argues, is the creation of a global network in which similar values, attitudes, and research goals are shared. Network participants have been instrumental in promoting feminism, environmentalism, and human rights as global issues. Berger cites the anti-smoking movement as a case in point: the movement began as an elite North American preoccupation in the 1970s and subsequently spread to other parts of the world—following the contours of academe's global network. As with Davos sophisticates, members of the transnational faculty club rely on English (primarily the American version learned in graduate school) to communicate with each other.

The anthropologists Ulf Hannerz and Arjun Appadurai have studied similar elites that operate on a global scale. Hannerz (1990) believes that a world culture emerged in the late twentieth century, stemming from the activities of "cosmopolitans" who nurture an intellectual appreciation for local cultures in the developing world. The new global culture, in this rendition, is based on the "organization of diversity" rather than "a replication of uniformity." By century's end, cosmopolitan elites had organized dozens of NGOs to help preserve cultural diversity in the developing world. Institutions such as Cultural Survival (located in Cambridge, Massachusetts) now operate on a world scale, drawing attention to indigenous groups that are encouraged to see themselves as "first peoples"—a new, global designation that emphasizes common experiences of exploitation. Appadurai (1997) focuses on highly educated, English-speaking professionals who trace their origins to South Asia. Elites of this nature create "diasporic public spheres" that cut across national borders; Appadurai claims that contemporary diasporas are not only transnational but "postnational"—meaning that people who operate in these spheres are oblivious to national borders and circulate in a social world that has multiple home bases.

Underlying these elite visions of globalism is a reluctance to define exactly what is meant by *culture*. This is not surprising, given that the concept of culture has become one of the most controversial issues in modern social sciences. During most of the twentieth century, anthropologists defined culture as a shared set of beliefs, customs, and ideas that held people together in recognizable, self-identified groups. Starting in the mid-1970s and culminating in the 1990s, however, scholars in many disciplines challenged the notion of cultural coherence as it became evident that members of close-knit groups held radically different visions of their social worlds. Culture is no longer perceived as a preprogrammed mental library—a knowledge system inherited from ancestors. Contemporary anthropologists, sociologists, and media specialists treat culture (if they use the term at all) as a set of ideas, attributes, and expectations that is constantly changing as people react to changing circumstances. This intellectual development reflects social life at the turn of the twenty-first century; the collapse of Soviet socialism and the rise of cybercapitalism has increased the perceived speed of social change everywhere.

The term *local culture* is commonly used in modern academic discourse to characterize the experience of everyday life in specific, identifiable localities. It reflects ordinary peoples' feelings of appropriateness, comfort, and correctness—attributes that define personal preferences and rapidly changing tastes. In this context, it is difficult to argue that an overarching, global culture actually exists. Jet-setting sophisticates may feel comfortable operating in a global network disengaged from specific localities, but the numbers involved are, as yet, insufficient to constitute a coherent cultural system. Where, for instance, do global operators maintain their families? What kind of kinship networks do they rely upon, if any? Is theirs a transitory lifestyle or a permanent condition?

For most people, place and locality still matter. Even the diasporics discussed by Appadurai are embedded in local communities (sometimes several) tied together by common perceptions of what constitutes an appropriate and fulfilling lifestyle. Many software engineers and Internet entrepreneurs who live and work in Silicon Valley, California, maintain homes (and strong social ties) in the Indian states of Maharashtra and Punjab.

Rather than searching for evidence that a world culture already exists, a more fruitful approach is to focus on aspects of life that are affected by the globalizing process. Recent research by anthropologists and media specialists makes clear that globalism is not an omnipotent, unidirectional force that levels everything in its path.

To comprehend cultural changes one must draw a distinction between *form* and *content*. Outward appearance and first impressions are almost always deceptive; what matters most is the internal meaning that people assign to a cultural innovation. Many theorists, including both opponents and proponents of globalism, project their own attitudes onto the people they claim to represent—assuming that all humans see the world in the same way. The perceived "sameness" of global culture often reflects the expectations of the analysts, rather than the perceptions of those who are the subjects of analysis. Misunderstandings of this nature abound in the literature devoted to globalism.

EXPERIENCING GLOBALIZATION: THE COLLAPSE OF TIME AND SPACE

Marshall McLuhan's "global village" thesis (first published in 1962) was one of the most influential ideas of the twentieth century. McLuhan argued that human society passed a critical threshold with the invention and popularization of electronic media, notably television. Accelerated communications produced an "implosion" of personal experience by bringing distant events to the immediate attention of people halfway around the world. Instantaneous communications, predicted McLuhan, would soon destroy power imbalances based on geography, create a global village, and thus bring an end to parochialism and nationalism.

This vision of cultural implosion resurfaced in late-twentieth-century theories of postmodernism. David Harvey, whose book *The Condition of Postmodernity* (1989) influenced a generation of scholars, argued that the postmodern condition is characterized by a "time-space compression" linked to inexpensive air travel and the ever present use of telephones, fax, and—more recently—e-mail.

There can be little doubt that people perceive the world today as a smaller place than it appeared to their grandparents. In 1969 an international telephone call from Hong Kong to Chicago cost nearly $10 per minute; in 2001 the same call varied from $1.20 to $4.00 per minute, depending upon carrier. In the 1960s and 1970s, immigrant workers in London relied on postal systems and personal letter carriers to send news back to their home villages in India and China; it took two months to receive a reply. Telephoning was not an option, even in dire emergencies. By the late 1990s, the grandchildren of these first-generation migrants carried cellular phones that linked them instantaneously to cousins in Calcutta, Singapore, and Shanghai. Awareness of time zones (when will people be awake? what time do offices open?) is now second nature to migrant workers; it is no longer a specialized skill cultivated by business travelers.

Meanwhile, foreign travel has become a routine experience for millions of middle- and working-class people. The dollar price of a trans-Pacific flight (not adjusted for inflation) has actually *declined* since the mid-1960s, while incomes on both sides of the Pacific have tripled. Diplomats, businesspeople, and ordinary tourists can feel "at home" in any city, anywhere in the world. In fact, the standardized hotel experience—pioneered by the Hilton Hotel chain—is difficult to avoid. Foreign travel no longer involves the necessity, or the challenge, of adapting to unfamiliar food and living arrangements. Western-style beds, toilets, showers, fitness centers, and restaurants now constitute the global standard. (A Japanese variant, featuring Japanese-style food and facilities, is available in most major cities.) One need not be a Davos sophisticate to wake up in familiar surroundings and have no idea where in the world one might be. An experience of this nature would have been nearly impossible in the 1960s, when the weather, aroma, and noise of the local society invaded one's hotel room. The very idea of a global culture was inconceivable prior to the universalization of air conditioning.

Television, Sports, and Globalization

McLuhan's notion of the global village presupposed the worldwide spread of television, which brings distant events into the homes of viewers everywhere. The spectacular growth of CNN (Cable News Network) is a case in point. Founded by media magnate Ted Turner in 1975, CNN has become an icon of globalism. Its American-style news programming is broadcast throughout the world, twenty-four hours a day. By the 1990s, CNN was an essential feature of the standardized hotel experience described above. Live broadcasts of the 1989 democracy demonstrations in Tiananmen Square, the fall of the Berlin Wall in 1989, and the Gulf War in 1991 illustrated the power of television to influence world opinion. Learning from such experiences, national governments now try to restrict international broadcasting, but satellite technology makes this increasingly difficult (as evidenced by events in Iraq during the spring of 2003).

McLuhan's implosion hypothesis is illustrated by a bizarre event that occurred on June 17, 1994, when CNN suddenly began to broadcast real-time images of Los Angeles police cars in pursuit of a white Ford Bronco (a sports utility vehicle). The Bronco was driven by O.J. Simpson, an American sports hero who was subsequently arrested as a murder suspect. Live coverage of the pursuit cut into regularly scheduled programming throughout CNN's worldwide system, presumably on the assumption that viewers everywhere would relate to the unfolding drama as meaningful news. Live broadcasts succeeded in transforming a parochial American drama into a world event. The subsequent trial drew a world audience and was covered exhaustively by CNN and other news networks.

The power of media giants to filter and present events as "news" makes television a logical target for criticism. A full-page advertisement appearing in the June 19, 2000, *New York Times* (funded by a consortium of environmentalist and anti-globalism NGOs) argued that television feeds homogenized images "directly inside people's brains" and is therefore "capable of unifying thoughts, feelings, values, tastes and desires" among billions of people. Critics cite, for example, a 1999 anthropological study (see Becker, Burwell, Gilman, Herzog, and Hamburg 2002) that linked the appearance of anorexia in Fiji to the popularity of American television programs, notably *Melrose Place* and *Beverly Hills 90210*. Both series featured the exploits of slender young actresses who, it was claimed, led Fijian women to question indigenous notions of the ideal body. Anti-globalism activists also argue that American soap operas have corrosive effects on local cultures by highlighting Western notions of beauty, individualism, and sexuality. Media surveys would seem to support such claims: In 1993, the American series *The Bold and the Beautiful* was ranked among the most popular soap operas in Egypt, India, Italy, and Lebanon.

American television programs sometimes have other, less predictable effects on local cultures, including changes that would surprise critics. In the northern Chinese province of Heilongjiang, for instance, anthropologist Yunxiang Yan (2000) discovered that *Hunter,* an American detective series, not only was the most popular television program in the early 1990s but also was changing local attitudes toward political authority. After watching the series week after week, an ordinary farmer protested loudly when local police did not produce an "arrest warrant" to support his detention for a minor altercation. The authorities in charge of the case, themselves avid fans of *Hunter,* were clearly unsettled by the experience. The *Hunter* case bolsters Thomas Friedman's argument (in *The Lexus and the Olive Tree* [2000]) that globalization is accompanied by the popularization of anti-authoritarian, democratic values.

The influence of television is nearly universal. Ninety-nine percent of American households had at least one functioning television receiver in 1998 (with 2.24 TVs in the average home). Per-capita television ownership figures for developing countries are rising rapidly (see Table 7.1). The total number of television receivers per capita is not, however, a reliable measure of viewership in many parts of the world. In the small towns of Guatemala, the villages of Jiangxi Province (south central China), and the hill settlements of Borneo, one television receiver—often a satellite system powered by a gasoline generator—may serve two or

Table 7.1. TELEVISION
RECEIVERS PER CAPITA, 1999

Brazil	0.223
Canada	0.714
China	0.319
Denmark	0.592
Egypt	0.119
France	0.591
Ghana	0.093
India	0.061
Japan	0.684
Mexico	0.270
Poland	0.337
Russia	0.405
South Africa	0.118
Thailand	0.189
United States	0.805

SOURCE: U.S. Bureau of Census (1999). Table 1371: Newspapers, radio, television by country. In *Statistical abstract of the United States, 1999.* P. 846.

three dozen viewers, each paying a small fee. A television-viewing business of this nature plays a central role in the 1999 hit film *The Cup* (featuring Tibetan Buddhist monks who become avid fans of World Cup soccer). Collective viewing in bars, restaurants, and teahouses was common during the early stages of television broadcasting in Indonesia, Japan, and Kenya (plus a long list of other societies). By the 1980s, video-viewing parlors had become ubiquitous in all but the poorest regions of the globe.

Live sports programs continue to draw the largest global audiences, perhaps because this form of entertainment requires minimal language skills. The 2002 World Cup soccer final between Brazil and Germany was watched by an estimated two billion people. National Basketball Association (NBA) championship playoff games are broadcast to over 140 countries. Michael Jordan, renowned for his basketball skills, became one of the world's most recognized public personalities in the late 1990s (see LaFeber 1999).

Basketball, unlike soccer, did not draw a world audience until the 1992 Olympic Games, when the so-called "Dream Team" of NBA stars electrified viewers who had never seen the sport played to American professional standards. NBA games have since become standard television fare in Australia, Israel, Japan, China, Germany, and Britain; basketball now rivals soccer as the world's most popular—and most played—sport. When state authorities banned NBA playoff games in retaliation for the May 1999 NATO bombing of the Chinese embassy in Belgrade, Beijing fans reacted with outrage, arguing that sports coverage has nothing to do with politics. Many of the Chinese students who threw rocks at the American embassy to protest the Belgrade incident were avid followers of Michael Jordan and his team, the Chicago Bulls (known in Chinese as the "Red Bulls").

Hollywood, Bollywood, and Trojan Horses

In 1994 *The Fugitive*, a Hollywood adventure film starring American actors Harrison Ford and Tommy Lee Jones, swept through China and generated an unprecedented demand for tickets. This was the first (recently produced) Western blockbuster to be distributed in China in forty years (although politically acceptable Western fare, such as the 1960 classic *Spartacus*, had been shown for decades). In 1998 the drama and special effects of *Titanic* created an even larger sensation. Chinese fans, especially middle-aged people, returned to the theater over and over—crying their way through the film. Enterprising hawkers soon appeared to sell packages of facial tissue outside Shanghai theaters. The theme song of *Titanic* became a best selling CD in China, as did posters of the young stars. Chinese consumers bought over twenty-five million pirated (and three hundred thousand legitimate) video copies of the film.

Jiang Zemin, president of China at the time, was so impressed by *Titanic* that he invited the entire Politburo of the Communist Party to a private screening. He justified his action by citing *The Art of War*, an ancient military classic: "Only through knowing the enemy . . . can we win a hundred battles." Jiang also argued that *Titanic* could be seen as a Trojan horse, carrying within it the seeds of American cultural imperialism.

Chinese authorities are not alone in their suspicions of Hollywood. In early 2000 Canadian government regulators ordered the CBC (Canadian Broadcasting Corporation) to stop showing Hollywood films during prime time and feature more Canadian-made programs. CBC executives protested that their viewers would stop watching their local network and turn to satellite reception for international entertainment. Such fears were well-grounded, given that 79 percent of English-speaking Canadians mentioned a U.S. program when asked to name their favorite television series in 1998.

Starting in the 1950s, a thriving local industry known as Bollywood developed in and around Bombay. By the mid-1990s, India had the most prolific film industry in the world, producing over eight hundred feature-length films a year. Primarily love stories with heavy doses of singing and dancing, Bollywood products are leading exports and draw enthusiastic audiences in Southeast Asia and the Middle East (see Jenkins, this volume). (State censors in Islamic societies often find the modest dress and subdued sexuality of Indian film stars acceptable for local viewers.)

In the late 1990s, Hollywood films such as *Jurassic Park* and *Speed* were cleared for public viewing in India, where they caused immediate sensations. *Jurassic Park* appeared in a dubbed Hindi version in 1994, making it the first American blockbuster accessible to a mass audience. The local appeal of Bollywood is still strong, but young people in India quickly developed an appreciation for the latest in special effects and computer graphics that enliven Hollywood films.

Mass Media as an Agent of Globalization?

Is Jiang Zemin right? Does exposure to *Titanic* cause people to become more like Americans? Anthropologists who study television and film are wary of such suggestions. Distinctions must be drawn between the production and the consumption of popular entertainment (see Jenkins, this volume). The process of globalization looks very different when one focuses on ordinary viewers and their efforts to make sense of what they see.

A case in point is Daniel Miller's pathbreaking study of television viewing in Trinidad, a country that produces little programming of its own. Miller discovered that Trinidadians had no trouble relating to the personal dramas portrayed in American soap operas, even though the lifestyles and material circumstances of the performers differed radically from anything experienced by viewers in Trinidad. In 1988, 70 percent of Trinidadians who had television watched daily episodes of

The Young and the Restless, a series that emphasized family problems, sexual intrigue, and gossip. Local people interpreted the televised dramas as commentaries on contemporary life in Trinidad; the portrayal of American material culture, notably women's fashions, was a secondary attraction. Miller concludes that it is a mistake to treat television viewers as passive recipients of global images over which they have no control. Trinidadians actively appropriated scenes from *The Young and the Restless* by reinterpreting the action to fit their own experience (see Miller 1992).

One might also ask why middle-aged Chinese fans of *Titanic* found themselves so emotionally involved with the exploits of two young Hollywood stars (Leonardo DiCaprio and Kate Winslet). Interviews in Shanghai revealed that many older people projected their own, long-suppressed experiences of lost youth into the film. From 1966 to 1976 the Cultural Revolution convulsed China and destroyed any possibility of educational or career advancement for millions of young people. Communist authorities also discouraged romantic love and promoted politically correct marriages based on class background and revolutionary commitment. Improbable as it might seem to Western observers, the story of lost love on a sinking cruise ship hit a responsive chord among Cultural Revolution veterans. Their enthusiastic, highly emotional response had almost nothing to do with the cultural system that framed the film. *Titanic* served as a socially acceptable vehicle for the public expression of regret by a generation of aging revolutionaries who had devoted their lives to building a form of socialism that had long since disappeared.

Global Food Networks and Consumer Expectations: The Standardization of Diet?

Food has always been a driving force for globalization, especially during earlier phases of European trade and colonial expansion. The American hot pepper (capsicum) was introduced to the Spanish court by Christopher Columbus in 1493 and rapidly spread throughout the colonial world. The capsicum and its by-products transformed cuisines and farming practices in Africa, Asia, and the Middle East. It is hard to imagine Korean culture without red kimchi or Szechuanese food without its fiery hot sauce—but both are relatively recent innovations (probably seventeenth century).

Other New World crops, such as maize, cassava, sweet potatoes, and peanuts, were responsible for agricultural revolutions in Asia and Africa, opening up terrain for farming that had previously been unproductive (see Mazumdar 1999). A century after the sweet potato was introduced into south China (mid-1600s), it was a dominant crop and was largely responsible for a population explosion that created what today is called Cantonese culture. It is the lowly sweet potato, not the more celebrated white rice, that sustained generations of southern Chinese farmers. Today the descendants of these Cantonese, Hokkien, and Hakka pioneers disdain the sweet potato as a "poverty food" that conjures up images of past hardships. In Taiwan, by contrast, independence activists (affluent members of the new Taiwanese middle class) have embraced the sweet potato as an emblem of identity, reviving old recipes and celebrating their cultural difference from "rice-eating mainlanders."

Global food networks, epitomized by the sweet potato saga, originated with the pursuit of exotic spices (black pepper, cinnamon, cloves, vanilla) that enlivened the bland cuisines of Medieval European courts. Today global food networks feature more prosaic commodities, such as soybeans, bananas, and oranges. Green beans are now grown in Burkina Faso, Central Africa, and shipped by express air cargo to Paris, where they end up on the plates of diners in four-star restaurants (Freidberg 1997). This particular exchange system is based on a "nontraditional" crop that was not grown in Burkina Faso until the mid-1990s; this small-scale agricultural revolution was encouraged by the World Bank to promote economic development. Central African farmers now find themselves in direct competition with other "counterseason" (with respect to European climates) producers of green beans in Brazil and Florida. African bananas, Chilean grapes, and California oranges have transformed consumer expectations everywhere in the world. Fresh bananas, for example, were expensive luxury items in Germany during the 1950s; today they are cheaper than local apples. Other commodities have reversed this general trend and have become more, rather than less, expensive (a case in point is the global traffic in tuna; see Bestor 2000).

Since the Second World War the pace of dietary globalization has increased dramatically. All nations are converging on a diet high in meat, dairy products, and processed sugars. A simultaneous movement away from grain and tuber starches correlates closely with a worldwide rise in affluence. The new "global diet," as it is called by some nutritionists, also involves a dramatic increase in energy supplied by fats—primarily animal fats. At the end of the twentieth century, Americans derived 60 percent of their energy from sugars and fats, which has led to a rise in obesity and diabetes. Japanese consumers have dramatically reduced their intake of rice and increased their consumption of high-fat dairy products. Similar dietary transitions are occurring whenever and wherever economic conditions permit higher percentages of household incomes to be invested in food. A new industry in children's food—emphasizing sweets and salty snacks—emerged in China during the early 1990s; prior to that time Chinese children ate essentially what adults ate (see Jing 2000). Rising levels of affluence and a corresponding decline in family size have turned children into discerning, sophisticated consumers whose tastes in food, toys, and entertainment drive global industries.

Vegetarians, environmental activists, and organic food enthusiasts have organized rearguard actions to reintroduce "traditional" dietary practices, but these efforts are concentrated among educated elites in industrial nations. The homogenization of human diet appears to be unstoppable. Is this global trend controlled by Western corporate interests?

The Fast-Food Revolution: Homogenization or Localization?

McDonald's, KFC (Kentucky Fried Chicken), and Coca-Cola are primary targets of anti-globalism demonstrators who are themselves organized into global networks via the Internet (see the discussion below). Food and beverage companies attract attention because they cater to the most elementary form of human consumption. We are what we eat, and when diet changes, notions of national and ethnic identity change accordingly. McDonald's has become a symbol of globalism for obvious reasons: on an average day the company serves nearly fifty million customers in over thirty thousand restaurants located in 118 countries. In the mid-1990s, a new McDonald's opened somewhere in the world every eight hours (the rate of expansion has subsequently slowed). Critics claim that the spread of American-style fast food undermines the integrity of indigenous cuisines, thereby promoting the homogenization of world dietary preferences. Anthropological research in Korea, Japan, and Hong Kong does not support this view (see Watson 1997a).

Close attention to cultural trends at the local level shows that the globalization process works both ways. Fast-food chains do indeed introduce innovations that sometimes change consumer behavior and preferences. In Japan, for example, using one's hands to hold and simultaneously eat prepared foods was considered a gross breach of etiquette before the popularization of McDonald's hamburgers. The company had such a dramatic impact on popular etiquette that it is now common to see Tokyo commuters eating in public, without chopsticks or spoons. In late-Soviet Russia, public rudeness had become a high art form among service personnel. Today consumers expect polite, smiling service when they visit Moscow restaurants, a social revolution initiated by McDonald's and its employee indoctrination programs (Caldwell 2004).

The social atmosphere in 1960s colonial Hong Kong was anything but genteel. Cashing a check, boarding a bus, or buying a train ticket required brute force. The majority of local residents were refugees from Maoist China, and they were not inclined to see the British colony as their home. To use a Cold War metaphor, Hong Kong was a borrowed place living on borrowed time (the ninety-nine-year lease on the colonial territory expired at midnight on June 30, 1997). Given this political environment, ordinary people did not feel compelled to participate in a civic culture that included standing in line for services. When McDonald's opened in 1975, customers clumped around the cash registers, shouting orders and waving money over the heads of people in front of them. The company responded by introducing queue monitors (young women) who channeled everyone into orderly lines. Queuing subsequently became a hallmark of Hong Kong's cosmopolitan, middle-class culture created by the children and grandchildren of refugees. Older residents credit McDonald's for introducing the queue, a critical element in this social transition (Watson 1997b).

Another innovation that has had a revolutionary effect on local cultures in Asia, Latin America, Europe, and Asia is the provision of clean toilets and washrooms. McDonald's was instrumental in setting new standards, and thereby raising consumer expectations, in cities that had never had public facilities. The significance of this innovation, especially for women, cannot be underestimated; wherever McDonald's sets up business, it rapidly becomes a haven for an emerging class of middle-income urbanites.

Have McDonald's and its rivals in the fast-food business had similar revolutionary effects on local dietary practices, as many nutritionists claim? Ethnographic research in East Asia suggests that self-service grocery stores, Western-style bakeries, and dairy firms are the primary agents of dietary change. The promotion of milk, yogurt, and ice cream is especially important. Fast-food chains, by contrast, have a surprisingly marginal effect on overall diet, as measured by total calories consumed per week. Critics argue, however, that it is the symbolic impact of fast food—rather than its total caloric input—that makes it such a powerful force for dietary change.

In developing markets, fast-food chains invest heavily in television advertising aimed directly at children. Largely as a consequence, American-style birthday parties have spread to many parts of the world where individual birth dates were not celebrated in the past. McDonald's and KFC became the leading venues for birthday parties throughout East Asia; special rooms and services are provided for the events (Lozada 2000). Fast-food chains also introduce practices that younger consumers may not experience at home, notably the chance to choose one's own food. Visits to McDonald's and KFC quickly become signal events for children who approach fast-food restaurants with a heady sense of empowerment. In this sense, therefore, American-style fast food has indeed had a global impact: it has changed the experience of childhood in many parts of the world.

Anti-Globalization Movements, Internet Technology, and the "Virtual State"

Anti-globalization activists often depict McDonald's, Disney, and Coca-Cola as agents of "cultural imperialism," a new form of domination that results from the export of popular culture from advanced capitalist societies to the developing world, where consumers presumably crave the trappings of global sophistication. The commodities involved in this exchange system are related to lifestyle, especially as experienced by young people: pop music, film, video, comics, fashion, fast foods, beverages, home decorations, entertainment systems, and exercise equipment (to name some of the more obvious examples). Critics of globalization argue that corporations that are capable of manipulating personal tastes will thrive as state authorities everywhere lose control over the distribution of goods and services.

Military force is perceived to be hopelessly out of step with this vision of world power; control of culture (and its production) is more important than control of borders. National boundaries are increasingly permeable, and any effort to exclude global pop culture only makes it irresistible to millions of young people who learn to "hack" their way through Internet firewalls and import barriers. "Information wants to be free" was the clarion call of software designers and Web aficionados in the 1990s. This code of ethics takes its most creative and anarchic form wherever governments try hardest to control the inflow of information (e.g., China and Iran).

The idea of a borderless world is also reflected in 1990s theories of the "virtual state," an emerging political condition that was said to reflect the essential chaos of late-twentieth-century capitalism. A leading proponent of this view is Richard Rosecrance (1999), who writes: "In its pure form . . . the virtual state [represents] an entirely new system of world politics. In the past . . . the main flow between countries consisted of armies. Future flows will be largely economic as capital, technology, manpower, and information move rapidly among states. In the long run, national access to international factors of production can replace the need to control additional land" (p. 2).

The American academic community had already begun to turn against such radical views by the time Rosecrance's book *The Virtual State* (1999) appeared. This shift was no doubt influenced by sobering developments in the Balkans (Serbia, Kosovo, Bosnia) and by the reappearance of xenophobic nationalisms in Russia and China. Martin Wolf, associate editor of the *Financial Times*, declared that "[as] the source of order and the basis of governance, the state will remain in the future as effective, and will be as essential, as it has ever been" (2001, p. 178). World developments since the September 11, 2001, terrorist attacks on the United States make Rosecrance's utopian vision seen strangely dated.

Nonetheless, arguments regarding the erosion of state sovereignty are particularly unsettling for elites who are consumers rather than producers of digital technology. Post-Soviet Russia, post-Mao China, and post-Gaullist France are obvious examples of Cold War giants that face uncertain futures in the emerging global system. French intellectuals and politicians have seized upon anti-globalism as an organizing ideology in the absence of other unifying themes. In his 2001 book, *France in an Era of Globalization*, French foreign minister Hubert Vedrine denounces the United States as a "hyperpower" that promotes "uniformity" and "unilateralism." Vedrine argues that France should take the lead in building a "multipolar world." Ordinary citizens are also concerned about a perceived loss of French national identity, particularly as the regulatory power of the European Union begins to affect everyday life. Sixty percent of respondents in a 1999 *L'Expansion* poll agreed that globalization represented the greatest threat to the French way of life (Meunier 2000). French politicians and journalists frequently use the term *Anglo-Saxon globalization* as a synonym for cultural disintegration and social anomie.

Food, especially haute cuisine, is commonly regarded (by French and non-French alike) as *the* core element of French culture—the one sure way to distinguish France from its less discerning neighbors. Not surprisingly, given these views, McDonald's has become a favorite target of European protest movements. In spite of its notoriety the corporation continues to expand in the very heartland of opposition: by the end of 2002 there were 973 McDonald's restaurants in France, employing over thirty thousand people (an increase of 60 outlets from 2001). The Big Mac may be a reviled symbol of cultural imperialism for French intellectuals, but the steady growth of fast-food chains demonstrates that anti-globalist attitudes do not always affect economic behavior, even in societies (such as France) in which such sentiments are nearly universal. Like their counterparts in the United States, French workers and office staff are increasingly pressed for time. The two-hour lunch is a thing of the past for most ordinary Parisians; by the mid-1990s, leisurely dining was reserved for intellectuals, politicians, and tourists.

French protesters are not alone in singling out American fast-food chains: from 1994 to 2003 McDonald's restaurants were subject to violent attacks (including bombings) in Rome, Macao, Rio de Janeiro, Prague, London, Karachi, Jakarta, Mexico City, Beirut, and Beijing—a complete list would fill most of this page. An international network of political activists emerged in the late 1990s to coordinate simultaneous protests at McDonald's restaurants around the world on a designated date in mid-October every year. The movement began with a now famous trial of anti-McDonald's demonstrators in London (known as the "McLibel" proceedings) and spread rapidly, via the Internet, to associated groups around the globe. By 2003 there were thousands of linked Web sites denouncing the corporation as an agent of cultural imperialism.

Anti-globalist organizers are, without doubt, among the world's most creative and sophisticated users of Internet technology (which, ironically, is one of the principal tools that makes globalization possible). An excellent illustration is the way Greenpeace, an environmentalist NGO originating in Europe and North America, organized a worldwide firestorm of protest against genetically modified (GM) foods during the early 2000s. Highly organized demonstrations appeared, seemingly overnight, in many parts of the world to denounce GM products as "Frankenfoods" that pose unknown (and undocumented) dangers to the environment. The bioengineering industry, supported by various scientific organizations, launched its own Web-based counterattack, but the response was too late and too disorganized to outflank Greenpeace and its NGO allies. Sensational media coverage had already turned millions of consumers against GM foods before the scientific community could enter the debate. (In Europe the fiasco associated with mad cow disease fueled suspicions that governments were withholding vital information about bioengineering and potential problems in the food chain.) The anti-GM food movement demonstrates the immense power of the Internet for organizing and orchestrating political protests. This power derives from the ability of a few determined activists to communicate with thousands (even millions) of potential allies in an instant—by simply clicking a mouse.

Web visionaries, notably those who wrote for *Wired* magazine during the 1990s, would embrace the Greenpeace anti-GM movement as a prophecy fulfilled. Kevin Kelly, former executive editor of *Wired* and author of the influential book *Out of Control* (1994), predicted that the Internet would gradually erode the power of governments to control citizens; advances in digital technology should allow people to follow their own interests and form interstate coalitions in cyberspace. Contributors to *Wired* also envisioned a world offering continuous, uninhibited access to information that would eventually undermine and render obsolete twentieth-century ideologies based on class, religion, and ethnicity. New, nonlocalized identities that defy easy classification or categorization would emerge first in advanced capitalist societies and spread gradually throughout the planet—and beyond. Utopian views of this nature are reminiscent of early Marxist dreams of a classless, stateless world devoid of religious and racial distinctions. Anthropological research on Internet subcultures is only beginning (at this writing), but preliminary results do *not* point to an evaporation of status hierarchies, social distinctions, or class sensitivities (see, e.g., Miller and Slater 2000). The total absence of (perceived) boundaries may, in fact, lead Web addicts to create virtual exclusivities—not the democratic cyber-communities envisioned by *Wired* digerati.

Clothing and Globalization

Clothing is an intriguing domain of globalization, precisely because outward appearances can be deceptive, disguising an amazing array of cultural diversities behind a facade of uniformity. The male business suit, with colored tie and buttoned shirt, is now universal, in the sense that it is worn (nearly) everywhere—even in parts of the world that try hard to avoid global trends, such as Saudi Arabia and Iran. Iranian parliamentarians wear the Western-style suit but forgo the tie; Saudi diplomats alternate Bedouin robes with tailored business suits, depending upon occasion.

World clothing fashions for both men and women swept through China after the 1976 death of Communist Party chairman Mao Zedong and the onset of economic liberalization. The androgynous gray or blue Mao suit gradually disappeared in the 1980s as Politburo members began to wear suits and ties in public. Communist patriarch Deng Xiao-ping and a handful of aging leaders continued to wear revolutionary-era suits until their deaths in the 1990s—by which time Mao suits had reappeared in Hong Kong and Shanghai boutiques as high-priced nos-talgia wear, saturated with postmodern irony.

The emergence of women's power suits in the 1980s is another obvi-ous feature of global standardization. Stylized pantsuits, with silk scarves and colorful blouses (analogues of the male business suit), are now worldwide symbols of modernity, independence, and com-petence. Similarly, military fashions were rapidly globalizing in the early 2000s, making it increasingly difficult to distinguish the national identities of troops in the field. The American military's adoption of a new helmet (an updated version of the German Second World War–era infantry helmet, which hangs low on the neck) caused conster-nation among many older Americans who associated this style with Nazism. By the 1990s, younger Americans and Europeans no longer made such connections. The modified helmet became truly global in 2001, when it appeared on elite Chinese troops marching in a parade in Beijing's Tiananmen Square. Today the only military units that follow alternative styles are anti-government rebel forces in Central Africa, South America, and the Balkans—and even these irregulars often affect what amounts to a uniform, inspired by the guerrilla garb that Holly-wood star Sylvester Stallone wore in his trilogy of *Rambo* films (1981–1988).

Religion, Family Life, and Globalization

Samuel Huntington, in his influential book *Clash of Civilizations* (1996), argues that the post–Cold War world is dissolving into regional alliances based on religious belief and historical attachment to var-ious civilizations. The most prominent of these formations are Western Christianity (Catholicism and Protestantism), Orthodox Christianity (Russian and Greek), Islam, Hinduism, and Confucianism. In Hunting-ton's view, the progress of globalization will be severely constrained by religiopolitical barriers, leading to a multipolar world as opposed to a standardized, global culture predicted by Internet pioneers and propo-nents of the virtual state.

The Huntington thesis appealed to many policy makers in Washington, no doubt because it offered a clear (critics called it a simplistic) vision of world politics at the dawn of the twenty-first century: "In the emerging era, clashes of civilizations are the greatest threat to world peace." By implication, the guardians of Western civilization must be prepared to defend their culture from internal dissenters (i.e., multiculturalists) and external enemies. (Huntington's book was a constant topic of discussion in the American media during the immediate aftermath of the September 11, 2001, terrorist attacks on the World Trade Center and the Pentagon.)

Ethnographic evidence gathered by anthropologists and sociologists does not support Huntington's model but points instead to a rapid diffusion of religious and cultural systems. Islam is an excellent case in point, given that it constitutes the fastest-growing religion in the United States, France, and Germany—supposed bastions of the Christian West. Thirty-five percent of students in the Dearborn, Michigan, public school system were Muslim in 2001; the provision of Halal (lawful under Islam) meals at lunchtime became a hot issue in local politics. Entire districts (arrondissements) of Paris are now dominated by Muslims, the majority of whom are French citizens born and reared in France. Muslims of Turkish origin constitute the fastest-growing sector of Berlin's population; and in northern England, the old industrial cities of Bradford and Newcastle are being revitalized by second- and third-generation descendants of Pakistani and Indian Muslims who immigrated during the 1950s and 1960s.

Christianity has, from its inception during the second century, been an aggressively proselytizing religion with a globalizing agenda. The Roman Catholic Church is arguably the first global institution, spreading rapidly throughout the European colonial world and beyond. Perhaps the fastest-growing religion in today's world is evangelical Christianity, a loose network of global movements that share little in common other than a preoccupation with missionary activities. By stressing each individual's personal experience of divinity, as opposed to priestly intercession, evangelism has wide appeal in developing countries. Pentecostal movements have swept through Latin America and sub-Saharan Africa, where they present serious challenges to established Catholic churches. In China unauthorized "house churches" are a major concern for Communist Party officials who attempt to control all religious activity through state-sponsored organizations (for Islam, Christianity, and Buddhism). Many of the unrecognized churches are syncretic in the sense that they combine aspects of local religion with Christian ideas, and are almost impossible to organize, let alone control. Peter Berger (1997), a sociologist of religion, argues that "there may be other globalizing popular movements [today], but Evangelicalism is clearly the most dynamic."

The boundaries between what Huntington calls Western Christianity and Orthodox Christianity are also eroding, notably in Russia following the collapse of Soviet power in 1991. Evangelical missionaries from the United States and Europe redirected much of their attention from Latin America and Africa to Russia during the 1990s and, in the process, alarmed leaders of the Russian Orthodox Church, which was also in the process of rebuilding after seventy-four years of Soviet repression. By 1997, under pressure from Orthodox clergy, President Boris Yeltsin proposed legislation to restrict the activities of religious organizations that had operated in Russia for less than fifteen years, effectively banning Western evangelical missionaries and their allies. The debate over Russian religious unity continues today, and if China is any guide, legislation will have little long-term effect on the outcome.

Huntington also assumes that the major societies in East Asia constitute an alliance of "Confucian" cultures that share a common heritage linked to the teachings of the ancient Chinese sage, Confucius (551–479 BCE). Early-twenty-first-century life in Tokyo, Seoul, Beijing, Taipei, and Hong Kong shows far more evidence of globalization than Confucianization. The reputed hallmarks of Confucianism—respect for parental authority and ancestral traditions—are no more salient in these cities than in Boston, Birmingham, or Berlin. This is a consequence of (among other things) a steady reduction in family size that has swept through East Asian societies since the 1980s. Late childbearing and marriage resistance among highly educated, working women has undermined the basic tenets of the Confucian family (Watson 2000). Birthrates in Singapore and Japan have fallen below replacement levels and are at record low levels in Hong Kong; birthrates in

Beijing, Shanghai, and other major Chinese cities are also declining rapidly. These developments mean that East Asia—like Europe—faces a major crisis as decreasing numbers of workers are expected to support an ever growing cohort of retirees. By 2025 China will have 274 million people over age sixty, more than the entire 1998 population of the United States. The prospects for other East Asian countries are far worse: 17.2 percent of Japan's 127 million people were over age sixty-five in 2000; by 2020 that percentage is expected to rise to 26.9, while the total population shrinks to 124 million.

Meanwhile Asia's "Confucian" societies face a concurrent revolution in family values: the conjugal family (centering on the emotional bond between wife and husband) is rapidly replacing the patriarchal joint family (focused on support of aged parents and grandparents). This transformation is occurring even in remote, rural regions of northwest China, where married couples now expect to reside in their own home (neolocal residence), as opposed to the house or compound of the groom's parents (patrilocal residence). The children produced by these conjugal units are very different from their older kin who were reared in joint families: today's offspring are likely to be pampered singletons (only children), known as "little emperors" or "little empresses." Contemporary East Asian families are characterized by an ideology of consumerism that is diametrically opposed to the neoauthoritarian, Confucian rhetoric promoted by leaders such as Singapore's Lee Kuan-yew and Hong Kong's Tung Chee-hwa.

Italy, Mexico, and Sweden (among other countries) also experienced dramatic reductions in family size and birthrates during the late twentieth century. Is the emergence of the conjugal family, and a widening generation gap, a necessary condition of globalization? Or does globalization generate the social conditions of conjugality? Questions of this nature are difficult to answer, given the complexities of kinship and family life in contemporary societies. Furthermore, new family formations are appearing faster than anthropologists can record them. A good example is the transnational household system common among American diasporics (see, e.g., Levitt 2001). Multidomiciled families were certainly evident before the advent of cheap air travel and cellular phones, but new technologies have changed the quality of life (much for the better) in diasporic communities. Thus, the globalization of family life is no longer confined to migrants from developing economies who work for low wages in advanced capitalist societies. The transnational family is increasingly a mark of high social status and affluence.

SPLASH-BACK AND THE ILLUSION OF A GLOBAL CULTURE

For hundreds of millions of (primarily urban) people the experience of everyday life has become increasingly standardized since the 1960s. Western-style toilets, showers, beds, furniture, kitchens, household appliances, utilities, and transportation facilities are nearly universal. In 1975 most residents of Asian and African societies had yet to see, let alone use, a flush toilet or a shower. Tables, chairs, and mattresses were symbols of elite status in rural China until the 1980s (most farmers slept on wooden planks and sat on stools). Today many rural households in China's southern provinces are equipped with what local people refer to as the accoutrements of modern life: color televisions, videocassette (or DVD) players, refrigerators, music systems, and boxspring beds. Air conditioning is fast becoming a standard measure of success in the Chinese countryside.

An interesting sidelight on the globalization of everyday life is the rapid spread of disposable diapers, an innovation that has transformed the experience of parenthood everywhere. Fifteen local manufacturers were competing with Procter and Gamble's Pampers for domination of the Chinese market by 2000. Until the mid-1980s, disposable diapers were largely unobtainable in most parts of China; today young Chinese parents cannot imagine life without such sanitary products.

Other technological marvels that North Americans and Europeans take for granted have had even more profound effects on the quality of life for billions of people in the developing world: hot water, cold beer, frozen fish, screened windows, bottled cooking gas, and refrigerators. It would be a mistake, however, to assume that these innovations have an identical, homogenizing effect wherever they appear. The introduction of refrigerators is a case in point: for most rural Chinese this appliance is still (at this writing) treated as a status symbol, used to cool beer, soft drinks, and fruit. It is considered unhealthy to refrigerate vegetables, meat, and fish. Furthermore, certain foods (notably bean curd dishes) are thought to taste better if they are cooked with coal or wood as opposed to bottled gas.

It is difficult to argue, therefore, that the globalization of technologies is making the world everywhere the same. The sameness hypothesis is sustainable only if one ignores the internal meanings that people assign to cultural innovations. The domain of popular music illustrates how difficult it is to unravel cultural systems in the contemporary world: Is rock and roll a universal language? Does reggae and ska have the same meaning to young people everywhere?

American-inspired rap (hip-hop) music swept through the Japanese pop scene in the 1990s, as it did in Brazil, Britain, France, Egypt, and China. Japanese rap artists developed their own, localized versions of this popular genre set to an African American urban ("gangsta rap") beat. The form of this music is defiantly anti-establishment, but the Japanese lyric content is decidedly mild, celebrating youthful solidarity and exuberance (Condry 1998). Much the same can be said of the Cantopop music originating in Hong Kong. Cantonese artists borrowed the essential form of early- to mid-1960s American rock and roll, drawing heavily on the ballads of Buddy Holly, Roy Orbison, and Elvis Presley. But, as with Japanese rap, Cantonese singers inserted their own cultural sensitivities and personal experiences into the lyric structure. Similar translations between form and content have occurred in the pop music of Indonesia, Mexico, and Korea. It is also obvious to any casual listener of American radio that Brazilian, South African, Indian, and Cuban forms have had profound effects on the contemporary American pop scene. The flow of popular culture is rarely, if ever, unidirectional (see Jenkins, this volume).

A key feature of contemporary globalization is the splash-back effect, involving cultural forms that were exported to other societies, transformed beyond recognition, and then reintroduced into the society of origin. A good example was the Pokemon craze (a Japanese card game based on surreal animals) that swept through American schools during the late 1990s, only to fizzle out by 2000. An earlier Japanese fad, the *Mighty Morphin Power Rangers* (a television show featuring young martial artists), may have had an even stronger influence on American children, to judge from the number of Halloween costumes the series inspired. Like the pop music systems discussed above, both Poke-mon and the Power Rangers ultimately derive from early-twentieth-century American cartoons (e.g., Mickey Mouse and Superman). By the time the Japanese forms appeared on American television, the cultural transformation was so thorough that the original Hollywood connection was apparent only to a handful of historians and culture studies specialists.

Global splash-back is also evident in the many immigrant cuisines that enliven the American diet: Hungarian paprika and Italian tomato sauce originated in Europe as New World imports. More recent examples abound in the fast-food industry. McDonald's may be the world's largest restaurant chain, but it is facing increasing competition in the American market, and not just from KFC and Burger King. Jollibee, a hamburger-and-ice-cream chain based in the Philippines, has branches in Hong Kong, Brunei, Indonesia, Kuwait, and Saudi Arabia. In the late 1990s, Jollibee moved into California, where it found itself competing with other foreign imports—including Cafe de Coral, Hong Kong's leading purveyor of Chinese-style fast food. Cafe de Coral is becoming a global chain with outlets in Canada, Poland, and the United States. Elephant Jump, a Thai fast-food chain promoted by the Thai government, is also planning a move into the American market.

All of these Asian competitors have borrowed key elements of McDonald's industrial system: logos, mascots, employee uniforms, and restaurant design. In the 1980s and 1990s imitations of the Golden Arches emerged in China (McDucks, Modornal), Korea (McKivers and McDonny's), South Africa (Macdonalds), India (MacFastFood), and Denmark (McAllan)—to name only a few obvious cases. Karl Marx would have appreciated the ironies of early-twenty-first-century capitalism: by inspiring non-Western competitors to "go global," American pop culture industries (music, fashion, food, film) may be creating the conditions of their own demise.

CONCLUSIONS: YOUTH CULTURES, GLOBALIZATION, AND EDUCATION

The utopian (or depending upon one's viewpoint, dystopian) idea of a global culture is primarily an illusion based on the uninformed—but nonetheless highly influential—judgments of scholars and journalists who are unable or unwilling to view the world from the perspective of people on the receiving end of globalization. The fact that residents of Moscow, Beijing, and New Delhi occasionally eat at McDonald's, watch Hollywood films, and wear (knockoffs of) Nike sneakers does not make them "global." The *appearance* of homogeneity is the most salient, and ultimately the most deceptive, feature of globalization. It is likely that standardization of everyday life will accelerate as digital technology finally manages to approximate the toaster in user-friendliness. But technological breakthroughs are not enough to create a world culture: people everywhere have an unquenchable desire to partake of the fruits of globalization while celebrating the inherent uniqueness of their own local cultures.

Meanwhile, what can be said about globalization's effect on education? Anthropologists would caution against the conclusion that young people everywhere are experiencing the world in uniform ways. The ethnographic case materials presented in this chapter demonstrate that even something as supposedly "uniform" or "homogenous" as a Big Mac is interpreted and assimilated in radically different ways, depending upon cultural conditions and local circumstances.

This skeptical view of globalization's homogenizing power is also reflected in the chapters by Henry Jenkins and Howard Gardner in this volume. Recognizing the profound impact that globalization has on children, teachers, and parents, Gardner concludes that it would be a mistake to expect that "local or national institutions, mores, and values will . . . necessarily disappear."

Recent anthropological research demonstrates that young people (aged three to eighteen) are playing an increasingly significant role in the development of future cultural systems (see Maira, this volume, and Jenkins, this volume). Children everywhere are becoming accomplished and demanding consumers. They have refined tastes, high expectations, and money to spend. If China is any guide, there will be increasing conflict between the demands of youth and the requirements of the aged (see, e.g., Fong 2002; Lozada 2000; Watson 2000). The education of a new generation of demanding youth will stretch the resources of state systems throughout the world, at precisely the time when medical costs for the elderly are growing.

It is often argued that globalization is like the weather: one can complain about it but not do anything to change it. But this is not true of teachers. Rather than wasting time, money, and energy attempting to hold back the rain, they can make a conscious decision to prepare young people for an increasingly globalized future. This new educational mission begins with the recognition that globalization is not an all-consuming, homogenizing force that destroys everything that is unique or valued in local cultures.

NOTE

This chapter is an expanded and updated version of my essay "Globalization and Culture," which appeared in the *Encyclopedia Britannica* (revised 15th print edition, 2002). Many of the ethnographic examples and the concluding theoretical discussion in this chapter do not appear in that shorter encyclopedia essay.

REFERENCES

Appadurai, A. (1997). *Modernity at large: Cultural dimensions of globalization*. Minneapolis: University of Minnesota Press.

Becker A. E., R. Burwell, S. Gilman, D. Herzog, and P. Hamburg (2002). Disordered eating behaviors and attitudes follow prolonged exposure to television among ethnic Fijian adolescent girls. *British Journal of Psychiatry* 180: 509–514.

Berger, P. L. (1997). Four faces of global culture. *National Interest* 49: 23–29.

Bestor, T. C. 2000. How sushi went global. *Foreign Policy* (November–December): 54–63.

Caldwell, M. L. (2004). Domesticating the french fry: McDonald's and consumerism in Moscow. In *The cultural economy of food*. J. L. Watson and M. L. Caldwell, eds. Oxford, UK: Basil Blackwell.

Condry, I. (1998). The social production of difference: Imitation and authenticity in Japanese rap music. In *The challenge of mass American culture*. U. Poiger and H. Fehrenbach, eds. Oxford, UK: Berghan Books.

Fong, V. L. (2002). China's one-child policy and the empowerment of urban daughters. *American Anthropologist* 104(4): 1098–1109.

Freidberg, S. (1997). Contacts, contracts, and green bean schemes: Liberalisation and agro-entrepreneurship in Burkina Faso. *Journal of Modern African Studies* 35(1): 101–128.

Friedman, T. (2000). *The Lexus and the olive tree*. New York: Anchor.

Hannerz, U. (1990). Cosmopolitans and locals in world culture. In *Global culture: Nationalism, globalization and modernity*. Mike Featherstone, ed. London: Sage Publications.

Harvey, D. (1989). *The condition of postmodernity.* Oxford, UK: Basil Blackwell.

Huntington, S. (1996). *Clash of civilizations and the remaking of world order.* New York: Simon & Schuster.

Jing, J., ed. (2000). *Feeding China's little emperors: Food, children, and social change.* Stanford, CA: Stanford University Press.

Kelly, K. (1994). *Out of control.* New York: Addison-Wesley.

LaFeber, W. (1999). *Michael Jordan and the new global capitalism.* New York: W. W. Norton.

Levitt, P. (2001). *The transnational villagers.* Berkeley: University of California Press.

Lozada, E. (2000). Globalized childhood? Kentucky Fried Chicken in Beijing. In *Feeding China's little emperors: Food, children, and social change.* J. Jing, ed. Stanford, CA: Stanford University Press.

Mazumdar, S. (1999). The impact of New World crops on the diet and economy of China and India, ca. 1600–1900. In *Food in global history.* Raymond Grew, ed. Boulder, CO: Westview Press.

McLuhan, M. (1962). *The Gutenberg galaxy: The making of typographic man.* Toronto: University of Toronto Press.

Miller, D. (1992). *The Young and the Restless:* A case of the local and the global in mass consumption. In *Consuming technologies: Media and information in domestic spaces.* R. Silverstone and E. Hirsch, eds. London: Routledge.

Miller, D., and D. Slater (2000). *The Internet: An ethnographic approach.* Oxford, UK: Berg.

Meunier, S. (2000). The French exception. *Foreign Affairs* 79(4): 104–116.

Rosecrance, R. (1999). *The rise of the virtual state: Wealth and power in the coming century.* New York: Basic Books.

Vedrine, H. (2001). *France in an era of globalization.* Washington, DC: Brookings Institution Press.

Waters, M. (1995). *Globalization.* London: Routledge.

Watson J. L., ed. (1997a). *Golden Arches East: McDonald's in East Asia.* Stanford, CA: Stanford University Press.

Watson, J. L. (1997b). McDonald's in Hong Kong: Consumerism, dietary change, and the rise of a children's culture. In *Golden Arches East: McDonald's in East Asia.* J. L. Watson, ed. Stanford, CA: Stanford University Press.

Watson, J. L. (2000). China's Big Mac Attack. *Foreign Affairs* 79(3): 120–134.

Watson, J. L., and M. Caldwell, eds. (2004). *The cultural economy of food.* Oxford, UK: Basil Blackwell.

Wolf, M. (2001). Will the nation-state survive globalization? *Foreign Affairs* 80(1): 178–190.

Yan, Y. (1997). McDonald's in Beijing: The localization of Americana. In *Golden Arches East: McDonald's in East Asia.* J. L. Watson, ed. Stanford, CA: Stanford University Press.

Yan, Y. (2000). The politics of consumerism in Chinese society. In *China briefing 2000: The continuing transformation*. T. White, ed. Armonk, NY: M. E. Sharpe.

Yan, Y. (2002). Managed globalization: State power and cultural transition in China. In *Many globalizations: Cultural diversity in the contemporary world*. P. Berger and S. Huntington, eds. Oxford, UK: Oxford University Press.

EIGHT

Carola Suárez-Orozco

FORMULATING IDENTITY
IN A GLOBALIZED WORLD

INTRODUCTION

Increasing globalization has stimulated an unprecedented flow of immigrants worldwide. These newcomers—from many national origins and a wide range of cultural, religious, linguistic, racial, and ethnic backgrounds—challenge a nation's sense of unity. Globalization threatens both the identities of the original residents of the areas in which newcomers settle and those of the immigrants and their children. Integrating immigrants and the subsequent generations into the receiving society is a primary challenge of globalization; failing to do so, however, will have long-term social implications. The ability to formulate an identity that allows comfortable movement between worlds will be at the very heart of achieving a truly "global soul" (Iyer 2000).

At the beginning of the new millennium, there are over 175 million immigrants and refugees worldwide. In the United States alone, 32.5 million, or approximately 11.5 percent of the population, are immigrants (U.S. Bureau of the Census 2000). This is not simply a U.S. phenomenon, however. In 2000, 4.2 percent of the population in the United Kingdom and 5.6 percent of the population in France, was foreign-born. In other nations the percentage of foreign-born is greater than in the United States: 11.8 percent in Sweden, 17.4 percent in Canada, and 23.6

percent in Australia (Migration Information 2003). In almost all these countries, this trend has been steadily increasing. It is important to note that these figures reflect only the first generation. If one considers the children of these immigrants—the second generation—clearly, many more individuals are involved in the task of negotiating a new identity that synthesizes elements of the culture of origin with those of the receiving culture.

The ever increasing flows of individuals from myriad backgrounds provide a number of aesthetic, cognitive, social, and marketplace opportunities. The ability to code-switch—to move fluidly between languages and cultures—has obvious social advantages. Bicultural and bilingual competence enables individuals to fluidly adapt themselves to evolving situations (Titone 1989). This skill has advantages for entering many professions in the business, diplomatic, and social service sectors. Sommer argues that bilingualism is essential for democracy as it "depends on constructing those miraculous and precarious points of contact from mismatches among codes and people" (Sommer 2004). Indeed, shortly after the last large wave of migration at the turn of the twentieth century, Stonequist argued that the marginality afforded to those individuals in between cultures could lead to individuals who play the essential role of cultural ambassadors adept at interpreting and bridging difference (Stonequist 1937). The cognitive flexibility that this multiple perspective taking requires is becoming an ever more essential trait for the global citizen (Gardner, this volume; Suárez-Orozco and Qin-Hilliard, this volume).

IMMIGRANT STRESS

Multiple pathways structure immigrants' journeys into their new homes. Immigrants and refugees are motivated by a variety of factors—relief from political, religious, or ethnic persecution (in the case of refugees); economic incentives; as well as the opportunity to be reunited with family members. Although for many immigrant families, migration results in substantial gains, it provides many challenges to the individuals involved. It removes individuals from many of their relationships and predictable contexts—extended families and friends, community ties, jobs, living situations, customs, and often languages.

Immigrants are stripped of many of their sustaining social relationships as well as the social roles that provide them with culturally scripted notions of how they fit into the world, resulting in acculturative stress (Berry 1997; C. Suárez-Orozco and M. Suárez-Orozco 2001).

Immigrant youth face particular challenges. They often immigrate not just to new homes but also to new family structures (C. Suárez-Orozco, Todorova, and Louie 2002). In our study of four hundred immigrant youth who came to the United States from a variety of origins, including Central America, China, the Dominican Republic, Mexico, and Haiti, we found that fully 85 percent of the youth in this project had been separated from one or both parents for periods of several months to several years (C. Suárez-Orozco et al. 2002). To compound this form of parental unavailability, many immigrant parents work long hours, rendering them relatively physically absent in the lives of their children. Further, depression and anger that may be associated with the migratory experience may make many immigrant parents psychologically unavailable to their children (Athey and Ahearn 1991). These forms of absence all too frequently leave immigrant children to their own devices long before it is developmentally ideal. Although in some cases it can lead to hyperresponsible children, in other cases it leads to depressed youth who are drawn to the lure of alternative family structures such as gangs—a particular risk for boys (Vigil 1988).

THE SECOND GENERATION

The challenges of the first generation are considerably different from those of the second generation. The first generation is largely concerned with surviving and adjusting to the new context. These immigrants may go through a variety of normative adverse reactions following the multiple losses of migration, including anxiety and depression. However, the first generation is protected from these psychological sequelae by several factors. The dual frame of reference by which immigrants can compare their current situation with that left behind often allows them to feel relatively advantaged in the new context (C. Suárez-Orozco and M. Suárez-Orozco 1995). Optimism is at the very heart of the immigrant experience: the possibility of a better tomorrow acts as both a tremendous motivator as well as a form of inoculation against encountered frustrations and barriers. Further, first-generation immigrants are often energized by the desire to support loved ones—by sending remittances home to those left behind, as well as by building the best possible life for their children. While not an easy road, it is one with a clear identity. Immigrants who arrive as adults maintain a sense of identity rooted deeply in their birthplaces. Many expatriates are, of course, quite comfortable in their new homeland. Nevertheless they tend to retain an outsider status as the cultural and linguistic hurdles are simply too high to be surmounted within one generation (C. Suárez-Orozco and M. Suárez-Orozco 2001).

The path for their children, the second generation, is less straightforward, offering a variety of pathways. For these youth, forging a sense of identity may be their single greatest challenge. Do they feel comfortable in their homeland? Do they feel accepted by the "native-born" of the host country? What relationship do they have with their parents' country of origin? Is their sense of identity rooted "here," "there," everywhere, or nowhere?

THE ARCHITECTURE OF CULTURAL IDENTITY

Stage versus Context

Erik Erikson (1968) argued that in the developmental stage of adolescence, identity is the critical maturational task. In forming an identity, youth attempt to create a self-identity that is consistent with how others view them. Identity is less challenging when there is continuity among the various social milieus youth encounter—home, school, neighborhood, and country. In the era of globalization, however, social spaces are more discontinuous and fractured than ever before.

A number of psychologists have claimed that identity goes through a variety of permutations during adolescence as the individual experiments with different identity strategies. Some argue that all youth move steadily from a stage of ethnic or "racial unawareness," to one of "exploration," to a final stage of an "achieved" sense of racial or ethnic identity (Marcia 1966). Others point out that the process of identity formation is, rather than being linear, more accurately described as "spiraling" back to revisit previous stages, each time from a different vantage point (Parham 1989).

Achieved and Ascribed Identities

Identity formation, I would argue, is not simply a process by which one passes through a variety of stages on the way to achieving a stable identity. Rather it is a process that is fluid and contextually driven. If raised in Beijing and immigrating as an adult, one may "discover" that one is "Asian" for the first time at age thirty. Prior to immigrating, that same individual in Beijing may never have considered her racial or ethnic identity (or if she did, it would be a neighborhood identity). In the Chinatown of the host society, the identity will be one of northern mainland Chinese origin (in contrast to Cantonese speakers from Hong Kong or Canton); but in the heartland of the host country the identity may become a more complex, "pan-Asian" construct. The social context is essential in predicting which identity is constructed (Suárez-Orozco 2000).

The tension between the dominant culture and minority newcomers lies at the heart of the ethnic and cultural identity formation drama of immigrants and their children (DeVos 1980). Youth are challenged to navigate between achieved identities and ascribed or imposed identities (C. Suárez-Orozco and M. Suárez-Orozco 2001). Achieved identity is the extent to which an individual achieves a sense of belonging—"I am a member of *this* group." An ascribed identity is imposed either by coethnics—"You are a member of *our* group"—or by members of the dominant culture—"You are a member of *that* group."

For some groups the imposed or ascribed identity is considerably stronger than for others. In the United States, for example, African identity is firmly ascribed, whereas Italian identity can be assumed at will. The degree to which ascribed origins are imposed may also evolve over time. At the turn of the twentieth century in Boston, having Irish origins had significant negative implications, whereas at the turn of the twenty-first century, being from Ireland merits little notice and can be articulated at will (for St. Patrick's Day events but not necessarily in a job interview).

Phenotypic racial features have considerable implications for the ease of assimilation. Historically, immigrants coming from Europe to the United States could more easily assimilate once they lost their accents and changed their names. The ability to join the mainstream unnoticed is more challenging when one is racially marked. Questions as to where one is "really from" or compliments made to Asian Americans who have been in the United States many generations on their English fluency lead to what law professor Frank H. Wu (2002) refers to as "perpetual foreigner syndrome." In this era of globalization, the fact that many immigrants of color originate in the developing world (Africa, Asia, the Caribbean, and Latin America) and enter postindustrial regions traditionally populated by Europeans (Europe, North America, Australia) makes "passing," or fully assimilating unnoticed, no longer possible for most new arrivals.

Contact with Cultures

Culture provides one with generally shared understandings and models for making meaning of one's experiences. Cultural beliefs present standards of behavior that are internalized over time, and cultural traditions offer a soothing sense of social safety. At the heart of these shared understandings are the interpersonal networks of relations in which one is embedded.

In order to maintain a sense of affinity with one's culture of origin, sustained contact is required. Regular visits back to the homeland—in what is described as a transnational existence—facilitates maintenance of the parent culture (Levitt 1996). Living in an ethnic enclave limits the opportunity for regular interaction with members of the mainstream culture. Ethnic communities, such as Chinatown in San Francisco, Mexican barrios in Los Angeles, the Dominican neighborhood in Washington Heights (in Manhattan), the Cuban enclave in Miami, and the like, nurture a sense of culture of origin without requiring return visits to the homeland. The strength of the effect of these ethnic neighborhoods and enclaves is determined by the density of the local ethnic population, the strength of the collective coethnic identity, the community's cohesiveness, and the availability of cultural role models.

If there is little contact with the culture of origin, however, then all of the "cultural lessons" fall upon the shoulders of the parents to teach. Parents are, no doubt, a critical source of information in the quest to form an identity. Immigration, however, undermines parents' ability to act as guides, by removing the "map of experience" necessary to successfully escort children in the new culture (Hoffman 1989). Without effortless proficiency in the new cultural expectations and practices, immigrant parents are less able to provide guidance in the ways of negotiating the currents of a complex society; in addition, they must rely on their children for cultural interpretations. As a seasoned immigrant comments to a prospective migrant in the novel *Accordion Crimes*, "the natural order of the world is reversed. The old learn from the children" (Proulx 1996).

The ease with which elements of the parent culture can be incorporated into the new culture will to some extent be affected by the "cultural distance" between the parent and new culture (Berry 1997). Youth growing up within dual contexts characterized by great degrees of dissimilarity between cultural beliefs and social practices are likely to suffer from greater identity confusion than those coming from more convergent cultural backgrounds (Arnett 2002). This would suggest that in the United States the children of rural Hmong in northern California (Fadiman 1998; Portes and Rumbaut 2001) or Yemeni immigrants in the Midwest would face more challenges than the children of Canadian immigrants in New England.

The fact that many immigrants enter highly segregated neighborhoods with large coethnic or minority populations complicates the potential for identification with mainstream culture. If there is little contact with the mainstream middle class in any form other than media representations encountered on television or in movies, identifying with the host culture becomes something of an abstraction.

Performing Identity

How does an individual demonstrate his ethnic affiliation? At the most basic level, the ethnic label an individual chooses signifies his identity (Maestes 2000; Waters 1996). Sociological research has used the self-selected label as a way of examining identity. Whether a second-generation person of Mexican origin calls herself Mexican or Mexican American, or Latina, or Chicana seems to be linked to quite different patterns of incorporation and engagement in schooling (Matute-Bianchi 1991; Portes and Rumbaut 2001; Waters 1996). Individuals who adopt a self-referential label that includes their parents' country of origin seem to do better in school than their counterparts who select a panethnicity (such as Hispanic or Latino) or who refer only to their country of residence (such as American). The same is true with self-selected labels adhered to by persons of Caribbean origin: Waters (1997) has demonstrated that Caribbean-origin youth who call themselves Jamaican American, for example, appear to have different perceptions of discrimination and opportunities than those who call themselves African American.

Feelings of belonging to rather than alienation from the various cultural groups an individual may be part of also has important implications (DeVos and Suárez-Orozco 1990). Whether or not one feels affiliation with and acceptance in the groups under consideration may be related to one's ability to incorporate elements of the culture into one's sense of self. Does the individual value his culture of origin? Does he feel accepted by other members of that culture? Is he drawn to the new culture (or cultures)? Does he feel welcome and incorporated into the new culture (or cultures)? Does he *wish* to be incorporated into the new culture, or does he find it alienating? These attitudes will have much to do with the fusion of culture that the individual internalizes (Maestes 2000).

Participation in a series of *ethnic activities,* as well as the *dominant culture's* activities and social practices, is one of the clearest ways in which cultural identity is performed (Maestes 2000). What language does the individual report feeling most comfortable using (Maestes 2000)? In what circumstances does she use the language of origin—spontaneously or under duress? What is the culture of the friends to whom she is drawn? Are these friends mostly persons of the individual's culture of origin, of the dominant culture, or of a range of origins? What religious practices are important, and to what degree? Do these practices occur on a daily basis, or are they more occasional, with a primarily social function? What foods does the individual most enjoy, particularly in social settings? What holidays does she celebrate? Are they largely those of the culture of origin, of the host society, or some combination? What entertainment choices does she make? Selections made in sports participation (baseball versus basketball versus soccer, for example), music (salsa versus rap versus pop), radio or television (ethnic versus mainstream), movies and videos (country of origin versus Hollywood versus an eclectic selection) can provide insight into relative comfort and affiliation with the points of cultural contact (Louie 2003).

The Ethos of Reception

The general social climate, or ethos of reception, plays a critical role in the adaptation of immigrants and their children (C. Suárez-Orozco and M. Suárez-Orozco 2001). Unfortunately, intolerance for newcomers is an all-too-common response all over the world. Discrimination against immigrants of color is particularly widespread and intense in many areas receiving large numbers of new immigrants, including Europe (Suárez-Orozco 1996), the United States (Espenshade and Belanger 1998), and Japan (Tsuda 2003). As today's immigrants are more diverse than ever before in ethnicity, skin color, and religion, they are particularly subject to the pervasive social trauma of prejudice and social exclusion (Tatum 1997).

The exclusion can take a structural form (when individuals are excluded from the opportunity structure) as well as an attitudinal form (in the form of disparagement and public hostility). These structural barriers and the social ethos of intolerance and racism encountered by many immigrants of color intensify the stresses of immigration. Although the structural exclusion suffered by immigrants and their children is tangibly detrimental to their ability to participate in the opportunity structure, prejudicial attitudes and psychological violence also play a toxic role. Philosopher Charles Taylor argues that "our identity is partly shaped by recognition or its absence, often by the misrecognition of others, and so a person or group of people can suffer real damage, real distortion, if the people or society around them mirrors back to them a confining or demeaning or contemptible picture of themselves" (Taylor 1994). How can youth of immigrant origin incorporate the notion that they are unwanted "aliens" who do not warrant the most basic rights of education and health care?

The Social Mirror

Child psychoanalyst D. W. Winicott suggests that a child's sense of self is profoundly shaped by the reflections mirrored back to him by significant others (Winicott 1971). Indeed, all human beings are dependent upon the reflection of themselves mirrored by others. "Others" include not just the mother (which was Winicott's principal concern) but also relatives, adult caretakers, siblings, teachers, peers, employers, people on the street, and even the media (C. Suárez-Orozco 2000). When the reflected image is generally positive, the individual (adult or child) is able to feel that she is worthwhile and competent. When the reflection is generally negative, it is extremely difficult to maintain an unblemished sense of self-worth.

These reflections can be accurate or inaccurate. When the reflection is a positive distortion, the response to the individual may be out of proportion to his actual contribution or achievement. In the most benign case, positive expectations can be an asset. In the classic "Pygmalion in the Classroom" study, teachers who believed that certain children were brighter than others (based on the experimenter randomly assigning some children that designation, unsubstantiated in fact) treated the children more positively and assigned them higher grades (Rosenthal and Feldman 1991). It is possible that some immigrant students, such as Asians, benefit somewhat from positive expectations of their competence as a result of being members of a "model minority"—though no doubt at a cost (Takaki 1993).

It is the negative distortions, however, that are most worrisome. What is the effect for children who receive mirroring from society that is predominantly negative and hostile? Such is the case with many immigrant and minority children (see Maira, this volume). Commenting on the negative social mirroring toward Muslim students after September 11, Iraqi American Nuar Alsadir eloquently stated: "The world shouldn't be a funhouse in which we're forced to stand before the distorting mirror, begging for our lives" (Alsadir 2002). W. E. B. Du Bois famously articulated the challenge of what he termed "double-consciousness"—a "sense of always looking at one's self through the eyes of others, of measuring one's soul by the tape of a world that looks on in amused contempt and pity" (Du Bois 1903/1989). When the expectations are of sloth, irresponsibility, low intelligence, and even danger, the outcome can be toxic. When these reflections are received in a number of mirrors, including the media, classroom, and street, the outcome is devastating (Adams 1990).

Research from the Harvard Immigration Project, a study of youth immigrating to the United States from China, Central America, the Dominican Republic, Haiti, and Mexico, suggests that immigrant children are keenly aware of the prevailing ethos of hostility in the dominant culture (C. Suárez-Orozco 2000). A sample of four hundred children were asked to complete the sentence "Most Americans think that [Chinese, Dominicans, Central Americans, Haitians, Mexicans—depending on the child's country of origin] are _____." Disturbingly, fully 65 percent of the respondents provided a negative response to the sentence-completion task. The modal response was "bad"; others—even more disconcerting—included "stupid," "useless," "garbage," "gang members," "lazy," and "we don't exist" (C. Suárez-Orozco 2000).

What meanings do youth construct from and how do they respond to this negative social mirror? One possible pathway is for youth to become resigned to the negative reflections, leading to hopelessness and self-depreciation that may in turn result in low aspirations and self-defeating behaviors. The general affect associated with this pathway is depression and passivity. In this scenario, the child is likely to respond with self-doubt and shame, setting low aspirations in a kind of self-fulfilling prophecy: "They are probably right. I'll never be able to do anything." Other youth may mobilize to resist the mirrors and injustices they encounter. I differentiate between two types of resistance. The first is a project infused with hope, a sense of justice, and faith in a better tomorrow. The other form of resistance is eventually overcome by alienation leading to anomie, hopelessness, and a nihilistic view of the future. In this latter case, youth may actively resist the reflections they encounter but are unable to maintain hope for change or a better future. Without hope, the resulting anger and compensatory self-aggrandizement may lead to acting-out behaviors including the kinds of dystopic cultural practices typically associated with gang membership.

For these youth, the response is "If you think I'm bad, let me show you just how bad I can be" (C. Suárez-Orozco and M. Suárez-Orozco 2001). The social trajectories of youth are more promising for those who are able to actively maintain and cultivate a sense of hope for the future. Whether they are resigned, oblivious, or resistant to the reflections in the social mirror, those who are able to maintain hope are in fundamental ways partially inoculated to the toxicity they may encounter. These youth are better able to maintain pride and preserve their self-esteem. In these circumstances, their energies are mobilized in the service of day-to-day coping. Some may not only focus on their own advancement but also harness their energies in the service of their communities by volunteering to help others, acting as role models, or advocating and mobilizing for social change. In this scenario, youth respond to the negative social mirror as a goad toward "I'll show you I can make it in spite of what you think of me" (C. Suárez-Orozco and M. Suárez-Orozco 2001).

Social Disparagement and Academic Outcomes

Children of color are particularly subject to negative expectations that have profound implications for their academic performance (Weinstein 2002). Cross-cultural data from research focused on a variety of disparaged minorities in a number of contexts all over the world suggest that exposure to a negative social mirror adversely affects academic engagement. This research provides insight into a number of critical questions: In ethnically diverse and increasingly transnational societies, how does schooling relate to hierarchies of inequality (Freire 1995)? Does the educational system reproduce inequalities by replicating the existing social order? Or does schooling help to overcome social inequalities by emerging as an avenue for status mobility?

What is the experience of self in cultures where patterned inequality shapes social interactions? Anthropological cross-cultural evidence from a variety of regions suggests that the social context and ethos of reception plays an important role in immigrant adaptation. Ogbu (1978) has argued that minorities who were originally incorporated against their will through conquest and enslavement are more likely to give up on educational avenues as a route to social mobility than are those of immigrant origin who enter a new society voluntarily. DeVos and M. Suárez-Orozco (1990) have demonstrated that a cultural and symbolic ethos of reception saturated with psychological disparagement and racist stereotypes has profound implications for the identity formation of minority and immigrant children, as well as for their schooling experiences.

In cases in which racial and ethnic inequalities are highly structured, such as for Algerians in France, Koreans in Japan, or Mexicans in California, "psychological disparagement" and "symbolic violence" may permeate the experience of many minority youth. Members of these groups not only are effectively locked out of the opportunity structure (through segregated and inferior schools and work opportunities in the least desirable sectors of the economy) but also commonly become the objects of cultural violence. The stereotypes of inferiority, sloth, and violence justify the sense that they are less deserving of full participation in the dominant society's opportunity structure. Facing such charged attitudes, which assault and undermine their sense of self, minority children may come to experience the institutions of the dominant society—especially its schools—as alien terrain reproducing an order of inequality (DeVos and M. Suárez–Orozco 1990). While all groups face structural obstacles, not all groups elicit and experience the same attitudes from the dominant culture. Some immigrant groups elicit more negative attitudes, encountering a more negative social mirror than others do. In U.S. public opinion polls, for example, Asians are seen more favorably than Latinos (Espenshade and Belanger 1998).

In past generations, assimilationist trajectories demonstrated a correlation between length of residence in the United States and better schooling, health, and income outcomes (Gordon 1964; M. Suárez-Orozco and Paez 2002). While assimilation was a goal and a possibility for immigrants of European origin, resulting in a generally upwardly mobile journey (Child 1943; Higham 1975), this alternative is more challenging for immigrants of color today. Further, increasing "segmentation" in the American economy and society is shaping new patterns of immigrant adaptation (Gans 1992; Portes and Rumbaut 2001; Rumbaut 1997; Waters 1999; Zhou 1997).

Certainly, a preponderance of evidence suggests that structural factors such as neighborhood segregation and poverty (see Massey and Denton 1993; Orfield and Yun 1999), as well as family-level factors (including parents' education and socioeconomic status), are significant predictors of long-term educational outcomes for children (Coleman et al. 1966). In a society powerfully structured by "the color line" (Du Bois 1903/1989), however, race and color are significant vectors for understanding the adaptations of immigrant youth of color.

Stanford University social psychologist Claude Steele has led new theoretical and empirical work on how "identity threats," based on group membership, can profoundly shape academic achievement. In a series of ingenious experimental studies, Steele and his colleagues have demonstrated that under the stress of a stereotype threat, performance goes down on a variety of academic tasks. For example, when high-achieving African American university students are told before taking an exam that the test has proven to differentiate between blacks and whites, in favor of whites, their performance was significantly worse than when they were not told that the test differentiated between groups (Steele 1997). Steele maintains that when negative stereotypes about one's group prevail, "members of these groups can fear being reduced to the stereotype" (Steele 1997, p. 614). He notes that in these situations, self-handicapping goes up. This "threat in the air" has not only an immediate effect on the specific situation that evokes the stereotype threat but also a cumulative erosive effect when events that evoke the threat continually occur. He argues that stereotype threat shapes both intellectual performance and intellectual identity.

How are identity and agency implicated in educational processes and outcomes? John Ogbu and his colleagues have done seminal work in the area of immigration, minority status, and schooling in plural societies (Matute-Bianchi 1991; Ogbu 1978, 1987). Inspired by George DeVos's comparative studies of social stratification and status inequality (DeVos 1973; DeVos and M. Suárez-Orozco 1990), Ogbu argued that parental and other socioeconomic factors explain only part of the variance; when these factors are controlled for, differences become evident. On one hand, immigrants tend to develop cultural models and social practices that serve them well in terms of educational adaptations and outcomes. On the other hand, "involuntary minorities," after generations of living with structural inequities and symbolic violence, tend to develop social practices and cultural models that remove them from investing in schooling as the dominant strategy for status mobility.

A number of theorists of the new immigration have begun to examine how race and color complicate the process of immigrant adaptation. Waters (1999) claims that in this "race conscious society a person becomes defined racially and identity is imposed upon [him or her] by outsiders" (p. 6). She reports that her black West Indian immigrant informants are shocked by the level of racism against blacks in the United States. Though they arrive expecting structural obstacles (such as discrimination in housing and promotions), what they find most distressing is the level of both overt and covert prejudice and discrimination. Black immigrants tend to bring with them a number of characteristics that contribute to their relative success in the new setting. For their children, however, "over the course of one generation the structural realities of American race relations and the American economy undermine the cultures of the West Indian immigrants and create responses among the immigrants, and especially their children, that resemble the cultural responses of African Americans to long histories of exclusion and discrimination" (Waters 1999, p. 6). While cross-sectional data have been used to identify this transgenerational pattern, preliminary data from the Harvard Longitudinal Immigrant Student Adaptation study suggest that among many immigrant youth of color, this process unfolds at a rapid pace within a few years of migration.

In response to marginalization they encounter in their ethnic homeland, for example, Japanese Brazilians resist assimilationist cultural pressures by strengthening their Brazilian national identity. Similar trends found among Haitians in Miami (Stepick 1997), Dominicans in Providence, Rhode Island (Bailey 2001), and Caribbean American youth in New York (López 2002) suggest that for many of today's new arrivals, the journey is a process of racial and ethnic self-discovery and self-authoring. New identities are crafted in the process of immigrant uprooting and resettlement through continuous feedback between the subjective sense of self and what is mirrored by the social milieu (Erikson 1968; C. Suárez-Orozco and M. Suárez-Orozco 2001).

Given that today nearly 80 percent of the new immigrants are of color, emigrating from the "developing world"—Latin America, the Caribbean, and Asia (Edmonston and Passel 1994; Fix and Passel 1994)—a pattern of racialization and adversarial identity formation within the school context is deeply concerning. In our increasingly globalized world, education becomes ever more crucial for functioning (Bloom, this volume; Suárez-Orozco and Qin-Hilliard, this volume). Formulating identities that allow individuals to move fluidly from context to context becomes critical to future functioning as global citizens.

IDENTITY PATHWAYS

Identities and styles of adaptation are highly context dependent and fluid. An immigrant youth might first gravitate toward one style of adaptation. Over time, as she matures and as her context changes, she may be drawn into new attitudes and social behaviors.

In some cases the identity that is forged is highly focused upon the culture of origin, with coethnics as the primary point of reference. In some of these cases, an identity that is adversarial to the dominant culture may emerge. In other cases youth of immigrant origin may embrace total assimilation and complete identification with mainstream American culture. In still other cases a new ethnic identity that incorporates selected aspects of *both* the culture of origin and mainstream American culture is forged. All of these identity styles have clear implications for adaptation to the new society, including the schooling experiences of immigrant youth. Within the same family, each child may adopt his or her own style, resulting in various siblings occupying very different sectors of the identity spectrum.

Coethnic Identities

Some immigrant-origin youth maintain a largely coethnic focus. Some may do so because they have limited opportunity to make meaningful contact with other groups in the host culture. Others may be responding to an understanding that a group with which they may have extensive contact is even more disparaged than they are as immigrants. Hence, Caribbean-origin individuals may distinguish themselves from African Americans in an attempt to ward off further disparagement (Waters 1999; Zéphir 2001).

Other youth of immigrant origin may develop an adversarial stance, constructing identities around rejecting—after having been rejected by—the institutions of the dominant culture. Princeton sociologist Alejandro Portes observes, "As second-generation youth find their aspirations for wealth and social status blocked, they may join native minorities in the inner city, adopting an adversarial stance toward middle-class white society, and adding to the present urban pathologies" (Portes 1993).

Immigrant children who find themselves structurally marginalized and culturally disparaged are more likely to respond to the challenges to their identities by developing an adversarial style of adaptation (Vigil 2002). These children of immigrants are responding in ways similar to those of other marginalized youth in the United States—such as many inner-city poor African Americans and Puerto Ricans (and elsewhere, such as Koreans in Japan or Algerians in France). Likewise, many of the disparaged and disenfranchised second-generation Italian American, Irish American, and Polish American adolescents of previous waves of immigration demonstrated a similar profile.

Today, some youth of immigrant origin respond to marginalization and the poisoned mirror by developing adversarial identities. Among children of immigrants who gravitate toward adversarial styles, embracing aspects of the culture of the dominant group is equated with giving up one's own ethnic identity (Fordham and Ogbu 1986). Like other disenfranchised youth, children of immigrants who develop adversarial identities tend to encounter problems in school and drop out, and consequently face unemployment in the formal economy.

Among youth engaged in adversarial styles, speaking the standard language of the host culture and doing well in school may be interpreted as a show of hauteur and as a wish to "act white." Navarrette, a Harvard-bound grandson of Mexican immigrants, recalls the taunts from his less successful peers in public schools. He remembers thinking, "They will call me 'Brain' as I walk through hallways in the junior high school. . . . They will accuse me, by virtue of my academic success, of 'trying to be white'" (Navarrette 1993). When adolescents acquire cultural models that make doing well in school a symbol of ethnic betrayal, it becomes problematic for them to develop the behavioral and attitudinal repertoire necessary for academic success.

The children of immigrants who are not able to embrace their own culture and who have formulated their identities around rejecting aspects of the mainstream society may be drawn to gangs. For such youth, gang membership, in the absence of other meaningful opportunities, becomes incorporated into their sense of identity. Gangs offer their members a sense of belonging, solidarity, protection, support, discipline, and warmth. Gangs also structure the anger many feel toward the society that violently rejected their parents and themselves. Although many second-generation youth may look toward gangs for cues about dress, language, and attitude, most remain on the periphery and eventually outgrow the gang mystique after working through the identity issues of adolescence. Others drawn to the periphery, and to the epicenter, of gangs are disproportionally represented in the penal system. The gang ethos provides a sense of identity and cohesion for marginal youth during a turbulent stage of their development while they are also facing urban poverty and limited economic opportunity, ethnic minority status and discrimination, lack of training and education, and a breakdown in the social institutions of school and family (Vigil 1988).

While many adversarial youth may limit their delinquent behavior to their immediate neighborhood, for others an adversarial stance may lead to extreme nationalism or radicalism. Again, the social mirror plays a critical role in this radicalized stance. Algerian-born Kamel Daoudi was raised in France and arrested on suspicion of being part of an al-Qaeda plot to blow up the American embassy in Paris. In an essay sent to TV network France 2, Daoudi wrote: "I became aware of the abominable social treatment given all those potential "myselves" who have been conditioned to become subcitizens, just good for paying pension for the real French. . . . There are only two choices left for me, either to sink into a deep depression, and I did for about six months, . . . or to react by taking part in the universal struggle against the overwhelming unjust cynicism" (Sciolino 2002).

Clearly, adversarial styles quite severely compromise the future opportunities of immigrant-origin youth who are already at risk of school failure because of poverty, inequality, and discrimination.

Ethnic Flight

The children of immigrants who shed their cultures structure their identities most strongly around the dominant mainstream culture (Berry 1997). Taking ethnic flight, these youth may feel most comfortable spending time with peers from the mainstream culture rather than with their less acculturated peers. For these youth, learning to speak standard English not only serves an instrumental function of communicating but also becomes an important symbolic act of identifying with the dominant culture. Among these youth, success in school may be seen not only as a route for individualistic self-advancement but also as a way to symbolically and psychologically move away from the world of the family and the ethnic group.

Often this identification with the mainstream culture results in a weakening of ties to members of one's own ethnic group. These young people all too frequently are alienated from their less acculturated peers, having little in common with them or even feeling superior to them. While they may gain access to privileged positions within mainstream culture, they must still deal with issues of marginalization and exclusion.

Even when immigrant-origin youth do not feel haughty toward their ethnic peers, they may find the peer group unforgiving of any behaviors that could be interpreted as "ethnic betrayal." It is not necessary for the child of an immigrant to consciously decide to distance himself from his culture. Among some ethnic groups, merely being a good student will result in peer sanctions. Accusations of "acting white" or being a "coconut," "banana," or "Oreo" (brown, yellow, or black on the outside and white on the inside) are frequent (Fordham and Ogbu 1986).

In an earlier era of scholarship, this style of adaptation was termed "passing" (DeVos 1992). While there were gains for the children of immigrants who "disappeared" into the mainstream culture, there were also hidden costs—primarily in terms of unresolved shame, doubt, and self-hatred. While passing may have been a common style of adaptation among those who phenotypically looked like the mainstream, it is not easily available to today's immigrants of color, who visibly look like the "other." Further, while ethnic flight is a form of adaptation that can be adaptive in terms of "making it" by the mainstream society's standards, it frequently comes at a significant social and emotional cost.

Transcultural Identities

Between the coethnic and ethnic flight gravitational fields, we find the large majority of children of immigrants. The task of immigration for these children is crafting a transcultural identity. These youth must creatively fuse aspects of two or more cultures—the parental tradition and the new culture or cultures. In so doing, they synthesize an identity that does not require them to choose between cultures but rather allows them to incorporate traits of both cultures while fusing additive elements (Falicov 2002).

For Latinos, this state is what Ed Morales refers to as "living in Spanglish." He defines "the root of Spanglish [as] a very universal state of being. It is displacement from one place, home, to another place, home, in which one feels at home in both places, yet at home in neither place. . . . Spanglish is the state of belonging to at least two identities at the same time, and not being confused or hurt by it" (Morales 2002, pp. 7–8). Such is the identity challenge of youth of immigrant origin— their developmental task requires crafting new cultural formations out of two systems that are at once their own and foreign. These children achieve bicultural and bilingual competencies that become an integral part of their sense of self.

Among youth engaged in bicultural styles, the culturally constructed social strictures and patterns of social control of their immigrant parents and elders maintain a degree of legitimacy. Learning standard English and doing well in school are viewed as competencies that do not compromise their sense of who they are. These youth network, with similar ease, among members of their own ethnic group as well as with students, teachers, employers, colleagues, and friends of other backgrounds. A number of studies in the past two decades have demonstrated a link between racial and ethnic identity pathways and academic outcomes (Gibson 1988; Ogbu and Herbert 1998). These studies suggest that those who forge transcultural identities are more successful academically.

Many who successfully "make it" clearly perceive and appreciate the sacrifices loved ones have made to enable them to thrive in a new country. Rather than wishing to distance themselves from parents, these youth come to experience success as a way to "pay back" their parents for their sacrifices. At times, they experience a form of "survivor guilt" as a result of the deprivation their parents and other family members have suffered in order to move to the new land. Among many such adolescents, success in school serves not only the instrumental function of achieving self-advancement and independence but also, perhaps even more important, the expressive function of making the parental sacrifices worthwhile through the son or daughter's "becoming a somebody." For such youth, "making it" may involve restitution by "giving back" to parents, siblings, peers, and other less fortunate members of the community.

A the transcultural identity is the most adaptive of the three styles. It blends the preservation of the affective ties of the home culture with the acquisition of instrumental competencies required to cope successfully in the mainstream culture. This identity style not only serves the individual well but also benefits the society at large. It is precisely such transcultural individuals whom Stonequist identified as being best suited to become the "creative agents" who might "contribute to the solution of the conflict of races and cultures" (Stonequist 1937, p. 15).

Transcultural identities are particularly adaptive in this era of globalism and multiculturalism. By acquiring competencies that enable them to operate within more than one cultural code, immigrant youth are at an advantage. The unilinear assimilationist model, which results in styles of adaptation I term ethnic flight, is no longer feasible. Today's immigrants are not unambivalently invited to join the mainstream society. The rapid abandonment of the home culture implied in ethnic flight almost always results in the collapse of the parental voice of authority. Furthermore, lack of group connectedness results in anomie and alienation. The key to a successful adaptation involves acquiring competencies that are relevant to the global economy while maintaining the social networks and connectedness essential to the human condition. Those who are at ease in multiple social and cultural contexts will be most successful and will be able to achieve higher levels of maturity and happiness.

Gendered Differences

An emerging body of literature reveals that boys from disparaged minority backgrounds seem to be particularly at risk of being marginalized, beginning in the educational system (Brandon 1991; Gibson 1988; J. Lee 2002; Portes and Rumbaut 2001; Qin-Hilliard 2003; Waters 1996). Consistent with this literature, data from the Harvard Immigration Project suggest that immigrant boys tend to demonstrate lower academic achievement (as measured by report card outcomes) and encounter more challenges in school than immigrant girls. Boys report feeling less support from teachers and staff and are more likely to perceive school as a negative, hostile, and racist environment (Qin-Hilliard 2003; Suárez-Orozco and Qin-Hilliard 2004).

A critical difference between boys and girls lies in the realm of social relationships. Research with nonimmigrant youth has consistently found that teacher support as well as peer support is critical for the academic achievement of both boys and girls (Roeser, Eccles, and Sameroff 1998). Relationships within schools provide several forms of support critical to academic outcomes—access to knowledge about academic subjects, college pathways, and the labor market, as well as role modeling, mentoring, advice, and advocacy. Stanton-Salazar (2001) finds that although Mexican American adolescent boys were equally likely to report family cohesiveness and supportive parental relationships as did girls, they reported that their school-based relationships were less supportive. Likewise, data from the Harvard Immigration Project reveal that immigrant-origin boys were more likely than girls to report they had no one to turn to for specific functions, including no one to help with homework (24 percent of boys versus 15 percent of girls), no one to tell their problems to (17 percent of boys versus 5 percent of girls), no one they trust to keep their secrets (15 percent of boys versus 8 percent of girls), and no one to turn to if they needed to borrow money (7 percent of boys versus 2 percent of girls). In addition, Qin-Hilliard and I found that girls were more likely to have at least one supportive adult relationship in their schools than were boys (49 percent of girls versus 37 percent of boys) (Suárez-Orozco and Qin-Hilliard 2004).

These findings suggest that gender differences in the quality of relationships in and out of school may help to explain the gender differences in academic outcomes. If boys are not receiving as much support (for school-related as well as non-school-related difficulties) and guidance in and out of school and are more likely to experience overt acts of hostility and low expectations from their teachers, they may find it much more difficult to achieve academically than girls (Suárez-Orozco and Qin-Hilliard 2004).

Several factors may contribute to this pattern. The negative social mirror that boys of color encounter appears to be significantly more distorting than that encountered by girls (López 2002). Boys of color are consistently viewed by members of the mainstream society they encounter as more threatening than are girls. Another factor that may help to explain boys' poorer school performance is peer pressure. Many researchers have noted that peer pressure to reject school is quite strong among boys (Gibson 1993; C. Suárez-Orozco and M. Suárez-Orozco 2001; Waters 1996). Furthermore, behaviors that gain boys respect with their peers often bring them into conflict with their teachers. Some researchers point out that immigrant boys are more pressured by their peers to reject school than immigrant girls from the same ethnic background (Gibson 1993; C. Suárez-Orozco and M. Suárez-Orozco 2001; Waters 1996). Gender differences in family responsibilities at home may also play a role in explaining differences in academic outcomes between girls and boys. Research findings consistently suggest that, compared with their brothers, immigrant girls have many more responsibilities at home (S. Lee 2001; Olsen 1997; Sarroub 2001; Smith 2002, Valenzuela 1999; Waters 1996). While these factors may account for this gendered pattern of academic engagement, more research is required to unpack the source of this trend.

EDUCATING THE GLOBAL CITIZEN

Globalization is contributing significantly to a world that is increasingly multicultural. On one hand, there is much to celebrate in this process while recognizing that diversification presents real challenges to both the individuals entering a new space as well as those living in receiving spaces. A primary danger of diversification, on the other hand, is an increase in intolerance and the threat of conflict. Diversity, however, presents a tremendous opportunity for individuals and cultures to search for commonalities of human experience that can be uniting.

Is there such a thing as a global identity? In recent decades, American youth culture has come to dominate the cultural scene among adolescents living in urban centers in Europe, Latin America, and Asia (C. Suárez-Orozco and M. Suárez-Orozco 2001). This pattern seems to be driven in large part by global media, including movies, television, music videos and recordings, and the Internet, as well as global marketing of such brands as Coca-Cola, McDonald's, and Nike (Arnett 2002). Whether this attraction to global brands translates into internalized cultural practices remains to be seen. Watson's (this volume) discussion of the ways in which families interact with McDonald's in China provides a glimpse into the possibility that the use of global symbols may not be as closely related to cultural change as some have hypothesized. The cultural contact may be more superficial than pervasive.

Psychologist Jeffrey Jensen Arnett, however, argues that globalization has clear implications for identity development among youth. He maintains that "most people in the world now develop a bicultural identity," which incorporates elements of the local culture with an awareness of a relation to the global culture (Arnett 2002, p. 777). As a result, he and others maintain that identity confusion may be increasing among youth (Nsamenang 2002). For many, however, the identity is less *bi*cultural than a "complex *hybrid*" (Arnett 2000, p. 778) or *trans*cultural (C. Suárez-Orozco and M. Suárez-Orozco 2001). Indeed, ethnic identity options may involve more than simply two cultures. For those who remain in the land of birth with a legacy of colonization, the challenge is to reconcile local traditions with the imported practices *and* globalized culture (Nsamenang 2002). In the words of Henry Louis Gates Jr.: "Today the ideal of wholeness has largely been retired. And cultural multiplicity is no longer seen as the problem but as a solution—a solution to the confines of identity itself. Double consciousness, once a disorder, is now a cure. Indeed, the only complaint we moderns have is that Du Bois was too cautious in his accounting. He'd conjured 'two souls, two thoughts, two unreconciled strivings.' Just two, Dr. Du Bois? Keep counting" (Gates 2003, p. 31).

The cultural challenges of globalization affect immigrants and native-born youth in different ways. For the children of immigrants, the task is to braid together into a flexible sense of self elements of the parent culture, the new culture they are navigating, and an emerging globalized youth culture. For those in the host society, the challenge is to broaden the cultural horizon to incorporate the changing perspectives, habits, and potentials of its diverse newcomers.

Many may struggle to manage the inconsistencies and ambivalences of multiple cultural menus (Nsamenang 2002). On one hand, the challenge may be particularly extreme when there is significant "cultural distance" between the country of origin and the host country (Berry 1997). For many children of immigrants, the diminished ties to any one cultural context "may result in an acute sense of alienation and impermanence as they grow up with a lack of cultural certainty, a lack of clear guidelines for how life is to be lived and how to interpret experience" (Arnett 2002, p. 778). On the other hand, harnessing the innate optimism of immigrant youth while providing adequate cultural interpreters, educational opportunities, and a reasonably welcoming reception in the new culture allows immigrant youth to quickly become successful members of their new society.

Developing a sense of belonging to a global culture has clear potential benefits:

> Because the global culture crosses so many cultural and national boundaries, in order to unify people across these boundaries, the values of the global culture necessarily emphasize tolerating and even celebrating differences. This means that the values of the global culture are defined in part by what they are not: They are not dogmatic; they are not exclusionary; they do not condone suppression of people or groups who have a point of view or a way of life that is different from the majority (Arnett 2001, p. 279).

As educators, we have a responsibility to place the tolerance—and even celebration—of cultural differences at the very core of our educational agenda. Such an end could serve to provide a core meaningful educational narrative that "envisions a future, . . . constructs ideals, . . .

prescribes rules of conduct, provides a source of authority, and above all gives a sense of continuity of purpose" (Postman 1995). Tolerance must be fostered not only in those who already reside in the receiving context but also among the widely diverse newcomers who are sharing the new social space. We must allow newcomers to retain a sense of pride in their cultures of origin while facilitating their entrance into the new milieu. Preparing youth to successfully navigate our multicultural world is essential to preparing them to be global citizens. Surely the implications for a more tolerant world are obvious.

REFERENCES

Adams, P. L. (1990). Prejudice and exclusion as social trauma. In *Stressors and adjustment disorders.* J. D. Noshpitz and R. D. Coddington, eds. New York: John Wiley and Sons.

Alsadir, N. (2002). Invisible woman. *New York Times Magazine,* November 17, p. 98.

Arnett, J. J. (2002). The psychology of globalization. *American Psychologist* 57(10): 774–783.

Athey, J. L., and F. L. Ahearn (1991). *Refugee children: Theory, research, and services.* Baltimore, MD: John Hopkins University Press.

Bailey, B. H. (2001). Dominican-American ethnic/racial identities and United States social categories. *International Migration Review* 35(3): 677–708.

Berry, J. W. (1997). Immigration, acculturation, and adaptation. *International Journal of Applied Psychology* 46: 5–34.

Brandon, P. (1991). Gender differences in young Asian Americans' educational attainment. *Sex Roles* 25(1–2): 45–61.

Child, I. L. (1943). *Italian or American? The second generation in conflict.* New Haven, CT: Yale University Press.

Coleman, J., et al. (1966). *Equality and educational opportunity.* Washington, DC: U.S. Government Printing Office.

DeVos, G. (1973). *Socialization for achievement: Essays on the cultural psychology of the Japanese.* Berkeley: University of California Press.

DeVos, G. (1980). Ethnic adaptation and minority status. *Journal of Cross-Cultural Psychology* 11(1): 101–125.

DeVos, G. (1992). The passing of passing. In *Social cohesion and alienation: Minorities in the United States and Japan.* G. DeVos, ed. Boulder, CO: Westview Press.

DeVos, G., and M. Suárez-Orozco (1990). *Status inequality: The self in culture.* Newbury Park, CA: Sage Publications.

Du Bois, W. E. B. (1989). *The souls of black folks.* New York: Bantam. (Original work published 1903).

Edmonston, B., and J. Passel, eds. (1994). *Immigration and ethnicity: The integration of America's newest arrivals.* Washington, DC: Urban Institute.

Erikson, E. (1968). *Identity: youth and crisis.* New York: W. W. Norton.

Espenshade, T., and M. Belanger (1998). Immigration and public opinion. In *Crossings: Mexican immigration in interdisciplinary perspective.* M. M. Suárez-Orozco, ed. Cambridge, MA: David Rockefeller Center for Latin American Studies.

Fadiman, A. (1998). *The spirit catches you and you fall down: A Hmong child, her American doctors, and the collision of two cultures.* New York: Farrar, Straus & Giroux.

Falicov, C. J. (2002). The family migration experience: Loss and resilience. In *Latinos: Remaking America.* M. M. Suarez-Orozco and M. M. Paez, eds. Berkeley: University of California Press.

Fix, M., and J. Passel (1994). *Immigration and immigrants: Setting the record straight.* Washington, DC: Urban Institute.

Fordham, S., and J. U. Ogbu (1986). Black students' school success: Coping with the burden of "acting white." *Urban Review* 18(3): 176–206.

Freire, P. (1995). *Pedagogy of the oppressed.* New York: Continuum.

Gans, H. (1992). Second-generation decline: Scenarios for the economic and ethnic futures of the post-1965 American immigrants. *Ethnic and Racial Studies* 15(April): 173–192.

Gates, H. L., Jr. (2003) Both sides now. *New York Times Book Review*, April 4, p. 31.

Gibson, M. A. (1988). *Accommodation without assimilation: Sikh immigrants in an American high school.* Ithaca, NY: Cornell University Press.

Gibson, M. A. (1993). Variability in immigrant students' school performance: the U.S. case. Unpublished manuscript. Washington, DC.

Gordon, M. M. (1964). *Assimilation in American life: The role of race, religion, and national origins.* Oxford, UK: Oxford University Press.

Higham, J. (1975). *Send these to me: Jews and other immigrants in urban America.* New York: Atheneum.

Hoffman, E. (1989). *Lost in translation: A life in a new language.* New York: Penguin Books.

Iyer, P. (2000). *The Global Soul.* New York: Vintage Press.

Lee, J. (2002). Racial and ethnic achievement gap trends: Reversing the progress toward equity? *Educational Researcher* 31(1): 3–12.

Lee, S. (2001). More than "model minorities" or "delinquents": A look at Hmong American high school students. *Harvard Educational Review,* 71(3): 505–528.

Levitt, P. (2001). *The transnational villagers.* Berkeley: University of California Press.

López, N. (2002). *Hopeful girls, troubled boys: Race and gender disparity in urban education.* New York: Routledge.

Louie, J. (2003). Media in the lives of immigrant youth. In *The Social worlds of immigrant youth: New directions for youth development.* C. Suárez-Orozco and I. Todorova, eds. New York: Jossey-Bass.

Maestes, M. (2000). *Acculturation and ethnic identity measures for Latinos and Asian Americans: Analyses of methodology and psychometrics*. Lincoln: University of Nebraska.

Marcia, J. (1966). Development and validation of ego-identity status. *Journal of Personality and Social Psychology* 3: 551–558.

Massey, D., and N. Denton (1993). *American apartheid*. Cambridge, MA: Harvard University Press.

Matute-Bianchi, M. E. (1991). Situational ethnicity and patterns of school performance among immigrant and non-immigrant Mexican descent students. In *Minority status and schooling: A comparative study of immigrant and involuntary minorities*. M. A. Gibson and J. Ogbu, eds. New York: Garland Publishing.

Migration Information (2003). *Global Data*. Retrieved January 3, 2003, from http://www.migrationinformation.org/GlobalData/countrydata/data.cfm.

Morales, E. (2002). *Living in Spanglish: The search for Latino identity in America*. New York: LA Weekly Books.

Navarrette, R. J. (1993). *A darker shade of crimson: Odyssey of a Harvard Chicano*. New York: Bantam.

Nsamenang, B. (2002). Adolescence in sub-Saharan Africa: An image constructed from Africa's triple inheritance. In *The world's youth: Adolescence in eight regions of the globe*. B. B. Brown, R. Larson, and T. S. Saraswathi, eds. New York: Cambridge University Press.

Ogbu, J. U. (1978). *Minority education and caste: The American system in cross-cultural perspective*. New York: Academic Press.

Ogbu, J. U. (1987). Variability in minority school performance: A problem in search of an explanation. *Anthropology and Education Quarterly* 18(4): 312–334.

Ogbu, J. U., and S. Herbert (1998). Voluntary and involuntary minorities: A cultural-ecological theory of school performance with some implications for education. *Anthropology and Education Quarterly* 29: 155–188.

Olsen, L. (1997). *Made in America: Immigrant students in our public schools*. New York: The New Press.

Orfield, G. (2002). Commentary. In *Latinos: Remaking America*. M. Suárez-Orozco and M. M. Paez, eds. Berkeley: University of California Press; Cambridge, MA: David Rockefeller Center for Latin American Studies.

Orfield, G., and J. T. Yun (1999). *Resegregation in American schools*. Cambridge, MA: The Civil Rights Project, Harvard University.

Parham, T. (1989). Cycles of psychological nigrescence. *Counseling Psychologist* 17(2): 187–226.

Portes, A. (1993). The "New Immigration." Press release, School of International Relations, Johns Hopkins University.

Portes, A., and R. G. Rumbaut (2001). *Legacies: The story of the second generation*. Berkeley: University of California Press.

Postman, N. (1995). *The end of education: Redefining the value of school*. New York: Alfred A. Knopf.

Proulx, E. A. (1996). *Accordion crimes*. New York: Scribners.

Qin-Hilliard, D. B. (2003). Gendered expectations and gendered experiences: Immigrant students' adaptation in U.S. schools. In *The Social worlds of immigrant youth: New directions for youth development*. C. Suárez-Orozco and I. Todorova, eds. New York: Jossey-Bass.

Roeser, R. W., J. S. Eccles, and A. J. Sameroff (1998). Academic and emotional functioning in early adolescence: Longitudinal relations, patterns, and prediction by experience in middle school. *Development and Psychology* 10: 321–352.

Rosenthal, D. A., and S. S. Feldman (1991). The influence of perceived family and personal factors on self-reported school performance of Chinese and Western high school students. *Journal of Research on Adolescents* 1: 135–154.

Rumbaut, R. (1997). *Passages to adulthood: The adaptation of children of immigrants in Southern California*. New York: Russell Sage Foundation.

Sarroub, L. K. (2001). The sojourner experience of Yemeni American high school students: An ethnographic portrait. *Harvard Educational Review* 71(3): 390–415.

Sciolino, E. (2002). Portrait of the Arab as a young radical. *New York Times*, September 22, p. A14.

Smith, R. (2002). Gender, ethnicity, and race in school and work outcomes of second-generation Mexican Americans. In *Latinos: Remaking America*. M. M. Suarez-Orozco and M. M. Paez, eds. Berkeley: University of California Press.

Sommer, D. (2004). *Bilingual aesthetics: A new sentimental education*. Raleigh, NC: Duke University Press.

Stanton-Salazar, R. D. (2001). *Manufacturing hope and despair: The school and kin support networks of U.S.-Mexican youth*. New York: Teachers College Press.

Steele, C. (1997). A threat in the air: How stereotypes shape intellectual identity and performance. *American Psychologist* 52(6): 613–629.

Stepick, A. (1997). *Pride against prejudice: Haitians in the United States*. Boston: Allyn & Bacon.

Stonequist, E. V. (1937). *The marginal man*. New York: Scribner and Sons.

Suárez-Orozco, C. (2000). Identities under siege: Immigration stress and social mirroring among the children of immigrants. In *Cultures under siege: Social violence and trauma*. A. Robben and M. Suárez-Orozco, eds. Cambridge, UK: Cambridge University Press.

Suárez-Orozco, C., and D. B. Qin-Hilliard (2004). The cultural psychology of academic engagement: Immigrant boys' experiences in U.S. schools. In *Adolescent boys in context*. N. Way and J. Chu, eds. New York: New York University Press.

Suárez-Orozco, C., and M. Suárez-Orozco (1995). *Transformations: Immigration, family life, and achievement motivation among Latino adolescents*. Stanford, CA: Stanford University Press.

Suárez-Orozco, C., and M. Suárez-Orozco (2001). *Children of immigration* (1st ed.). Cambridge, MA: Harvard University Press.

Suárez-Orozco, C., I. Todorova, and J. Louie (2002). Making up for lost time: The experience of separations and reunifications among immigrant families. *Family Process* 41(4): 625–643.

Suárez-Orozco, M. M. (1996). Unwelcome mats. *Harvard Magazine* 98: 32–35.

Suárez-Orozco, M. M., and Paez, M. M. (2002). *Latinos: Remaking America.* Berkeley: University of California Press.

Takaki, R. (1993). *A different mirror: A history of multicultural America.* New York: Little, Brown.

Tatum, B. (1997). *"Why are all the black kids sitting together in the cafeteria?" and other conversations about race.* New York: Basic Books.

Taylor, C. (1994). *Multiculturalisim: Examining the politics of recognition.* Princeton: Princeton University Press.

Titone, R. (1989). The bilingual personality as a metasystem: The case of code switching. *Canadian Society for Italian Studies* 3: 55–64.

Tsuda, T. (2003). *Strangers in the ethnic homeland: Japanese Brazilian return migration in transnational perspective.* New York: Columbia University Press.

U.S. Bureau of the Census (2000). *Current population reports.* Washington, DC.

Valenzuela, A. (1999). Gender roles and settlement activities among children and their immigrant families. *American Behavioral Scientist* 42(4): 720–742.

Vigil, J. D. (1988). *Barrio gangs: Street life and identity in Southern California.* Austin: University of Texas Press.

Vigil, J. D. (2002). Community dynamics and the rise of street gangs. In *Latinos: Remaking America.* M. M. Suarez-Orozco and M. M. Paez, eds. Berkeley: University of California Press.

Waters, M. (1996). The intersection of gender, race, and ethnicity in identity development of Caribbean American teens. In *Urban girls: Resisting stereotypes, creating identities.* B. J. R. Leadbeater and N. Way, eds. New York: New York University Press.

Waters, M. (1999). *Black identities: West Indian dreams and American realities.* Cambridge, MA: Harvard University Press.

Waters, M. (1997). Ethnic and racial identities of second-generation black immigrants in New York City. *International Migration Review* 28(4): 795–820.

Weinstein, R. (2002). *Reaching higher: The power of expectations in schooling.* Cambridge, MA: Harvard University Press.

Winicott, D. W. (1971). *Playing and reality.* Middlesex, UK: Penguin.

Wu, F. H. (2002). *Yellow: Race in America beyond black and white.* New York: Basic Books.

Zéphir, F. (2001). *Trends in ethnic identification among second-generation Haitian immigrants in New York City.* Westport, CT: Bergin & Garvey.

Zhou, M. (1997). Growing up American: The challenge confronting immigrant children and children of immigrants. *Annual Review* 23: 63–95.

NINE

Sunaina Maira

IMPERIAL FEELINGS

Youth Culture, Citizenship, and Globalization

INTRODUCTION

Youth culture is often taken to be the exemplary manifestation of globalization, a testament to its possibilities and excesses, highlighting the deep anxieties and desires it evokes. Nike-clad or henna-painted, underground or hypervisible, apathetic or idealist, anarchist or apolitical, youth culture seems to be a primary site onto which the dualities used to structure the popular discourse of globalization are projected. This binarism of globalization's meanings, of course, is a gross oversimplification of the complex effects of transnational flows of culture, capital, media, and labor, but images of youth culture represent the tensions associated with the economic and social shifts of late capitalism. In particular, the "monstrous" figure of the adolescent seems to embody fears about cultural homogenization and balkanization, commodification and co-optation. John and Jean Comaroff (2001) write, "Is it surprising, then, that . . . the standardized nightmare of the genteel mainstream is an increasingly universal image of the adolescent, a larger-than-life figure . . . beeper tied to a global underground economy—in short, a sinister caricature of the corporate mogul? Perhaps because of its fusion of monstrosity, energy, and creativity, this figure also subsumes some of the more complex aspects of millennial capitalism, if in the manner of a grotesque" (p. 19). I argue that this symbolic use of youth, and youth culture, to capture the anxieties and desires associated with globalization both reveals the ideological work done by the notion of the liminal category of "youth" and limits the integration of youth culture research into studies of globalization.

In the sections below, I explore some of the conjunctures and disjunctures between theories of globalization and youth culture and offer the notion of "youthscapes" (Maira and Soep, 2004) as a new framework for a more critical, interdisciplinary approach to link both areas of research. I will also draw on my recent research on notions of citizenship among South Asian immigrant youth to argue that the experiences of young people are central to debates about neoliberal modes of consumer citizenship and transnationalism. This study highlights the importance of thinking about the meanings of nationalism for different groups of young people, especially given the resurgent nationalism of the "new Cold War" United States, but also in light of the fact that immigrant youth increasingly cross national borders as migrant workers. However, while these immigrants think of themselves as transnational citizens, U.S. borders are being reinvested with xenophobia and state surveillance, especially since the events of September 11, 2001. The ongoing assault on immigrant and civil rights shows that discourses of citizenship are linked to practices of labor by the globalization and transformation of both citizenship and labor.

Given that *globalization* has by now come to mean so much, and so little, I will discuss globalization specifically as a mode of empire, as an imperial project that has historically operated simultaneously through domestic and foreign policy while obscuring the connections between both spheres. Looking at everyday life in the heart of empire and at the responses of young people at local, national, and transnational scales allows for an approach that would help advance a critical understanding and methodology for studying globalization.

WHY THE BARRICADES?

Youth, or at least, young activists, seem to be ever present at the barricades of anti–World Trade Organization (WTO) protests and flock annually to the World Social Forum in Porto Alegre, Brazil (see Shepard and Hayduk 2002). However, research on globalization has not inter-sected deeply enough with that on youth culture, whether in education, the social sciences, or cultural studies, particularly in works that focus on macrolevel processes or at least on adult actors. While "youth" are sometimes present in this research as young immigrants or consumers of globalized culture, theorists have not taken seriously enough the actual cultural productions or lived experiences of young people, which is what I mean by "youth culture."[1] There is a large and growing body of work that deals with culture and globalization (see, for example, Appadurai 1996; Basch, Glick Schiller, and Szanton Blanc 1994; Crane, Kawashima, and Kawasaki 2002; Canclini 2001; Gupta and Ferguson 1997; Hannerz 1996; Jameson and Miyoshi 1998; Massey 1994; D. Miller 1998; Morley and Robins 1995; Wilson and Dissanayake 1996), and many of the shifts in cultural processes that are discussed in this lit-erature shape the lives of, if they are not partly produced by, young people in various local and national contexts. For example, the trans-national circulation of cultural objects and expressive forms and the production of the globalized cultural imaginaries described by Arjun Appadurai (1996) are very evident in youth cultures around the globe, as are attempts at localizing and indigenizing global popular culture (for example, Gross, McMurray, and Swedenburg 1996; Jenkins, this volume; Larkin 2002; Olwig and Hastrup 1997; Watson, this volume). Issues of youth culture seep into studies of globalization by way of their attention to popular culture, media, and cultural change, but there is much less focus directly on youth per se, and particularly on the ways young people *themselves* understand or grapple with globalization. At the same time, youth culture studies in the United States has not drawn explicitly enough on critical theory and research in the areas of global-ization, social movements, and citizenship. There seems to be an episte-mological barricade, or at least a chain-link fence, between the two areas.

Why have scholars of globalization not engaged adequately with questions of youth culture, and why have not more youth culture schol-ars theorized globalization? I think that a partial answer lies in these very social meanings attached to youth, an association that seems to follow youth across various national contexts, even across historical periods, and that is both part of the cultural construction of youth *and* a reason why they are not sufficiently acknowledged by scholars of globalization. The most salient of these constructions is the portrayal of youth as inadequately formed adults, as subjects lacking in the presumably desired qualities of adulthood, rather than as subjects in their own right with specific (even if they are not always unique) needs and concerns. Much work on globalization and transnationalism has tended to focus largely or explicitly only on adults, and youth are assumed to be less fully formed social actors or subjects less able to exert the agency in the face of globalization that some scholars are, rightly, eager to document. To be sure, youth are engaged in an ongoing process of social and cognitive development (see the chapters by Gardner and C. Suárez-Orozco in this volume) and do, in fact, acquire more rights and responsibilities as they move into adulthood. However, there is often an assumption in traditional work on youth and citizenship, for example, that young citizens—to the extent that they have rights, which are often limited—must be socialized into adult norms of political involvement rather than being considered thinking agents who may express important critiques of citizenship and nationhood (Buckingham 2000, p. 13).

For example, to return to the image of the youth at the barricades, the widely publicized 1999 blockage of the WTO meetings in Seattle, Washington (Cockburn and St. Clair 2000), is very revealing of these underlying concerns about young people and globalization. Coverage of those events revealed a striking ambivalence that goes to the heart of the duality projected onto youth: the suspicion that young people are not mature citizens who can act effectively and, simultaneously, the fear that they are actually citizens with the power to effect change that some may not desire. This kind of deeper social ambivalence has, of course, long existed as moral panics about youth, who come to symbolize a given society's anxieties and hopes about its own transformation (Cohen 1972). Without veering into a functionalist analysis, it might be safe to say that these anxieties are projected onto young people because of the association of youth with liminality, in anthropological terms, so that societies both reject as "deviant" those who critique their norms, and also tolerate, even incorporate, them as liminal citizens (Dannin 2002, p. 16).

The notion of youth as unformed citizens is embedded in developmental assumptions about youth that actually tie youth culture analyses in interesting ways to the study of globalization. Adolescent psychology, in the tradition of theorist Erik Erikson (1968), is based on the premise that identity is the defining question of adolescence. Stage models of identity assume that development is, if not a linear, at least a teleological process; there is an implicit tenet that youth are proceeding toward a desirable end goal, which is to be realized only and always in adulthood. Globalization, too, is often framed in the context of arguments about "progress"; even if these arguments are discussing economic and political, and not psychological, development, they still are embroiled in debates about the desired end goals. By now, of course, most scholars and critics concede that globalization is not a linear process but is inherently and deeply uneven (see, for example, Inda and Rosaldo 2002; Bloom, this volume; Watson, this volume; see also M. Suárez-Orozco and Qin-Hilliard, this volume). The processes of *both* globalization and youth, and the conjunctures and disjunctures between them, need to be considered together. The flows of people, goods, capital, and media images across national borders are embedded in, and produce, social and material inequalities that in turn drive further immigration and displacement (Appadurai 1996; Basch et al. 1994; Sassen 1998). Youth are necessarily caught in this loop, in this movement of people and mobilization for justice and equity, and in this cycle of production and consumption (Buroway 2000; Tam 2001).

Globalization theorists need to pay more careful attention to youth studies and include them not just as examples of other processes but as areas that contain their own processes of responding to or even creating globalized culture. At the same time, youth culture and education researchers need to move beyond approaches that are largely local or national in focus, or even universalist in their assumptions, to be able to link schooling and youth development to a globalized context. This need not entail moving outside the school or the local contexts of youth culture, but it does mean having a wider analytic frame that can take account of issues such as immigration, economic shifts, or media consumption that impact the lives of children and students in very tangible ways (Jenkins, in this volume). Given popular culture's link to global processes of production and consumption, the transnational context is often at least implicit within youth culture studies, and in fact some may argue that youth culture scholars have been studying globalization for years.[2] At the same time, though, this work has traditionally theorized the daily experiences and cultural productions within a local or national frame of reference (for examples of compelling exceptions, see Lipsitz 2001; Simonett 2001).

THEORIZING YOUTH CULTURE

The theoretical framework that pioneered an incisive analysis of the ideological construction of youth as a social category, and of the cultural productions of youth themselves as responses to a particular social and historical context, is that of the Birmingham school of subculture theorists. According to John Clarke, Stuart Hall, Tom Jefferson, and Brian Roberts in their classic work *Resistance through Rituals,* youth belong to a subculture when "there is a shared set of social rituals that define them as a group instead of a mere collection of individuals" (1976, p. 47). The Birmingham school deliberately used the term *subculture* instead of simply *youth culture* because they argued that the notion of subculture, in their framework, highlighted a deeper structural analysis linking youth to youth industries, such as music and fashion, that had created a "teenage [consumer] market" (p. 16). These theorists drew on the Chicago school of sociology's work on subcultures and youth delinquency and also on the Frankfurt school's approach to mass culture,[3] but their intervention—in the context of social transitions in Britain, particularly for working-class males—aimed at understanding the meanings that youth make for themselves through the use of popular culture. Their seminal theory of youth subcultures drew on both semiotic and structural analyses, looking at the symbolic work of youth subculture in helping youth ideologically resolve the paradoxes they confront in different social spheres.

Of course, this theory outlines only a representational solution to the crises of youth, and critics have also argued that the Birmingham school theorists, such as Dick Hebdige (1979), overinterpreted the symbolic meanings of youth culture in terms of resistance, failing to take into account young people who were not involved in these spectacular subcultures, and that they projected their own politics onto the youth they were studying (Cohen 1997; Gelder 1997; Turner 1996). Feminist critics have also argued that this early work neglected the experiences of girls and young women and the more private expressions of youth sub-cultures (McRobbie and Garber 1994; McRobbie 1991). Yet I think the Birmingham school's framework remains influential in the United States because it takes seriously the responses of youth at a collective level and focuses on young people in their everyday settings—including schools (see the influential studies of Foley 1994 and Willis 1977)—as well as embedded in a larger political or social context. The strength of this incipient interdisciplinary approach is its emphasis on thinking simultaneously about "structures, cultures, and biographies," thus offering a theoretical lens for thinking about the links between youth culture and globalization that is very relevant to education (for example, the significant contributions made by Flores 2000 and Lipsitz 1994).

Youth culture studies, I believe, demands an interdisciplinary approach if it is to address both issues of individual meaning making and social-historical context. Yet in the United States, at least, it seems that youth research tends to be based either on empirical methods of interviewing, ethnography, and surveys or textualist approaches drawing on literary and media or film studies. The Birmingham school approach to studying "structures, cultures, and biographies" has been transplanted to the United States, some argue, through the division of academic labor between political economy/sociology, cultural anthropology, and literary criticism (Grossberg 1996). The context of knowledge production in the U.S. academy is thus partially responsible for the lack of interdisciplinary programs or departments that can train students to integrate social and interpretive analyses and can support more collaborative interdisciplinary research. These structural issues related to higher education are, I think, one reason for the disjuncture between youth culture studies and work on globalization.

In trying to develop a more adequate framework theorizing the link between the two areas, Elisabeth Soep and I are coediting a collection, titled "Youthscapes," to redress the undertheorizing of youth as key players within globalization and the use of the field of youth culture studies as the epistemological folk devil of academic knowledge production (Maira and Soep 2004). We developed the notion of "youthscapes" to offer an approach that would provide an analytic and methodological link between youth culture and nationalizing or globalizing processes.

Appadurai (1996), in his model of cultural globalization, used the term *scape* to describe dimensions of global cultural flows that are fluid and irregular, rather than fixed and finite. Ethnoscapes comprise the shifting circuits of people who animate a given social world; technoscapes draw attention to high-speed channels connecting previously distant territories; financescapes encompass new systems for accumulating and moving money; mediascapes involve the dispersal of images and texts; and ideoscapes embody the "imagined worlds" produced through intersections between and among all of the above.

"Youth" is a social category that belongs to all five of Appadurai's categories, so a youthscape is not a unit of analysis but a way of thinking *about* youth culture studies, one that revitalizes discussions about youth cultures and social movements while simultaneously theorizing the political and social uses of youth. The process of conceptualizing a site for local youth practice as embedded within national and global forces is what we mean by *youthscape*. *Youthscape* suggests a site that is not just geographic or temporal but social and political as well, a "place" that is bound up with questions of power and materiality (Dirlik 2001/2002, Soja 1989). In the section that follows, I draw on my current research on South Asian immigrant youth after 9/11 to illustrate a particular youthscape that highlights national as well as transnational discourses of belonging and exclusion, work and mobility, and that has important implications for education in a globalized world.

MUSLIM IMMIGRANT YOUTH
AND CULTURAL CITIZENSHIP AFTER 9/11

In the wake of the September 11, 2001, attacks and the subsequent war in Afghanistan, questions of citizenship and racialization have taken on new, urgent meanings for South Asian immigrant youth. Many South Asian Americans, Arab Americans, and Muslim Americans, or individuals who appeared "Muslim," have been victims of physical assaults and racial profiling.[4] My ethnographic study focuses on working-class Indian, Pakistani, and Bangladeshi immigrant students in the public high school in Cambridge, Massachusetts, since fall 2001. Cambridge is an interesting site for this research, for while media attention and community discussions of racial profiling were primarily focused on South Asians in the New York–New Jersey area, there were hundreds of incidents around the country in places where South Asians have not been as visible in the public sphere or as organized, including incidents in the Boston area. It is also interesting to focus on communities, such as Cambridge, that are known to be more politically progressive in order to understand what such a setting both allows and does not allow at a time of national crisis, and what youth might say about political events when they are, in a sense, allowed to say it.

The Cambridge public high school has an extremely diverse student body, reflecting the city's changing population, with students from Latin America, the Caribbean, Africa, and Asia. Students from India, Pakistan, Bangladesh, and Afghanistan constitute the largest Muslim student population in the school, followed by Muslim youth from Ethiopia, Somalia, and Morocco.[5] The South Asian immigrant student population at the high school is predominantly working to lower-middle class, recently arrived (within the last one to five years), mostly from small towns in South Asia, and with minimal to moderate fluency in English. The majority of the Indian immigrant youth are from Muslim families, most from Gujarat, and several of them are actually related to one another, as their families have immigrated as part of an ongoing chain migration. The parents of these youth generally work in low-income jobs in the service sector, and they themselves work after school, up to twenty hours a week, in fast-food restaurants, gas stations, and retail stores and as security guards.

Cultural Citizenship

I found that in nearly all my conversations with these youth, as well as with their parents, the discussion would inevitably turn to citizenship for this was an issue of deep concern to them that had profoundly shaped their lives and driven their experiences of migration. The concept of citizenship is at the heart of discussions of democracy, multiculturalism, and transnationalism in the United States, all questions that are being debated anew after 9/11. Research on youth and citizenship is meager and generally tends to come out of the traditions of developmental psychology or functionalist socialization theory, both of which assume that young people must emulate existing adult models of "good citizenship," liberally defined, and must adjust to the status quo (Buckingham 2000, pp. 10–11). This assumes a limited definition, too, of what constitutes the "political"; more recent work challenges these assumptions and pays attention to young people's own understandings of politics and the ways they negotiate relationships of power in different realms of their everyday life (Bhavnani 1991, p. 172; Buckingham 2000, p. 13).

Citizenship has traditionally been thought of in political, economic, and civic terms, but increasingly, analyses focus on the notion of cultural citizenship as multiethnic societies are forced to confront questions of difference that undergird social inequity (Coll 2002; Rosaldo 1997). Cultural citizenship—cultural belonging in the nation, or the cultural dimensions of citizenship more broadly—is a critical issue for immigrant communities and minority groups, for the rights and obligations of civic citizenship are mediated by race, ethnicity, gender, and sexuality (Berlant 1997; T. Miller 2001; Rosaldo 1997), as well as by religion. The concept of cultural citizenship has been developed by Latino studies scholars Renato Rosaldo (1997) and William Flores and Rita Benmayor (1997), who use it as a category that can activate a particular political project focused on immigrant and civil rights by redefining the "basic social contract of America." It has also been developed, in a different vein, by cultural theorists, such as Aihwa Ong, who are concerned with citizenship as a regulatory process and who define cultural citizenship as "a dual process of self-making and being-made within webs of power linked to the nation-state and civil society" (Ong 1996, p. 738). Some, like Toby Miller, have been skeptical about the possibility of using citizenship as the collective basis for radical political transformation—given its increasingly individualized, privatized definition—but are still open to its potential; T. Miller (1993, p. 12) writes:

> The citizen is a polysemic category, open to contestation; an avatar for all parts of the spectrum. . . . It is a technology that produces a "disposition" [among citizens] not to accept the imposition of a particular form of government passively, but to embrace it actively as a collective expression of themselves.

My work bridges these two major approaches, the Foucauldian view that is skeptical about working within a politics defined by the state's disciplining power, not to mention that of capital, and the view oriented to social movements that sees possibilities for revitalizing a democratic vision by paying attention to everyday struggles. I am interested in the critical possibilities of cultural citizenship for galvanizing struggles for civil and immigrant rights, particularly for young immigrants, but within the limits of both increasing privatization of public services and the inequities of global capital (T. Miller 1993; Hutnyk 2000).

South Asian immigrant youth construct understandings of citizenship in relation to both the United States and one or more nations in South Asia, for as others have pointed out, migrant or diasporic subjects construct cultural citizenship that connects them to multiple nation-states, not just one (Siu 2001). But I also think we need to go beyond simply affirming this notion of transnational cultural citizenship—by now well documented—to look at its different manifestations in specific contexts and at particular historical moments. Taking a cue from Toby Miller's notion of polysemic citizenship, I think we need to explore the different *kinds* of cultural citizenship in everyday life, in all their subtlety and contradiction, as well as the ways in which issues of economic or legal citizenship spill over into cultural citizenship. In my research, I have found that these categories are more blurred than some theorists of cultural citizenship have acknowledged; it is important not to lose sight of the continuing salience of the traditional bases of citizenship even as they are being transformed. Preliminary findings from this study suggest that there are three ways in which South Asian immigrant youth understand and practice cultural citizenship: *flexible citizenship, multicultural/polycultural citizenship,* and *dissenting citizenship.* These three categories also point to the ways in which the questions of citizenship facing these youth not only go beyond debates about cultural rights to questions of economic, civil, and human rights but also point to the limitations of rights-based discourses. In this chapter, in the interest of space, I discuss only the last two forms of citizenship among immigrant youth; however, it is worth noting that ideas about multiculturalism in education and more critical, polyculturalist notions inform ideas of transnational and dissenting citizenship (Maira 2004).

Flexible Citizenship

My research suggests that these South Asian immigrant youth are living a new kind of transnational adolescence, increasingly common among what are called "transmigrants" (Glick Schiller and Fouron 2001, p. 3), due to the international division of labor that forces immigrant youth to cross national borders—with or sometimes without their families—as economic or political refugees (Hondagneu-Sotelo 2002; C. Suárez-Orozco, this volume). Nina Glick Schiller and Georges Fouron, in their brilliant ethnography of long-distance nationalism, make the subtle distinction between transnational migrants and "transborder citizens" who cross national borders but "do so in the name of only one nation" (2001, p. 25). In my study, it is not as easy to categorize the national affiliations of these immigrant youth as singular or multiple, partly because as adolescents they express their national identifications through practices that are somewhat different than those of adults, given that the decision to cross national borders is generally taken by adult members of their families, and partly because they seem to express different kinds of national affiliations, and anxieties and desires linked to nation, in different sites. Moreover, my study suggests that the transnational, or transborder, adolescence of these South Asian Muslim immigrant youth is a condition in which these youth are forced to confront both the limits of any one state to provide for or protect them and the ability of nationalism to be decoupled from legal citizenship as it crosses the territorial boundaries of states.

Most of these young immigrants desired and had applied for U.S. citizenship, since they came here sponsored by relatives who already were permanent residents or citizens, in some cases fathers who had migrated alone many years earlier.[6] About half have green cards already; the others are a mix of citizens and undocumented immigrants. For them, citizenship is part of a carefully planned, long-term, family-based strategy of migration in response to the economic pressures on those living in, or at the edge of, the middle class in South Asia. This strategy is what some researchers call the "flexible citizenship" of migrants who use transnational links to provide political or material resources not available to them within a single nation-state (Basch et al.

1994), as has been argued for affluent Chinese migrants by Aihwa Ong (1999). They desired U.S. citizenship because of what they perceived as its civic and also economic benefits: a few stated that they wanted to be able to vote, and several said that they wanted to be able to travel freely between the United States and South Asia in order to be mobile in work and family life. After 9/11, of course, citizenship seemed to become less a matter of choice for immigrants, particularly Muslims and South Asian and Arab Americans, than a hoped-for shield against the abuses of civil rights.

Working-class South Asian migrants, too, seem to be enacting a version of flexible citizenship, if at greater cost to themselves and their children. At least two boys had been separated from their fathers for about fifteen years; Faisal said his father had left Pakistan for the United States right after he was born and in effect missed his son's childhood while he was working in the United States to support him and his family till they could be reunited. By the time Faisal came to the United States, however, his older brother was too old to enroll in high school and had to struggle to get a GED (general equivalency diploma) and find a job with limited English skills. A Bangladeshi boy and his brothers and sisters lived with a relative, separated from their parents and from some siblings who were still in Bangladesh. These youth did not speak readily in public about the meaning of these separations and reunions, seeming to take these transnational family arrangements as a fact of their lives (see C. Suárez-Orozco, this volume, for a related discussion), but some spoke longingly of the friends and familiar places they had left behind. Riyaz, a Gujarati Muslim boy who came to the United States in fall 2002, spoke with anguish and almost disbelief at his uprooting from his village, his companions, his routine. He did not speak much English when he first came, but when asked to bring an image he associated with the place he had left behind to a school workshop, he drew a broken heart; a Pakistani immigrant boy scribbled "India" and "America" next to each of the jagged halves of Riyaz's. Rizwan's uncle was an agent who helped people migrate to the Persian Gulf states from their home town of Valsar, underscoring that the United States was just one node for labor migrants in the vast Gujarati diaspora.

Some of these immigrant youth imagine their lives spanning national borders and speak of returning to South Asia, at least temporarily, once they have become U.S. citizens. Some of their parents hope to retire there, and many families engage in transnational marriage arrangements. Sohail, who worked as a computer assistant after school, wanted to set up a transnational high-tech business so that he could live part-time in Gujarat and part-time in Boston while supporting his parents. He saw this as a development strategy for nonresident Indians (NRIs) to fulfill their obligations to the home nation-state, using the benefits of U.S. citizenship. Sohail said,

> The thing is, this place doesn't need me more than my country, because in my country, there's a lot of poor people who need help, and our education, if we study here, then we'll go back to our country, open up some kind of companies or something, that'll be really good for them, because our economy is really down right now, you know.

It seems that these young immigrants' notion of flexible cultural citizenship are based on two kinds of processes of "self-making and being-made," to use Aihwa Ong's framework, in relation to the various nation-states with which they affiliate. The first process involves transnational popular culture, for the identification of these youth with India or Pakistan is based largely on Bollywood (Hindi) films, Indian television serials, and Indian music that they access through video, satellite TV, and the Internet. Most of these young people do not have the time or resources to participate in U.S. public culture; they hardly ever go to films in local theaters and don't attend music concerts. In this, their experiences seem very different from the "pop cosmopolitan" consumers of global media described by Henry Jenkins (this volume) who watch anime films at MIT or make forays into "ethnic neighborhoods" in search of manga comics. In contrast, the immigrant students in my study are rooted in their (low-income or immigrant) neighborhoods, and it is their consumption of popular culture from their country of origin that marks them as "transnational" (I return later to the question of cosmopolitanism). The South Asian boys surf the Web for Bollywood stars—in some cases, even "Lollywood," or films from Lahore—and for Hindi film and music Web sites. Some of the girls regularly watch episodes of Hindi TV serials on DVD or on cable TV, and they all watch Indian films on video. Jamila, a Bangladeshi immigrant girl, talked of visiting Internet chat rooms for diasporic Bangladeshi youth, as well as youth in Bangladesh, and alluded to a transnational identification, commenting that Bangladeshis "in London, they're like, they're almost the same as me."

Mona, a Gujarati girl who worked evenings with her sister in a relative's convenience store in Waltham, often borrowed videotapes of Indian television serials, such as *Kusum*, from the store to watch at home and knew all the details of the intricate family and social relationships of the serials' extended families. Many of these youth do find themselves living in reconstituted extended families, spread across apartment buildings or city blocks in Cambridge. Tellingly, too, large-screen televisions and entertainment centers seemed to be the point of pride in almost all the homes I visited; given that few of these families went to movie theaters, the home is an important site for consuming Indian films on video or DVD and, with the installation of AT&T's link to the South Asian Zee-TV channel, watching daily news programs in Gujarati or Urdu. This private construction of national identity, based on popular culture consumption, resonates with the work of Nestór García Canclini, who argues that "for many men and women, especially youth, the questions specific to citizenship, such as how we inform ourselves and who represents our interests, are answered more often than not through private consumption of commodities and media offerings than through the abstract rules of democracy or through participation in discredited legal organizations" (2001, p. 5). Flexible cultural citizenship can be constructed in and through popular culture, a dimension that Ong does not adequately explore.

Transnational popular culture practices also seem to be an important component of the equation of cultural citizenship because of the role they play in relation to the labor of working-class immigrant youth. These young immigrants base their cultural citizenship on institutional practices of labor and education that are both regulated by the state and articulated with the global economy. Their participation in U.S. public culture, in fact, is largely as workers in the low-wage, low-skill service sector, working at chain stores such as Dunkin Donuts and Star

Market, with other immigrant or young workers, or at family-owned convenience stores. These youth have come to the United States, in some sense, as migrant workers; even though they often do not explicitly assume this identity, it profoundly shapes their relationships to the city and interactions with others. Waheed lamented that he could never get to go out in the city with his friends because they all worked on different schedules and it was almost impossible for them to have a night off together, given that he worked night shifts at his weekend job. Karina, who had just migrated from a village in Gujarat and was working at McDonald's, commented on the gendered shift in wage labor outside the home, saying, "In my country, the women don't work, and here you have to work. And here life is so busy." Karina's lament about her stressful life in the United States was a common refrain among these immigrant youth, who rushed from school, to part-time jobs, to homework and household chores.

Compared to more affluent or highly credentialed South Asian immigrants, these working-class immigrant youth are more ambiguously positioned in relation to what Ong calls the neoliberal ideology of productivity and consumption in the United States that emphasizes "freedom, progress, and individualism" (1999, p. 739). They see the limits of this self-reliant consumer-citizen in their own lives and in that of their families. Soman, who works in his family's Indian restaurant in Central Square after school and often waits on South Asian students from MIT, says, "In India, I felt like a free bird without a home. Here, I'm in a golden cage. I see the wealth of America but I can't reach it. It's like looking at the moon." A Nepali immigrant girl said, "It's difficult being an immigrant because it's hard to become a citizen. If you don't have a green card, you do things you don't want to do, take jobs that you don't want to take." The idea of productive citizenship is necessarily predicated on legal-juridical regulations of citizens and workers and on the need for a low-wage, undocumented/noncitizen labor pool. The work of citizenship as a disciplining technology of the state is very evident after 9/11, with the ongoing arrests and deportations of immigrant workers and the greater fear among noncitizens who have transnational ties, political or familial (see Vimalassery 2002).

South Asian immigrant youth fulfill a niche in the labor market for jobs in low-end retail and fast-food restaurants with low pay and no benefits, jobs that are often occupied by young people in the United States (Newman 1999; Tannock 2001), but unlike nonimmigrants who also provide this cheap labor, they can perform the economic citizenship required of the neoliberal citizenship but cannot win cultural citizenship. They may be fulfilling the American ethos of "hard work" and productivity, but it is in their turn to consumption of South Asian popular culture that they construct themselves as subjects with national affiliation. And yet even these affiliations, as I have hinted, are understood as identifications with nation through family or transnational youth culture, rather than as nationalistic pride per se. This, too, is perhaps increasingly common for young immigrants who see the nation-state not as a benefactor but as a place of familiarity and belonging—often a very local "home," a specific neighborhood where they lived or street where they used to hang out in their village or town—suggesting a *translocal* identification as much as a transnational affiliation.

The school is also obviously a site where immigrant youth are socialized into sometimes competing definitions of citizenship or nationalism and where they try to obtain credentials for work and class mobility (Foley 1994; Smith 2002; C. Suárez-Orozco, this volume). For example, I was struck that one of the South Asian immigrant boys in the school said he was channeled into taking "Garage" as a vocational education class for two years. Although the students in the course are trained not just to do auto repair but to use computerized technology, Osman, whose father was a taxicab driver, was not interested in working in the auto industry and hoped to get a "computer job." These youth may not have the social capital or networks to get the "right" kind of jobs, but they are acutely aware that they don't have them. At a workshop on careers, most said that they wanted jobs in high tech and some in business or engineering, yet none of them seemed to have any idea of how to get an internship or even an office job. Osman ended up getting a job at an MIT library, but when Faisal, another Pakistani immigrant boy, noted that he worked at a convenience store, other boys laughed and yelled "gas station," leaving him feeling hurt and annoyed.

In the school, immigrant students slowly begin to confront the hierarchies of cultural and economic citizenship in the United States, even though teachers in the bilingual program, among others, remain strong advocates and mentors of immigrant students. Attitudes toward immigrants have, of course, taken on an even more xenophobic edge in the aftermath of 9/11, as evident in the charged debates in the city, and state, about the (euphemistically named) "English for the Children" campaign. Aimed at replacing bilingual education with English immersion and backed by multimillionaire Ron Unz, this proposal was on the Massachusetts ballot after having passed in California (see Orellana, Ek, and Hernández 2000). These immigrant youth and their parents very much *want* to learn English, but even if they are ambivalent about the merits of different bilingual education approaches as they are presented or distorted in the media, they also do not want to be considered second-class citizens because they speak another language. Yet parents who are not citizens cannot vote on this issue that will affect the lives and future of their children and their community; the ballot question eliminating bilingual education was overwhelmingly approved in Massachusetts in the fall 2002 elections, though it was defeated in Cambridge. Clearly, cultural citizenship cannot be easily separated from legal, political, and economic citizenship.

It also became apparent that these young immigrants thought about citizenship in ways that were themselves flexible, shifting, and contextual. In some cases, religious identity seems actually to prompt youth to think of themselves as belonging to the United States or at least identifying with its concerns, if not identifying as "American." Sohail said to me in the fall of 2001, "Islam teaches [us that] what country you live in, you should support them. . . . See, if I live in America, I have to support America; I cannot go to India, all right, I'm Indian now." This, of course, is the same boy who said that he ultimately wanted to return to India and support its development. But these statements are not as contradictory as they first appear; Sohail is able to draw on Islam to help him think through questions of loyalty at a moment in the United States when Muslims are being framed as noncitizens *because* of a particular construction of Islam. Sohail instead uses Islam to counter this technology of exclusion and to support a flexible definition of citizenship that will help him reconcile his national allegiances. Sohail's strategy is part of a rather sophisticated understanding of citizenship as necessarily mobile, as drawing on different ideological resources to respond to the exigencies of diverse moments and places.

Dissenting Citizenship

Many have pointed out that the post-9/11 moment has "facilitated the consolidation of a new identity category" in the United States that conflates "Arab/Muslim/Middle Eastern" with "terrorist" and "noncitizen" (Volpp 2002). This identity category that casts Muslim Americans outside the nation is not new, but Leti Volpp is right to point out that a "national identity has consolidated that is both strongly patriotic and multiracial" (2002, p. 1584), absorbing some African Americans, East Asian Americans, and Latino(a)s. However, it seems to me that some immigrant youth are articulating a critique of the U.S. state that some middle-class South Asian community leaders are not willing to voice. All the students I spoke to had a thoughtful and astute analysis of the events of 9/11 and the U.S. government's bombing of Afghanistan, speaking of it in terms of culpability and justice and resisting the nationalization of 9/11 and the U.S. response. Amir, a Pakistani boy, said to me in December 2001, "You have to look at it in two ways. It's not right that ordinary people over there [in Afghanistan], like you and me, just doing their work, get killed. They don't have anything to do with . . . the attacks in New York, but they're getting killed. And also the people in New York who got killed, that's not right either." Jamila said, "I felt bad for those people [in Afghanistan] . . . because they don't have no proof that they actually did it, but they were all killing all these innocent people who had nothing to do with it." Aliyah, a Gujarati American girl who could very easily pass for Latina in large part because of her style, chose to write the words "INDIA + MUSLIM" on her bag after 9/11. For her, this was a gesture of defiance responding to the casting of Muslims as potentially disloyal citizens; she said, "Just because one Muslim did it in New York, you can't involve everybody in there, you know what I'm sayin'?"

After an anti-Muslim incident in the high school, the director of the bilingual program organized a student assembly where three South Asian Muslim students delivered eloquent speeches condemning racism to an auditorium filled with their peers. Even though these working-class youth do not have the validation of, or time to participate in, community or political organization, they have taken a stance in local race politics and have become spokespersons in the public sphere willing to voice dissent. I do not want to suggest here that these youth are somehow a hidden political vanguard; not all these youth are rushing to the microphone, and in the present climate of surveillance and paranoia, some of them are understandably hesitant to speak about political issues in public spaces. Even those who are legal citizens are worried, given that we live with the USA PATRIOT Act and Operation TIPS (Terrorist Information and Prevention System) in an era that some have likened to a new McCarthyism (see Chang 2002; Cole and Dempsey 2002).

Yet even in this climate, I have found these Muslim immigrant youth to be engaged in a practice of dissenting citizenship, a citizenship based on a critique and affirmation of human rights that means one has to stand apart at some moments, even as one stands together with others who are often faceless, outside the borders of the nation. This practice echoes what Paul Clarke has called "deep citizenship," an ethics of care that is fundamentally about a moral and political engagement with the world that extends beyond the state (1996, p. 4). These Muslim American youth have been forced, by historical events, to engage politically with the world, which they understand both locally and globally; this is perhaps a moment of making what Clarke calls "citizen selves." Youth are a category of citizens whose rights and representations, in the media but also in policy and in public discourse, are always primarily negotiated for them by others, such as institutional authorities or family adults. Yet vis-à-vis their families, these immigrant youth model a version of deep citizenship that is not always available to their parents as some students have become spokespersons about race and religion in the public sphere.

Dissenting citizenship is not coeval with cosmopolitanism, at least not in this instance (see Henry Jenkins, this volume, for an analysis of "pop cosmopolitanism").[7] Clearly, the perspective of these working-class youth is very different from those of cosmopolitan elites, such as privileged tourists, affluent business families, or especially the "Davos class" (Bauman 1998, pp. 77–102; Giddens 2000; Ong 1999), whose migrancy is rooted in privilege and whose crossing of nation-state borders stems from very different investments in transnational citizenry. But even notions of cosmopolitanism that account for its particularity (as opposed to universalism), plurality of form, and imbrication with nationalism (Clifford 1998; Robbins 1998) do not quite capture the specific political critique being waged here. The critique of these Muslim immigrant youth is both far more attached to regional and religious identity, and far more critical in their appraisal of U.S. nationalism and state powers, than some liberal theorists of cosmopolitanism allow (Nussbaum 2002). The perspective of Muslim immigrant youth is very much rooted in their identities *as* Muslims, who are targeted as such by the state, and also sheds light on U.S. national policy as a manifestation of imperial policy at this moment. In this, I argue, the critique goes beyond the debate between liberal and conservative appraisals of cosmopolitanism's possibilities (Nussbaum and Cohen 1996/2002), because it raises an issue that is not emphasized enough by these critics: that of cosmopolitanism and, related, of globalization, as an *imperial feeling*. I use the term *imperial feeling* to capture an emerging acknowledgment of U.S. policy on the global stage as linked to economic and military dominance, a cautious acknowledgment which is generally expressed not as full-blown critique in the mass media but as an emerging sentiment in the public sphere, a growing "feeling," often an anxiety, that the United States is occupying the role of a new "empire."[8] While it is clear that the relations among nation, state, and capital have been transformed since earlier eras of imperialism (Aronowitz and Gautney 2003; see also Coatsworth, this volume), the role of U.S. economic and military power—increasingly tied to a unilateral foreign policy and national interests—is not to be underestimated, particularly after the demise of Soviet communism and especially after the events of 9/11, which have led to an increasingly authoritarian exercise of U.S. state power both at home and abroad (Marable 2003, p. 6).

The tension between human rights and national sovereignty that Seyla Benhabib (2002) argues is constitutive of nationalisms is heightened in the case of practices of U.S. citizenship because imperial nationalism threatens the sovereignty as well as the human rights of *other* nations and national subjects (see Aronowitz and Gautney 2003). Contrary to Michael Hardt and Antonio Negri's (2001) amorphous theory of decentered "empire," I argue that it is, in fact, *imperialist* power that is at work, even if it has been transformed by the new logic of global capital and the weakened link between the state and the economy.

Similarly, I differ from Mohammed Bamyeh (2000), who has suggested that capital has become decoupled from politics and that the "new imperialism" is a "self-referential system of power" that has "only an irrational attachment to the principle of hegemony," existing in various nations as diverse "local" imperialisms (pp. 12, 15). While it is obvious that imperial power no longer necessarily requires direct governance of colonized states and that the power of the state itself has generally declined (Glick Schiller and Fouron 2002), it is also evident that the power of the U.S. state to exercise the globality of violence and globality of economy characterizes this new mode of empire, to draw on Alain Joxe's (2002) framework. There is also, of course, much work analyzing what Juan Flores (2000) calls "imperialism lite," or the penetration of popular culture, a vigorously debated issue in globalization studies. My point here is that to link globalization to U.S. imperial power is to grapple with ways to respond to the everyday emergency that is life in the post-9/11 empire.

The dissenting views of Muslim immigrant youth implicitly critique the imperial feeling of U.S. nationalism after 9/11 through their linking of warfare *within* the state to international war. It is this conjoining of the domestic and foreign that makes this an important mode of dissent, because the imperial project of the new Cold War, as in earlier times, works by obscuring the links between domestic and foreign policies. Kathleen Moore points out that even before the post-9/11 curtailment of civil liberties, the Anti-Terrorism and Effective Death Penalty Act and the Illegal Immigration Reform and Immigrant Responsibility Act (1996) narrowed the definition of the "civil community" in response to the "heightened sense of insecurity required to maintain a restructured, wartime regulatory state after the primary security target disappears. . . . The regulatory state perpetuates essentialized understandings of the self (as citizen) and the other (as alien) and will continue to distribute rights and therefore power hierarchically as long as a heightened sense of insecurity persists" (Moore 1999, p. 95; see also Cole and Dempsey 2002 for documentation of abuses of civil liberties and profiling of Muslim Americans after the 1996 acts). Moore (1999) underscores that the distinction between citizens and noncitizens is used in political discourse to support foreign policy and justify the military campaigns and domestic priorities of the U.S. state, such as the battles over "welfare, affirmative action, and immigration reform" (p. 87). This is even more true when the illusion of a "peacetime economy" is discarded for a nation at war as in the present moment, which is actually an extension of the "war on immigrants" waged since the late 1980s.

The dissent of Muslim immigrant youth is not vanguardist, because it does not need to be; these youth are simply—but not merely—subjects of both the wars on terror *and* the war on immigration, and so their exclusion from processes of being-made as citizens, and their emergent political subject making, highlight the ways in which civic consent is secured by imperial power. The process of dissenting citizenship is not without its wrinkles, for it seems that these young immigrants implicitly understand the limits of a state-based notion of citizenship, in its economic, cultural, and political senses. As "transmigrants" they strategically use citizenship as they manage the failures of both home and host states to guarantee protection and equal rights to Muslim subjects.[9] However, it is the links between legal, economic, and cultural citizenship that are so important for U.S. empire. Jean and John Comaroff (2001) argue that the neoliberal mode of "millennial capitalism" increasingly obscures the workings of labor and highlights instead processes of consumption, so that citizenship is re-created as consumer identity, echoing García Canclini's insights. The immigrant youth in this study are not outside of this process; they understand themselves as consumers too, of, among other things, a lifestyle or education that compelled their parents to migrate from South Asia.

CONCLUSION

The forms of citizenship that have emerged from this study—flexible, multicultural and polycultural, and dissenting—are responses that these immigrant youth simultaneously express in response to the condition of living a transnational adolescence; the forms are not mutually exclusive nor do they exist in some kind of hierarchy of political or personal efficacy. These citizenship practices are used by adults as well, but it is clear that young people, such as immigrant students, have to negotiate particular concerns due to their positioning in the family and social structure and their participation in education. While they have to deal with the migration choices of their parents or the demands of being both students and workers, it is clear that their lives are also shaped by the state and economic policies that drive their parents to cross national borders. My research shows not just that the flexibility of capital evokes strategies of flexible citizenship but also that the state, of course, is flexible in its regimes of governmentality. Immigrant youth are forced to respond to new and shifting measures to limit their civil rights, some of which measures are not publicized widely, creating more uncertainty and terror. The Bush administration has implemented new policies for regulating workers and disciplining citizens since 9/11, from stripping due process rights from any persons deemed to be associated with "terrorism" to mass arrests of Muslim immigrant men complying with new "special registration" requirements that target citizens by religion and national origin (Chang 2002; Cole and Dempsey 2002). As a result, both undocumented and legal immigrants are terrified because of the sweeping surveillance and detention powers appropriated by the Bush-Ashcroft regime. The loss of immigrant rights terrorizes noncitizens, who are vulnerable, some have argued, to hyperexploitation by employers after 9/11 and to fear of simply living "ordinary" lives; in my research, I heard several such stories from youth in Cambridge, from an undocumented immigrant girl unable to enroll in a community college and continue her education to a high school graduate confused about whether she could marry an undocumented immigrant and terrified that he would be deported.

Yet it is important to remember that this state of emergency, this crisis of civil rights and its concomitant mode of dissenting citizenship, is in fact not exceptional in the United States (Ganguly 2001), for the post-9/11 moment builds on measures and forms of power already in place; this is a state of everyday life in empire. There are important continuities before and after 9/11 that are not acknowledged enough publicly. My use of *post-9/11* is meant to signify not a radical historical or political rupture but rather a moment of renewed contestation over ongoing issues of civil rights and immigrant rights, terrorism and militarism, nationalism and belonging. While I share the skepticism of new theorists of empire and globalization toward a state-bound notion of citizenship, I am interested in the "decolonization of citizenship" as part of a project of radical democracy[10] that is grounded in the specific, not abstracted, struggles of ordinary people. We need an ethnography of the new empire to undergird the theories of globalization being produced and debated; a youthscapes approach, as I have argued here, could help us provide such a critical intervention by taking seriously the experiences of youth as actors on a global stage.

Looking at youth culture and citizenship through a youthscapes approach allows an analysis of both structural and cultural issues that is critical for an understanding of education in a globalized twenty-first century. My research demonstrates that it is impossible to respond adequately to the concerns of immigrant students today unless we have a theory and methodology that take into account the lives of young people both inside and outside schools and the ways these span national borders—without romanticizing the possibilities for spatial mobility to translate into social mobility. It is crucial that we, as educators, have a theory of youth cultural practice and understand the relationships among education, labor, popular culture, and family life, some of the major arenas that youth traverse on a daily basis. During my fieldwork for this project, I was involved in a volunteer-run program at the high school that organized regular workshops on academic, cultural, and political issues for South Asian immigrant youth on topics ranging from immigrant and civil rights and job hunting to popular culture and gender. Through our informal and integrative curriculum, we were able to provide an important space that acknowledged the transnational adolescence of these youth and allowed them to express their struggles with racial and religious profiling as much as their fondness for Bollywood films. We were fortunate that the high school was very supportive of such open discussions with youth at a time when many felt particularly vulnerable; indeed staff at the school initiatated many such discussions and forums themselves (see Maira 2004).

Many of the essays in this volume point to the varied levels at which educational institutions can respond to the increasingly complex lives of youth and new notions of citizenship in a globalized world, and underscore the ways in which questions of pedagogy cannot be considered outside the domestic and foreign political contexts in which the lives of young people are embedded. Schools are considered crucibles for socialization into citizenship and a democratic society, yet clearly issues of national identity, civil rights, and freedom of expression are always deeply contested. My research shows that these contestations cannot be divorced from questions of globalization nor from experiences of youth. The current moment presents renewed challenges to these ongoing struggles over civil rights and immigrant rights, nationalism and belonging, and local and global affiliations that deeply affect young immigrants. Talking to these young people has helped me see the value of reactivating a notion of citizenship that lies between the state and an amorphously cosmopolitan "humankind," for their notion of citizenship is deeply engaged with questions of power and justice at local, state, and transnational scales.

NOTES

The ethnographic research on which this paper is based was funded by the Russell Sage Foundation and the Institute for Asian American Studies at the University of Massachusetts–Boston and supported by my dedicated research assistants, Palav Babaria and Sarah Khan. I wish to thank Marcelo Suárez-Orozco for his invaluable support and Desirée Baolian Qin-Hilliard for her always gracious assistance.

1. Youth culture studies, according to the most widely accepted intellectual genealogy, emerged incisively at the Center for Contemporary Cultural Studies in Birmingham, England, in the 1970s, which brought serious attention to the meanings of youth subcultures at a time of social transition in postwar Britain. The center's work was based, for the most part, on ethnographic studies that focused on the rituals that youth create within the context of popular culture and consumption and performance practices (Clarke, Hall, Jefferson, and Roberts 1976). This early intervention tended to see youth subcultures primarily as mirrors for larger cultural and material concerns while acknowledging the notion of "youth" as itself socially constructed by dominant ideologies and marketing campaigns (Cohen 1997; Gelder 1997; Turner 1996).

2. See, for example, the valuable contributions of scholars such as Juan Flores (2000), Robin Kelley (1997), Lauraine Leblanc (1999), Angela McRobbie (1999, 1994), Tricia Rose (1994), and Sarah Thornton (1996).

3. See Thornton (1996) for more on this theoretical genealogy.

4. There were seven hundred reported hate crimes against South Asian Americans, Arab Americans, and Muslim Americans, including four homicides (two involving South Asian American victims), in the three weeks following September 11, 2001 (Coen 2001). At least two hundred hate crimes were reported against Sikh Americans alone (Lampan 2001). The Council on American-Islamic Relations reported that it had documented 960 incidents of racial profiling in the five weeks after September 11, with hate crimes declining and

incidents of airport profiling and workplace discrimination on the increase (Associated Press 2001).

5. There are currently about sixty students of South Asian origin who belong to this age category in the high school, almost evenly split between first-generation/immigrant students and second-generation South Asian Americans.

6. Transnational family structures are increasingly common for immigrant youth, according to Carola Suárez-Orozco (this volume).

7. I focus here less on the implications of cultural cosmopolitanism via media consumption, which Jenkins addresses in his fascinating essay, than on the political meanings of cosmopolitanism for ideas of nationalism and citizenship.

8. For example, among other articles in the liberal mass media, a recent issue of a widely distributed Boston arts and entertainment newspaper—alternative in its cultural reportage but fairly conservative on foreign policy—featured at least three commentaries that referred to the United States within the framework of "colonial powers," "imperial powers," and "empire-building" (Kennedy 2003). See also the cover story of a recent issue of *Harper's Magazine*, titled "The Economic of Empire" (Finnegan 2003).

9. It is possible, although so far not many of the Indian immigrant youth seem ready or willing to speak about this, that the state-condoned anti-Muslim massacres in Gujarat, India, in spring 2002 have raised questions about their belonging and their rights to equal protection under the law in India itself. This is understandably a difficult subject for even their parents to speak about, but one Indian Muslim immigrant told me that in "private spaces," Muslim immigrants express the vulnerability that they feel both in the United States and at "home." At the least, perhaps, there is a sense that their cultural citizenship and loyalties are in question in both nations.

10. Lao Montes, A. (2003). Personal communication. February.

REFERENCES

Appadurai, A. (1996). *Modernity at large: Cultural dimensions of globalization*. Minneapolis: University of Minnesota Press.

Aronowitz, S., and H. Gautney. (2003). The debate about globalization: An introduction. In *Implicating empire: Globalization and resistance in the 21st century world order*. S. Aronowitz and H. Gautney, eds. New York: Basic Books.

Associated Press (2001). Hate crime reports down, civil rights complaints up. October 25.

Bamyeh, M. A. (2000). The new imperialism: Six theses. *Social Text* 62 (18): 1–29.

Basch, L., N. Glick Schiller, and C. Szanton Blanc, eds. (1994). *Nations unbound: Transnational projects, postcolonial predicaments, and deterritorialized nation-states*. Amsterdam: Gordon and Breach.

Bauman, Z. (1998). *Globalization: The human consequences*. New York: Columbia University Press.

Bhavnani, K. K. (1991). *Talking politics: A psychological framing for views from youth in Britain.* Cambridge, UK: Cambridge University Press.

Benhabib, S. (2002). *The claims of culture: Equality and diversity in the global era.* Princeton: Princeton University Press.

Berlant, L. (1997). *The Queen of America goes to Washington city: Essays on sex and citizenship.* Durham, NC: Duke University Press.

Buckingham, D. (2000). *The making of citizens: Young people, news, and politics.* London: Routledge.

Buroway, M., J. A. Blum, S. George, Z. Gille, T. Gowan, L. Haney, et al. (2000). *Global ethnography: Forces, connections, and imaginations in a postmodern world.* Berkeley and Los Angeles: University of California Press.

Chang, N. (2002). *Silencing political dissent: How post–September 11 anti-terrorism measures threaten our civil liberties.* New York: Seven Stories/Open Media.

Clarke, P. A. (1996). *Deep citizenship.* East Haven, CT: Pluto Press.

Clarke, J., S. Hall, T. Jefferson, and B. Roberts. (1976). Subcultures, cultures, and class. In *Resistance through rituals: Youth subcultures in post-war Britain.* S. Hall and T. Jefferson, eds. London: Hutchinson/Centre for Contemporary Cultural Studies, University of Birmingham.

Clifford, J. (1998). Mixed feelings. In *Cosmopolitics: Thinking and feeling beyond the nation.* P. Cheah and B. Robbins, eds. Minneapolis: University of Minnesota.

Cockburn, A., and J. St. Clair. (2000). *Five days that shook the world: Seattle and beyond.* London: Verso.

Coen, J. (2001). Hate crimes reports reach record level. *Chicago Tribune,* October 9.

Cohen, S. (1972). *Folk devils and moral panics: The creation of the mods and rockers.* Oxford, UK: Basil Blackwell.

Cohen, S. (1997). Symbols of trouble. In *The subcultures reader.* K. Gelder and S. Thornton, eds. London: Routledge.

Cole, D., and J. Dempsey. (2002). *Terrorism and the constitution: Sacrificing civil liberties in the name of national security.* New York: The New Press.

Coll, K. (2002). *Problemas y necesidades: Latina Vernaculars of Citizenship and Coalition-Building in Chinatown, San Francisco.* Paper presented at Racial (Trans)Formations: Latinos and Asians Remaking the United States, Center for the Study of Ethnicity and Race, Columbia University, March.

Comaroff, J., and J. Comaroff. (2001). Millennial capitalism: First thoughts on a second coming. In *Millennial capitalism and the culture of neoliberalism.* J. and J. L. Comaroff, eds. Durham, NC: Duke University Press.

Crane, D., N. Kawashima, and K. Kawasaki, eds. (2002). *Global culture: Media, arts, policy, and globalization.* London: Routledge.

Dannin, R. (2002). *Black pilgrimage to Islam.* New York: Oxford University Press.

Dirlik, A. (2001/2002). Colonialism, globalization, and culture: Reflections on September 11. *Amerasia Journal* 27(3)/28(1): 81–92.

Erikson, E. H. (1994). *Identity: Youth and crisis.* New York: W. W. Norton (Original work published 1968).

Finnegan, W. (2003). The Economics of Empire. *Harper's Magazine,* May 2003, pp. 41–54.

Foley, D. E. (1994). *Learning capitalist culture: Deep in the heart of Tejas.* Philadelphia: University of Pennsylvania Press.

Flores, J. (2000). *From Bomba to hip-hop: Puerto Rican culture and Latino identity.* New York: Columbia University Press.

Flores, W. V., and R. Benmayor, eds. (1997). *Latino cultural citizenship: Claiming identity, space, and rights.* Boston: Beacon Press.

Ganguly, K. (2001). *States of exception: Everyday life and postcolonial identity,* Minneapolis: University of Minnesota Press.

García Canclini, N. (2001). *Consumers and citizens: Globalization and multicultural conflicts.* Minneapolis: University of Minnesota Press.

Gelder, K. (1997). Introduction to part three. In *The subcultures reader.* K. Gelder and S. Thornton, eds. London: Routledge.

Giddens, A. (2000). *Runaway world: How globalization is reshaping our lives.* New York: Routledge.

Glick Schiller, N., and G. Fouron. (2001). *Georges woke up laughing: Long-distance nationalism and the search for home.* Durham, NC: Duke University Press.

Gross, J., D. McMurray, and T. Swedenburg. (1996). Rai, rap, and Franco-Maghrebi identities. In *Displacement, diaspora, and geographies of identity.* S. Lavie and T. Swedenburg, eds. Durham, NC: Duke University Press.

Grossberg, L. (1996). Toward a genealogy of the state of cultural studies: The discipline of communication and the reception of cultural studies in the United States. In *Disciplinarity and dissent in cultural studies.* C. Nelson and D. P. Gaonkar, eds. New York: Routledge.

Gupta, A., and J. Ferguson. (1997). After "peoples and cultures." In *Culture, power, place: Explorations in critical anthropology.* A. Gupta and J. Ferguson, eds. Durham, NC: Duke University Press.

Hannerz, U. (1996). *Transnational connections: Culture, people, places.* London: Routledge.

Hardt, M., and A. Negri. (2001). *Empire.* Cambridge, MA: Harvard University Press.

Hebdige, D. (1979). *Subculture: The meaning of style.* London: Methuen.

Hondagneu-Sotelo, P. (2002). Families on the frontier: From braceros in the fields to braceras in the home. In *Latinos: Remaking America.* M. M. Suárez-Orozco and M. M. Páez. Berkeley: University of California Press and Cambridge, MA: David Rockefeller Center for Latin American Studies, Harvard University.

Hutnyk, J. (2000). Stephen Corry and Iris Jean-Klein versus Richard Wilson and John Hutnyk (GDAT debate no. 10). In *The right to difference is a fundamental human right.* P. Wade, ed. Manchester, UK: Group for Debates in Anthropological Theory, University of Manchester.

Inda, J. X., and R. Rosaldo, eds. (2002). *The anthropology of globalization.* Malden, MA: Blackwell.

Jameson, F., and M. Miyoshi, eds. (1998). *The cultures of globalization.* Durham, NC: Duke University Press.

Joxe, A. (2002). *Empire of disorder.* Los Angeles and New York: Semiotext(e).

Kelley, R. D. (1997). *Yo' mama's dysfunctional! Fighting the culture wars in urban America.* Boston: Beacon Press.

Kennedy, D. (2003). Waging post-warfare. *Boston Phoenix*, April 25–May 1, pp. 16–18.

Lampan, J. (2001). Under attack, Sikhs defend their religious liberties. *Christian Science Monitor*, October 31.

Larkin, B. (2002). Indian films and Nigerian lovers: Media and the creation of parallel modernities. In *The anthropology of globalization.* J. X. Inda and R. Rosaldo, eds. Malden, MA: Blackwell.

Leblanc, L. (1999). *Pretty in pink: Girls' gender resistance in a boys' subculture.* New Brunswick, NJ: Rutgers University Press.

Lipsitz, G. (1994). *Dangerous crossroads: Popular music, postmodernism, and the poetics of place.* London: Verso.

Lipsitz, G. (2001). *American studies in a moment of danger.* Minneapolis: University of Minnesota Press.

Maira, S. (2004). Planet Youth: Asian American youth cultures, citizenship, and globalization. In *New directions for Asian American studies.* K. Ono, ed. Malden, MA: Blackwell.

Maira, S., and E. Soep, eds. (2004). *Youthscapes: Popular culture, national ideologies, global markets.* Philadelphia: University of Pennsylvania Press.

Marable, M. (2003). 9/11: Racism in a time of terror. In *Implicating empire: Globalization and resistance in the 21st century world order.* S. Aronowitz and H. Gautney, eds. New York: Basic Books.

Massey, D. (1994). *Space, place, and gender.* Minneapolis: University of Minnesota Press.

McRobbie, A. (1991). *Feminism and youth culture: From Jackie to Just Seventeen.* London: Macmillan.

McRobbie, A. (1994). *Postmodernism and popular culture.* London: Routledge.

McRobbie, A. (1999). *In the culture society: Art, fashion, and popular music.* London: Routledge.

McRobbie, A., and J. Garber. (1970). Girls and subcultures: An exploration. In *Resistance through rituals: Youth subcultures in post-war Britain.* S. Hall and T. Jefferson, eds. London: Routledge.

Miller, D., ed. (1998). *Material cultures: Why some things matter.* Chicago: University of Chicago Press.

Miller, T. (1993). *The well-tempered subject: Citizenship, culture, and the postmodern subject.* Baltimore: Johns Hopkins University Press.

Miller, T. (2001). Introducing . . . cultural citizenship. *Social Text* 19(4): 1–5.

Moore, K. (1999). A closer look at anti-terrorism law: *American Arab Anti-Discrimination Committee v. Reno* and the construction of aliens' rights. In *Arabs in America: Building a new future.* M. Suleiman, ed. Philadelphia: Temple University Press.

Morley, D., and K. Robins, eds. (1995). *Spaces of identity: Global media, electronic landscapes, and cultural boundaries.* London: Routledge.

Newman, K. S. (1999). *No shame in my game: The working poor in the inner city.* New York: Alfred A. Knopf and the Russell Sage Foundation.

Nussbaum, M. C. (2002). Patriotism and cosmopolitanism. In *For love of country.* J. Cohen, ed. Boston: Beacon Press.

Nussbaum, M. C., and J. Cohen. (2002). *For love of country.* Boston: Beacon Press.

Olwig, K., and K. Hastrup, eds. (1997). *Siting culture: The shifting anthropological subject.* London: Routledge.

Ong, A. (1996). Cultural citizenship as subject-making: Immigrants negotiate racial and cultural boundaries in the United States. *Cultural Anthropology* 37(5): 737–762.

Orellana, M. F., L. Ek, and A. Hernández. (2000). Bilingual education in an immigrant community: Proposition 227 in California. In *Immigrant voices: In search of educational equity.* E. Trueba and L. I. Bartolomé, eds. Lanham, MD: Rowman & Littlefield.

Robbins, B. (1998). Introduction, Part I: Actually existing cosmopolitanism. In *Cosmopolitics: Thinking and feeling beyond the nation.* P. Cheah and B. Robbins, eds. Minneapolis: University of Minnesota Press.

Rosaldo, R. (1997). Cultural citizenship, inequality, and multiculturalism. In *Latino cultural citizenship: Claiming identity, space, and rights.* W. F. Flores and R. Benmayor, eds. Boston: Beacon Press.

Rose, T. (1994). *Black noise: Rap music and black culture in contemporary America.* Hanover, NH: Wesleyan University Press.

Sassen, S. (1998). *Globalization and its discontents: Essays on the new mobility of people and money.* New York: The New Press.

Shepard, B., and R. Hayduk. (2002). *From Act Up to the WTO: Urban protest and community building in the era of globalization.* London: Verso.

Simonett, H. (2001). *Banda: Mexican musical life across borders.* Middletown, CT: Wesleyan University Press.

Siu, L. (2001). Diasporic cultural citizenship: Chineseness and belonging in Central America and Panama. *Social Text* 69(19)4: 7–28.

Smith, R. C. (2002). Gender, ethnicity, and race in school and work outcomes of second-generation Mexican Americans. In *Latinos: Remaking America.* M. M. Suárez-Orozco and M. M. Páez, eds. Berkeley: University of California Press and Cambridge, MA: David Rockefeller Center for Latin American Studies, Harvard University.

Soja, E. (1989). *Postmodern geographies: The reassertion of space in critical social theory.* London: Verso.

Tannock, S. (2001). *Youth at work: The unionized fast-food and grocery workplace.* Philadelphia: Temple University Press.

Tam, H, ed. (2001). *Progressive politics in the global age.* Cambridge, UK: Polity and Oxford, UK: Blackwell.

Thornton, S. (1996). *Club cultures.* Cambridge, UK: Polity Press.

Turner, G. (1996). *British cultural studies: An introduction.* 2nd ed. London: Routledge.

Vimalassery, M. (2002). Passports and pink slips. *SAMAR (South Asian Magazine for Action and Reflection)* 15: 7–8, 20.

Volpp, L. (2002). The citizen and the terrorist. *UCLA Law Review* 49: 1575–1600.

Willis, P. (1977). *Learning to labor: How working-class kids get working-class jobs.* New York: Columbia University Press.

Wilson, R., and W. Dissayanake, eds. (1996). *Global/local: Cultural production and the transnational imaginary.* Durham, NC: Duke University Press.

Howard Gardner

HOW EDUCATION CHANGES

Considerations of History, Science, and Values

THE GLACIAL PACE OF INSTITUTIONAL CHANGE
UNDER NORMAL CONDITIONS

The transmission of knowledge and skills to the next generation, the process of education in formal and informal settings, is inextricably bound with the emergence of Homo sapiens over the last several hundred thousand years (Bruner 1960; Donald 1991; Tomasello 2000). Formal schools, however, are just a few thousand years old; and the notion of universal education, in which all young persons in a society receive several years of competent schooling, is still a distant dream in many corners of the globe (Bloom and Cohen, 2001; Bloom, this volume).

For the most part, institutions change slowly. Such gradual change may be a positive element. The practices associated with an institution tend to be worked out by trial and error over long periods of time. While such experimentation does not guarantee a stronger and more effective institution, at least the most problematic structures and procedures are eliminated. When it comes to educational institutions—which have come to bear a primary responsibility for the intellectual and moral health of the next generation—such conservatism is especially to be recommended. We do not—or at least we should not want to—

sacrifice our children to the latest fad. On occasion, shock treatments are administered to an educational system—for example, consider the dramatic changes that took place in Japan after the Second World War or in China following the Communist Revolution in 1949. Such changes may achieve their initial goal. But less welcome consequences can also occur; for example, hiding large parts of history in the case of Japan, alienating children from their parents in the case of the Cultural Revolution in China.

Education stands out in one crucial way from most other societal institutions. Put directly, education is fundamentally and primarily a "values undertaking," and educational values are perennially in dispute. Members of a society can reach agreement with relative ease about the purpose of medicine—to deliver high-quality health care to all citizens; nor need the purposes of the military or the monetary system be perennially disputed. However, except for certain fundamentals, the purposes of education, and the notion of what it means to be an educated person, are subjects about which individuals—both professional and lay—hold distinctive and often conflicting views. Clearly, the values that undergirded the educational system in imperial Japan or China differed radically from those that came to motivate the system in a fledgling democratic society like Japan in 1950 or an experimental socialistic society in China at the same time. As I once put it whimsically, "in the United States of 2000, how could we possibly create an educational system that would please the three Jesses—conservative North Carolina senator Jesse Helms, charismatic African American leader Jesse Jackson, and flamboyant Minnesota wrestler-turned-governor Jesse Ventura?"

While the gradual change of educational institutions can readily be justified, we must also ask what can, and should, happen to educational institutions when dramatic alterations take place in the ambient society. Such changes can take place as a result of a shift in values: that is what prompted changes in East Asia a half century ago. However, changes can also take place as a result of scientific findings that alter our understanding of the human mind or because of broader historical forces, like globalization, that affect regions all over the world. At such times, the tension between the pace of institutional change, on one hand, and the pace of scientific discoveries and historical forces, on the other, can become acute.

THE EVOLUTION OF FORMAL EDUCATION
FROM RELIGIOUS TO SECULAR AUTHORITY

For much of its relatively short history, formal schooling has been characterized by a religious orientation. Teachers were typically members of a religious order; the texts to be read and mastered were the holy books; and the lessons of school were ethical and moral in character. (The madrasas of the Islamic world, the cheders that have accompanied the Jewish diaspora in recent decades, and the rise of fundamentalist schools in the United States would have seemed much less anomalous a few centuries ago.) Religious instruction, or a state religion, is still common in many European countries, while the "state religion" of communism is only gradually waning as an educational staple on the Chinese mainland. (It remains alive and well in Cuba.)

Yet, despite the persistence of such religious or quasi-religious strains, most of the developed world, and much of the developing world, has converged on a form of precollegiate education that is largely secular in thrust. The major burden of the first years of school—the primary grades—is threefold: (1) to introduce children to the basic literacy systems of the ambient culture—the "three R's," to use the English parlance; (2) to acclimate youngsters to the milieu of decontextualized learning, where—in contradistinction to the learning that is most readily accomplished by human beings—one learns about events and concepts outside of their naturally occurring contexts (Bruner, Olver, and Greenfield 1966; Resnick 1987); (3) to give children the opportunity to play and work together civilly with those individuals with whom they can expect to grow and eventually spend their adult years. While such processes used to begin around the age of six or seven, it is notable that many countries now attempt to inculcate these skills in the preschool years, sometimes as early as the fourth or fifth year of life.

A century ago, only a small percentage of the population received even this much education before those with "basic education" returned to the farm or proceeded to the factory. Bloom and Cohen note that in "recent decades, progress towards universal education has been unprecedented. Illiteracy in the developing world has fallen from 75% of people a century ago to less than 25% today" (2001, p. 1). Still the amount of education in the developing world is modest: the "average number of years spent in school more than doubled between 1965 and 1990, from 2.1 to 4.4, among those age 25 and over in developing countries" (Bloom and Cohen 2001, p. 1). In contrast, in the developed world, nearly all youngsters receive education at least through some secondary school, and in some lands, a third to a half or even more receive some form of postsecondary education.

Following the years of primary school, the burden of education shifts. Complementing the missions stated above, most formal educational institutions also strive to help students obtain fluency in the basic literacies, so that they can deal readily with all manner of texts; assist them in mastering the fundamentals of several key disciplines, particularly mathematics and the sciences; and provide tools so that students can understand and participate in the formal and informal social, economic, and political systems of their country. This latter goal is achieved both through direct instruction in history, literature, and civics and through a demonstration of these processes in the manner in which the school operates. Specifically, in authoritarian cultures, almost all of the processes of education are dictated by a central authority, such as the Ministry of Education or the dominant religious order. In more democratic cultures, students and teachers have considerable say in the governance and activities of the school, and sometimes even curricular choices are left to the local educational establishment.

It would be an exaggeration to claim that education across the developed world is centrally orchestrated. Vast and gritty differences exist across and even within nations. Yet there is surprising convergence in what is considered a reasonable precollegiate education in Tokyo or Tel Aviv, in Budapest or Boston. Following ten to thirteen years of school, students are expected to have studied several sciences, mastered mathematics through beginning calculus, know a good deal about the history and governance of their own country, be able to read and write fluently in their native language. Most nations have or are moving toward standardized curricula and assessments in these areas—another indication of globalization's momentum. Countries differ notably in the extent to which they require mastery of languages other than the native tongue(s), knowledge of the history and culture of other parts of the world, and acquaintance with "softer" subjects like the arts or literature. International comparisons, such as the International Mathematics and Science Survey (TIMMS), exert increasingly strong pressures in the planning chambers of educational ministries. And programs like the International Baccalaureate are spreading rapidly to many countries—developing as well as developed—throughout the world (Walker, 2002a).

From this description, it may seem that large parts of the world have managed to strip education not only of its religious moorings but also of a clash among competing values. To some extent, this characterization has validity. There is little dispute across the globe that future citizens need to be literate, numerate, capable of scientific thought, and knowledgeable about the history, traditions, and governmental system of the nation in which they are being educated. Yet the specter of values still looms large in two respects. First, competence in science, mathematics, engineering, and technical subjects has come increasingly to be valued, perhaps overvalued, in comparison, say, to the arts, literature, moral education, or philosophy. In this sense, a technical education is equally important to fundamentalist Muslims, Hindus, Christians, and Jews; piano or calligraphy lessons take place after school or on weekends for those who can afford it. Second, especially within democratic societies, there are large and unresolved disputes about what competence means. Thus, within the sciences, competence can mean mastery of large bodies of factual information, familiarity with laboratory procedures, in-depth understanding of selected key concepts, and/or the ability to make new discoveries or raise new questions. And educational policy makers disagree about whether future citizens should know political or social history, embrace triumphalist or critical accounts of their own history, learn to support or to critique the status quo. The sphere of values remains alive and well in education.

Until thirty years ago, even students who received the highest-quality education typically left school during adolescence. Nowadays, however, some form of tertiary education is becoming common, even expected, especially in developed countries. The American option of some years of "liberal arts" is exceptional—and may be an endangered species even in the United States; it is (perhaps reasonably in some countries) assumed that sufficient liberal arts were conveyed in the precollegiate years and that the tertiary years should focus on professional or at least preprofessional training, again with an emphasis on technical professions. Whether or not tertiary education occurs at the end of adolescence, it is widely recognized that some forms of adult or "lifelong" learning will be necessary across the occupational spectrum. Which institutions should handle such an education and what value systems will be embodied are questions that will need to be addressed in the coming years.

THE EMERGING IMPACT OF SCIENTIFIC FINDINGS ON EDUCATIONAL PRACTICE

For centuries, significant changes in the educational system have been due largely to historical events. The emergence of large cities in Europe gave rise to the universities of the late Middle Ages. The invention of the printing press made possible wide-scale literacy and allowed individuals increasingly to take charge of their own education ("Just give me a library card, please"). The changing status of women both allowed more young girls into the educational system and ultimately conferred career options beyond teaching on large numbers of capable adult women.

Since the rise of psychology and other social sciences in the latter part of the nineteenth century, educational policy makers have sought to base their recommendations on emerging knowledge about human beings. Note that this is itself a values statement: the claim that scientific discoveries about human nature ought to be a basis for educational changes might seem bizarre in an educational milieu where sacred considerations are dominant.

With little question, in recent years the largest impact on educational policy making has come as a result of psychometrics. Testing has a long history, but its rationale took a sharp turn in the early twentieth century. The impetus for this turn came from the growing belief that individuals differed from one another in intellectual potential and that psychologists could measure these differences reliably through an IQ (intelligence quotient) test.

Interestingly, the test makers initially embraced a range of political and social positions. Alfred Binet, the French psychologist who created the first intelligence tests, sought to identify individuals with potential learning difficulties so that these persons could achieve special help and support. American progressives who embraced intelligence tests saw them as ways of improving education generally by placing it on a more scientific basis: as Lord Kelvin famously pointed out, measurement is the key component of any scientific practice (Lemann 1999). However, testing has also been embraced by those with a contrasting political and social agenda. For many scientists and policy makers in the early twentieth century, testing was a scientifically validated way of selecting those with talent and consigning those who scored poorly to the backwaters of school and society (Gould 1981).

Contributing strongly to educational policy and practice have been the models of human learning that have emerged in psychology. Each of the principal models has antecedents that date back to earlier philosophical positions, but each has been reinforced by researchers who draw on data and scientific ways of thinking. For example, B. F. Skinner (1938), the behaviorist, drew on studies with animals and human beings to argue that learning is best effected by a careful schedule of rewards and punishments (more technically, schedules of reinforcement). This epistemological position—which dates back to the empiricist philosophers of the seventeenth and eighteenth centuries—called for carefully calibrated curricula that guided learners smoothly from one concept or practice to the next, slightly more complex one—in a way as error free as possible.

Consider two contrasting pictures of human nature that derived from the psychology of cognitive development. Drawing on the famed Swiss psychologist Jean Piaget (1983), many educators have called for a system in which young individuals discover for themselves the laws that govern the physical, biological, and social worlds. According to this position, which reverberates with Rousseauian sentiments, attempts to inculcate facts and concepts directly are ill-advised: only superficial learning can result. Students are better off if—like Rousseau's Emile—they can explore for themselves the operations of, say, a lever, an abacus, or the rules that govern a billiard ball and figure out the operating principles. While not rejecting the Piagetian perspective in toto, the influential Russian psychologist Lev Vygotsky (1978) added two important components. First, he noted that there is a great deal of knowledge about such concepts already circulating within the society and that the challenge of education is to help students internalize what has already been established by previous generations. Second, he showed that proper support, or scaffolding, for the learning child is always advisable and sometimes necessary if the child is to achieve more sophisticated understandings and skills. It is illusory to believe that children can on their own figure out the major ideas that have slowly emerged in the scholarly disciplines, even though they may be able to master certain universal understandings without explicit tutelage.

Even though most educators have not read Binet or Skinner, Piaget or Vygotsky in the original (and most parents have not heard of these authorities), the legacies of these intellectual giants have exerted an impact on education around the world. The belief in formal tests as means of selecting and comparing has proved an incredibly powerful twentieth-century virus. Behaviorist methods are widely used, particularly with populations that exhibit cognitive or emotional problems. But discovery methods are also prominent in many scientific and mathematics classes, while concern with the proper forms of support or scaffolding permeate discussions about education, ranging from Head Start programs to apprenticeships in scientific laboratories or medical schools.

THE CHALLENGE POSED BY NEW DISCOVERIES

Just as generals often fight the last war, many educators base their well-intentioned practices on outmoded ideas about human cognition. In the past quarter century, I have had the opportunity to observe two major changes in how scientists think about human learning and to anticipate the emergence of a third. In each case, these paradigm shifts could have major educational implications, ones that remake how teachers work with students. In tracing the course and fate of these understandings, we can gain important insights into what happens when scientific discoveries meet educational practices.

From Intelligence to Intelligences

Let me begin with the example of intelligence. For nearly a century, a consensus has obtained among those who are charged with thinking about intelligence. Put succinctly, the consensus stipulates that there is a single thing called human intelligence; individuals differ from birth in how smart they are; one's intellectual potential is largely determined by one's biological parents; and psychologists assess a person's intellect by administering a test of intelligence. These views date back to the claims of Charles Spearman (1904) and Lewis Terman (1916) at the turn of the century, and they have been espoused in recent years by such experts as the British psychologist Hans Eysenck (1987) and the American social scientists Richard Herrnstein and Charles Murray (1994).

While this consensus was challenged from early on by both scholars (Thurstone 1938) and commentators (Lippmann 1922–1923/1976), only recently has there been a more concerted critique by scientists of various stripes. Among scholars of artificial intelligence, there is a growing recognition that notions such as "general problem solving" are not well-founded and that successful computer programs contain specific knowledge about specific forms of expertise. Among neuroscientists, there is agreement that the brain is not a general, equipotential organ: rather, specific capacities (e.g., language, spatial orientation, understanding of other people) are associated with specific regions of the brain and have evolved over the millennia to entail specific kinds of information processing (for relevant references, see Gardner 1983/1993a, 1985). Among anthropologists and psychologists, an increasingly vocal minority has proposed the existence of several relatively independent forms of intelligence (Battro, this volume; Goleman 1995; Mithen 1996; Rosnow, Skedler, Jaeger, and Rin 1994; Salovey and Mayer 1990; Sternberg 1985; Tooby and Cosmides 1991).

In a formulation developed two decades ago, I argued that human beings are better thought of as possessing half a dozen or more separate sets of capacities that I termed multiple intelligences (Gardner 1983/1993a). As currently construed, the list stipulates eight intelligences (linguistic, logical mathematic, spatial, musical, bodily-kinesthetic, interpersonal, intrapersonal, and naturalist), with a possible ninth, or existential, intelligence. Each intelligence embodies a separate form of information processing, and while intelligences readily operate in synchrony in normal individuals, there is no necessary relation between one intelligence and another.

"MI theory," as it has come to be called, has two fascinating and complementary facets, and both of these can play out in the educational sphere. The first implication is that all of us possess these several intelligences: they make us human, cognitively speaking. Thus any teacher faced with youngsters who are not totally impaired can assume that the students possess all of these intelligences. If one chooses, it is possible to teach to the specific intelligences, to develop them, to draw on them in conveying consequential educational materials.

The second facet is that each individual possesses a distinctive profile of intelligences. Even identical twins—literally clones of one another with the same genetic profile—may each exhibit a characteristic "scatter" of intellectual strengths and weaknesses. These differences are due, presumably, to several factors: for example, even when two individuals have identical genetic information, they don't undergo the identical experiences in the world (or even in the womb); and two individuals who appear indistinguishable on a physical basis may be strongly motivated to distinguish themselves from one another.

The assertion that we possess a range of intelligences, with each person's profile as idiosyncratic, immediately poses a fascinating educational dilemma. One horn of that dilemma proclaims that we should ignore these differences or even try to erase them. The opposing horn holds that we should recognize these differences and try, insofar as possible, to turn them to our educational advantage.

It is fascinating to realize that throughout most of human history, differences among individuals have been considered a nuisance factor in educational circles. We have favored uniform schools—in which each person is treated the same as every other one. Moreover, this "equal treatment" appears on the surface to be fair, since no favoritism has apparently been shown.

However, one can also argue—as I have—that such "uniform" schools are actually unfair (Gardner 1993b, 1999a). They privilege one profile of intelligences—almost always the blend of language and logic that is probed in intelligence tests—and ignore or minimize the other ones. It would be possible to take entirely the opposite tack—one that I have labeled "individually centered education." In this alternative philosophy, one finds out as much as possible about each student and then crafts an education that helps each student learn as much as possible, in ways that are congenial to that student. I believe that such individualized education will come to fruition very soon. This outcome will occur not because of my theory or my preaching but because technology will make it possible to individualize education as much as we want to. And once it becomes clear that algebra or French or economics or music theory can be presented in many ways, then it will constitute malpractice to perseverate in using the methods of uniform education (see Turkle 1997, this volume).

The case of MI theory makes it clear that scientific findings can readily yield educational implications. Indeed, once MI theory had been enunciated, educators in many parts of the world began to claim that they were refashioning their classes or schools in the light of the theory. I was pleased that these ideas—psychological ones—had stimulated their thinking. But it soon became clear that MI theory was like an inkblot test—an ambiguous stimulus that could be interpreted in highly idiosyncratic ways. Some educators saw MI theory as a rationale for arts education or special education; others saw it as a pretext for creating tracks, in terms of the various intelligences; still others considered MI theory as a suggestion to teach seven to eight topics and/or to do so in seven to eight different ways. Even the psychometricians got into the act: I was approached by several publishing companies and asked if I wanted to develop a battery of tests, one for each intelligence!

The decisions one makes in such instances clearly reflect one's own value system. One can never proceed directly and unambiguously from a scientific finding to an educational practice. Indeed, this stricture pertains even to the traditional view of intelligence. I had a chance to discuss the findings of *The Bell Curve* with its senior author, Richard Herrnstein, before his untimely death. Herrnstein and I agreed that if one premise of the book was correct—that it is difficult to change IQ—one may draw two diametrically opposite inferences. The Herrnstein-Murray inference is that it is not worth trying to raise IQ and that one should simply accept these differences and make the best of them. But an opposite, more optimistic inference is that one should devote all one's energies in an attempt to raise IQ and one might well hit upon a method that is successful.

The embracing of MI theory, at least at a nominal level, is an example of how a scientific finding can be readily validated by the educational community. However, such a friendly reception is not always the case.

The Challenges of Disciplinary Understanding

Once one has acquired the basic literacies, the next educational milestone entails mastery of various subjects or disciplines. While the list of valued disciplines differs across societies, in general it features a number of sciences (biology, physics, chemistry), several branches of mathematics (algebra, geometry, precalculus), as well as a smattering of more humanistic pursuits (history, geography, one or more art forms). If the literacies represent the consensual curricula for the elementary grades, disciplinary mastery and understanding is the curriculum of choice for secondary schools and perhaps college as well.

Let me say a word about each of these terms. When I speak of *disciplines,* I intend a distinction between subject matter (learning the names, facts, and concepts of a particular subject) and discipline (mastering the distinctive ways of thinking that characterize a scientist, historian, humanist, or artist). Both scientists and historians offer explanations of events, but the nature of the data that they examine and the kinds of explanations that they offer are distinctively and instructively different. When I speak of *understanding,* I venture well beyond the simple capacity to recall what one has read or heard about. An individual who understands a disciplinary topic can apply that understanding to new situations, ones that she has never encountered before. In the absence of such performances of understanding, acquired knowledge remains inert—incapable of being mobilized for useful purposes.

In the past, both traditionalists and progressives woefully underestimated the difficulties entailed in disciplinary understanding. Traditionalists saw disciplinary study chiefly as the mastery of factual and definitional information drawn from various subject matters; and such mastery entailed chiefly repetition, drill, and preconfigured problem sets (Bereiter and Engelmann 1966; Hirsch 1987, 1996). Progressives believed that disciplinary understanding flowed naturally from the opportunity to explore topics in depth, in natural settings, at one's own pace (Bruner 1960; Dewey 1964; Jervis and Tobier 1988). Just as literacy should arise as a matter of course following opportunities to practice in a literate environment, so disciplinary mastery should arise naturally from deep immersion in the relevant subject matter.

Alas, both of these educational perspectives have proved wrong. A large body of research from the cognitive sciences over the last few decades has documented an alarming state of affairs. It turns out that the understanding of the principal ideas in the various disciplines has proved much more challenging than most educators have believed. The smoking gun can be found in the study of the sciences. Even students who get high grades in the sciences at leading secondary schools and universities turn out to have very tenuous understanding of the principal ideas in various subject areas. This result has been ascertained by examining such students outside of their classroom environment. Not only are most students inadequate in applying properly what they have learned in class, but in many cases, they give the same answers to problems and questions as are given by students who have not even taken the course in the first place! (For a summary of the relevant literature, see Gardner 1991, 1999b.) Thus, for example, even our high-scoring high school and college students fail to evince understanding of evolution, or the laws of motion, or the principles of economics when they are questioned outside a text-test context.

In *The Unschooled Mind* I have laid out this state of affairs in some detail. Whether one looks at the physical sciences, the natural sciences, the human sciences, mathematics, history, or the arts, the same picture emerges: most students prove unable to master disciplinary content sufficiently so that they can apply it appropriately in new contexts. For the most part they have simply memorized facts and definitions and can parrot back this "inert knowledge." Perhaps their teachers were asking them to do only this, so that in such cases, low expectations may well be at work. However, considerable evidence now documents strong cognitive forces that stand in the way of disciplinary understanding.

Why does this happen? I have argued that in the early years of life, young persons develop very powerful theories about the world: theories about objects, physical forces, living beings, life and death, other persons, the nature of the mind, and the like. These theories are based largely on common sense, though they may bear traces of both our biological heritage and the folk theories that young persons hear enunciated around them. Sometimes these theories turn out to be essentially correct; sometimes they are charming, to boot; but more often than not, they are simply erroneous misconceptions. To the extent that they are aware of them (and often they are not!), parents and teachers would like simply to eradicate these erroneous theories. Such mind transformation turns out not to be easy to do, however. In my view we have underestimated *both* the strength of these early theories *and* the amount of scaffolding, challenging, and consolidating that is needed to replace intuitive, unschooled theories with a new and superior understanding.

Again, the recognition of new data about the human mind should prove provocative to educators, but in this case it does not immediately dictate commensurate educational practices. One could, for example, simply dodge the challenge of disciplinary mastery and remain at the level of Gradgrindian (or Hirschian) factual mastery. One could decide to challenge directly the misconceptions of the young and see whether the proper conceptions can readily arise in their place. One could let the misconceptions play out, see where they are inadequate, and let youngsters themselves contrive better understandings. One could develop targeted curricula that provide support for specific forms of disciplinary understanding. It hardly needs to be remarked that the kind of local and national assessment instruments in play will exert a powerful impact on the educational strategy that is followed. If the instrument calls for a great deal of coverage—spanning the proverbial terrain from Plato to NATO in a world history course—then any chance of eradicating misconceptions will be undercut. And in my view, the latter scenario is what has happened so far. Few educators are willing to face the serious implication of the finding that genuine disciplinary understanding is rarely found, even among our most successful students.

Beyond Disciplinary Understanding—History Marches On

In the fall of 2002, both the Rhodes Scholarship and the Marshall Scholarships were announced at Harvard University. Seven students won these coveted awards, which provide support for study at a British university. What caught my eye was the fact that all seven of these students had undertaken interdisciplinary study while undergraduates. One student was enrolled in history and literature, a second was in physics and biochemistry, a third was in philosophy and international relations. All three of these individuals were also seriously involved in the arts.

While it has rarely been written about in the popular media, a major sea change has occurred in the academy over the last fifty years. A large number of interdisciplinary centers, programs, projects, and departments have sprung up all over the educational landscape, from middle school, through college and university curricula, all the way to advanced think tanks in the sciences, the humanities, and policy studies. This trend has reflected a variety of forces, ranging from the sober (so many contemporary problems demand input from a number of disciplines) to the mundane (it is attractive for a faculty member to have her own center, in which she can explore issues of interest to her in the ways she finds congenial with colleagues of her own choosing). And the actual work carried out under the rubric of interdisciplinarity has ranged from pathbreaking to self-absorbed to trivial.

For the last few years, my colleagues and I, complementing our studies of disciplinary understanding, have been exploring the nature of interdisciplinary work (Boix-Mansilla and Gardner 1997; Gardner and Boix-Mansilla 1994). There is no question that interdisciplinarity is in the air and that much work is being carried out under its banner. What has struck us is the astonishing lack of standards for what counts as adequate or appropriate interdisciplinary work. While standards are in place for judging the quality of work in the traditional disciplines, there has not been time—and perhaps there has not been motivation—to set up analogous kinds of indices for quality work in various interdisciplinary amalgams. Thus one is thrown into an uncomfortable situation: either accept all the work uncritically ("if it is interdisciplinary, it must be meritorious"); apply indices from the disciplinary world that may not be appropriate; or try to assess the impact of the work—which may not necessarily reflect its quality. (As the cases of cold fusion and Alan Sokal's spoof of postmodernist analysis remind us, the best scholarship is not necessarily the brand that gets the most attention, at least in the short run.)

The rise of interdisciplinary studies is not a scientific phenomenon; rather it is a historical fact of our time. Trends in our increasingly globalized society have brought interdisciplinary concerns to the fore. Issues like poverty reduction, anti-terrorism, privacy, prevention of disease, energy conservation, ecological balance—the list could be expanded at will—all require input from and syntheses of various forms of disciplinary knowledge and methods. Educational institutions seek, in their ways, to respond to the demand for this kind of skill; and the more adventurous students are attracted to studies that call for a blend of disciplinary expertises. Yet in a world that still believes in one kind of intelligence and that has not appreciated the difficulty of understanding even a single discipline, we are hardly in a position to mount interdisciplinary programs and feel confident about evaluating their success. Perhaps it will be necessary to institute psychological studies of the synthesizing or interdisciplinary mind.

EDUCATIONAL OPTIONS IN AN ERA OF GLOBALIZATION

Nearly everyone recognizes that the youth of today are being prepared for a world that is different in fundamental ways from the world of 1900, 1950, perhaps even 1975. In addition to the obvious differences in political alignments and technological sophistication, youth today partake of a powerful hegemonic cultural message emanating from the United States, as well as strong and divergent cultural countercurrents streaming in from major societies. Any student growing up in such a world needs to be able to navigate among these diverse and powerful messages (see Friedman 2000; Giddens 2000; also see Jenkins, Maira, and Watson, this volume). Yet there is not even the beginning of a synthesis of how this altered world should impact education, particularly education at the primary and secondary levels (see Suárez-Orozco and Qin-Hilliard, this volume). Here, I put forth some suggestions for a curriculum suitable to the era of globalization. I do so with the explicit awareness that all educational recommendations presuppose a certain set of values. Mine are based on an education that is suitable for a democratic society, in which individuals have a fair degree of say in where they live and how they live; in which the use of one's mind to the fullest is a prominent value; and in which all able-bodied individuals are expected to contribute not only to the security and well-being of their families but also to the health of the broader communities in which they live.

Beginning on a conservative note, I believe that we should not turn our backs on those methods and procedures that have been worked out over long periods of time. Though there is always room for improvement, we know a great deal about how to develop the literacies in young persons, both those who can learn in normal ways and those who have specific learning problems—for example, in the decoding of written alphabetic text.

Once we come to the mastery of disciplines, however, we can no longer afford business as usual. Now that we know the difficulties of disciplinary mastery, we need to recognize that this concern must occupy a large proportion of our pedagogical energies. My recommendation in this area is to cut down radically on the number of subjects to master in precollegiate education: I would favor all students learning at least one science, one area of history, one art form, expression and appreciation in their own language, and especially in countries where the principal language is not widely spoken beyond its borders, expression and appreciation of English.

Once a sharper focus has been adapted, it is indeed possible to teach for disciplinary understanding. Such teaching is best done by focusing on the principal deep ideas in the discipline and approaching them from many different angles (Blythe 1998; Cohen, McLaughlin, and Talbert 1993; Wiske 1998). A depth-over-breadth engagement with a limited number of topics and disciplines is most likely to undermine the misconceptions and to establish deep and robust forms of understanding. Interestingly, the idea of multiple intelligences can be used here. For if one focuses sharply on a limited number of concepts, it is possible to approach these concepts in several ways, exploiting our various human intelligences. Such a multiperspective approach yields two dividends: it reaches more students and it exemplifies what it means to have expertise (Gardner 1999b). After all, the expert is the individual who can think of a topic in lots of different ways.

My focus on a few key disciplines reveals that I believe in the idea of a core curriculum. In that sense I am a traditionalist. But I am completely open to the presentation of the curriculum along any number of pathways and to the assessment of mastery in several different ways. In matters of pedagogy and assessment, I am a pluralist. These ideas clash with those who want to revert to the ideal of uniform schools; they are congenial to those who see themselves as helping each student to realize his or her full potential in ways that are congenial.

Because of my fealty to the disciplines, I have been a strong believer that interdisciplinary work should await the mastery of a number of individual disciplines. We would not take seriously a claim of bilingualism unless a person had mastered more than one language; and so I reason that one should not evoke the term *interdisciplinary* until one has exhibited mastery of more than one discipline. Pursuing this line, disciplinary education becomes the challenge of secondary education, interdisciplinary education the superstructure associated with tertiary and postgraduate education.

Recently, however, I have softened this line. Because interdisciplinary work has become so important in our world, it may not be practical to withhold its practice until complete mastery of specific disciplines has coalesced. Perhaps it will be possible for an individual to achieve sufficient mastery of one discipline so that he can become part of a multi-discipline team. The challenge for this new team member is to bring a particular disciplinary perspective to bear on a problem and to gain enough expertise so that he can appreciate the contributions of the other disciplines, pose insightful questions, and integrate the answers into his understanding. I see no reason why novices should not be allowed to observe these interdisciplinary exchanges and benefit from them. However, it is vital that such novices understand that ultimately one will not be able to participate in a legitimate way in an interdisciplinary team unless one has paid one's disciplinary dues.

Membership in such teams points up another vital desideratum for participation in a global society. Simply being the smartest person in one's discipline will no longer suffice. Individuals need to be able to work effectively and in a civil manner with individuals who have different expertises and who come from different cultural backgrounds (Murnane and Levy 1996; Resnick 1987; Suárez-Orozco and Qin-Hilliard, this volume). We might say that such individuals need to develop interpersonal intelligence and multicultural understanding.

While there is a place for direct instruction in these realms, there is little question that youngsters are most powerfully affected by the examples that they see around them each day. To the extent that parents, teachers, and their respective communities exhibit strong forms of personal relations and cultural sensitivity, we can expect that youngsters will be equipped to participate effectively in working and playing teams. If, however, such forms of sensitivity have not been exhibited regularly by those who are closest to the young, then educational or work institutions face a daunting challenge.

Many have proposed that in our highly competitive global society, creativity, originality, thinking "outside the box" are at a premium. Silicon Valley represents eloquent testimony to the importance—as well as the risks—of a highly creative ambience. Yet it is questionable whether the enhancing of creativity should be a task of the schools. Much depends on whether the lessons of creativity are manifest "on the street" and in commercial enterprise—as they are in Silicon Valley or Hong Kong—or whether the conformism and tradition encountered daily on the streets and in the home need to be countered boldly in the educational system.

TOWARD ONE POSSIBLE EDUCATIONAL REGIME
FOR A GLOBAL ERA

I propose that precollegiate education in the future encompass the following relatively new skills and understandings (see Suárez-Orozco and Qin-Hilliard, this volume). These need not be transmitted by schools or by schools alone, but unless they are passed down via other sectors of the society, their transmission will become the challenge par excellence for the precollegiate educational system.

1. *Understanding of the global system.* The trends of globalization —the unprecedented and unpredictable movement of human beings, capital, information, and cultural life forms—need to be understood by the young persons who are and will always inhabit a global community. Some of the system will become manifest through the media; but many other facets—for example, the operation of worldwide markets—will need to be taught in a more formal manner.

2. *Capacity to think analytically and creatively within disciplines.* Simple mastery of information, concepts, and definitions will no longer suffice. Students will have to master disciplinary moves sufficiently so that they can apply them flexibly and generatively to deal with issues that could not be anticipated by the authors of textbooks.

3. *Ability to tackle problems and issues that do not respect disciplinary boundaries.* Many—perhaps most—of the most vexing issues facing the world today (including the issue of globalization!) do not respect disciplinary boundaries. AIDS, large-scale immigration, and global warming are examples of problems in need of interdiscplinary thinking. One could take the position that it is first necessary to master individual disciplines; moving among or beyond disciplines then becomes the task of tertiary or professional education (Gardner 1999b). However, there is much to be said for beginning the process of interdisciplinary work at an earlier point in education—as is done, for example, in the "theory of knowledge" course required of students in the International Baccalaureate or the courses in "problem-based learning" taught at the Illinois Mathematics and Science Academy. How best to begin to introduce rigorous multiperspective thinking into our classrooms is a challenge that we have only begun to confront; and as noted, our psychological understanding of the mind of the synthesizer has yet to coalesce.

4. *Knowledge of and ability to interact civilly and productively with individuals from quite different cultural backgrounds—both within one's own society and across the planet.* Globalization is selecting for interpersonal competencies, including the ability to think and work with others coming from very different racial, linguistic, religious, and cultural backgrounds (see Maira, this volume; C. Suárez-Orozco, this volume). Mastery and cultivation of these competencies will be the cornerstone of educational systems in the most successful democracies of the twenty-first century (see Suárez-Orozco and Qin-Hilliard, this volume).

5. *Knowledge of and respect for one's own cultural tradition(s).* The terrorists who crashed into the Twin Towers of the World Trade Center privileged the scientific and technical knowledge and cognitive skills that globalization has to offer. At the same time, they despised the Western, and especially the American, values, ethos, and worldview that in many regions of the world—including much of Western Europe—pass as globalization's underside. Soci-

eties that nurture the emergence of the instrumental skills needed to thrive *while* not subverting or undermining the expressive domains of culture—values, worldviews, and especially, the domain of the sacred—will endure and may even have the edge in globalization's new regime. Managing the dual process of convergence (in the instrumental domains of culture) and divergence (in the expressive domains of culture) may well be among the most critical tasks of education for globalization. Societies that can manage this psychic jujitsu will thrive.

6. *Fostering of hybrid or blended identities.* Education for globalization will select for the crafting and performing of hybrid identities needed to work, think, and play across cultural boundaries (see C. Suárez-Orozco, this volume). These will be increasingly indexed by multilingual competencies and transcultural sensibilities that will enable children to traverse discontinuous cultural meaning systems; to metabolize, decode, and make meaning in distinct, sometimes incommensurable cultural spaces and social fields. Societies that privilege transculturation and hybridity will be in a better position to thrive, while societies that enforce a regime of compulsive monoculturism and compulsive monolinguism are likely to lose out under globalization's emerging regime.

7. *Fostering of tolerance.* Education for globalization will give those societies that tend to (1) tolerate or, better yet, privilege dissent, (2) foster doubt (in Francis Bacon's sense), and (3) provide equality of opportunity will have a powerful edge over societies that tend to privilege reflex-like consent and inequality of access to opportunity due to various ascribed qualities. More ominously, our world is unlikely to survive unless we become far more successful at fostering tolerant attitudes within and across nations.

CONCLUDING NOTE

Though many may wish that they would go away, the main lines of globalization are here to stay. It is difficult to envision a world in which the economic trends, communication technologies, movements of population, and cultural messages of the past few decades will somehow be reversed. Even events as epochal as those of September 11, 2001, are likely to modulate the forces of globalization rather than derail them in a fundamental way.

Yet local or national institutions, mores, and values will not necessarily disappear. Indeed the very power of the forces of globalization will in many cases prompt strong reactions, sometimes violent, sometimes effective. Those newly emerging institutions that can respond to the forces of globalization while at the same time respecting the diversities of cultures and belief systems are most likely to have a long half-life.

Chief among those institutions will be educational systems, with those charged with precollegiate education assuming enormous importance for the foreseeable future. Educational systems are inherently conservative institutions, and that conservatism is in many ways justified. Still, just as educational systems eventually adapted to the agricultural and industrial revolutions, just as they eventually responded to the decline of religion and the invention of print and audiovisual technologies, they will have to adapt as well to the facts of the globalized, knowledge-centered economy and society. In doing so, they will have to somehow integrate the new scientific findings, their multiple (and sometimes seemingly contradictory) educational implications, with past and present historical trends, and to do so in light of their most cherished values. This task may take one hundred years or more; but as a French military leader once famously remarked, "In that case, we had better begin today."

NOTE

I wish to thank the participants of the Harvard-Ross Retreat (April 2002) and Seminar (October 2002) on Education and Globalization for their valuable suggestions, and Marcelo Suárez-Orozco and Desirée Baolian Qin-Hilliard for their skillful editing. Work described in this paper was supported by the Atlantic Philanthropies, Jeffrey Epstein, and Courtney S. Ross-Holst, to whom thanks are due.

REFERENCES

Bereiter, C., and S. Engelmann (1966). *Teaching the disadvantaged in the preschool.* Englewood Cliffs, NJ: Prentice Hall.

Bloom, D. E., and J. E. Cohen (2001). *The unfinished revolution: Universal basic and secondary education.* Paper presented at the American Academy of Arts and Sciences, Cambridge, MA, July 2001.

Blythe, T. (1998). *The teaching for understanding guide.* San Francisco: Jossey-Bass.

Boix-Mansilla, V., and H. Gardner (1997). Of kinds of disciplines and kinds of understanding. *Phi Delta Kappan 78*(5): 381–386.

Bruner, J. S. (1960). *The process of education.* Cambridge, MA: Harvard University Press.

Bruner, J. S., R. Olver, and P. M. Greenfield (1966). *Studies in cognitive growth.* New York: John Wiley and Sons.

Cohen, D., M. McLaughlin, and J. Talbert (1993). *Teaching for understanding.* San Francisco: Jossey-Bass.

Dewey, J. (1964). *John Dewey on education.* R. Archambault, ed. Chicago: University of Chicago Press.

Donald, M. (1991). *Origins of the modern mind.* Cambridge, MA: Harvard University Press.

Eysenck, H. (1986). The theory of intelligence and the psychophysiology of cognition. In *Advances in the psychology of human intelligence,* Vol. 3. R. Sternberg, ed. Hillsdale, NJ: Lawrence Erlbaum.

Friedman, T. (2000). *The Lexus and the olive tree: Understanding globalization.* New York: Anchor Books.

Gardner, H. (1985). *The mind's new science: A history of the cognitive revolution.* New York: Basic Books.

Gardner, H. (1991). *The unschooled mind.* New York: Basic Books.

Gardner, H. (1993a). *Frames of mind: The theory of multiple intelligences.* New York: Basic Books (Original work published in 1983).

Gardner, H. (1993b). *Multiple intelligences: The theory in practice.* New York: Basic Books.

Gardner, H. (1999a). *Intelligence reframed: Multiple intelligences for the 21st century.* New York: Basic Books.

Gardner, H. (1999b). *The disciplined mind: Beyond facts and standardized tests: K–12 education that every child deserves.* New York: Simon & Schuster.

Gardner, H., and V. Boix-Mansilla (1994). Teaching for understanding in the disciplines—and beyond. *Teachers College Record 96*(2): 198–218.

Giddens, A. (2000). *Runaway world: How globalization is reshaping our lives.* New York: Routledge.

Goleman, D. (1995). *Emotional intelligence.* New York: Bantam.

Gould, S. J. (1981). *The mismeasure of man.* New York: W. W. Norton.

Herrnstein, R. J., and C. Murray (1994). *The bell curve.* New York: The Free Press.

Hirsch, E. D. (1987). *Cultural literacy.* Boston: Houghton Mifflin.

Hirsch, E. D. (1996). *The schools we need and why we don't have them.* New York: Doubleday.

Jervis, K., and A. Tobier (1988). *Education for democracy.* Weston, MA: The Cambridge School.

Lemann, N. (1999). *The big test.* New York: Farrar, Straus & Giroux.

Lippmann, W. (1976). Readings from the Lippmann-Terman debate (Original work published in 1992–1993). In *The IQ controversy: Critical readings.* N. J. Block and G. Dworking, eds. New York: Pantheon.

Mithen, S. (1996). *The prehistory of the mind.* London: Thames & Hudson.

Murnane, R., and F. Levy (1996). *Teaching the new basic skill: Principles for educating children to thrive in a changing economy.* New York: The Free Press.

Piaget, J. (1983). Piaget's theory. In *Handbook of Child Psychology,* Vol. 1. P. Mussen, ed. New York: John Wiley.

Resnick, L. (1987). *Education and learning to think.* Washington DC: National Academy Press.

Rosnow, R., A. Skedler, M. Jaeger, and B. Rin (1994). Intelligence and the epistemics of interpersonal acumen: Testing some implications of Gardner's theory. *Intelligence* 19: 93–116.

Salovey, P., and J. Mayer (1990). Emotional intelligence. *Imagination, Cognition and Personality* 9: 185–211.

Skinner, B. F. (1938). *The behavior of organisms.* New York: Appleton Century Crofts.

Spearman, C. (1904). General intelligence, objectively determined and measured. *American Journal of Psychology* 15: 201–293.

Sternberg, R. J. (1985). *Beyond IQ.* New York: Cambridge University Press.

Terman, L. (1916). *The measurement of intelligence.* Boston: Houghton Mifflin.

Thurstone, L. L. (1938). *Primary mental abilities.* Chicago: University of Chicago Press.

Tomasello, M. (2000). *The cultural origins of cognition.* Cambridge, MA: Harvard University Press.

Tooby, J., and L. Cosmides (1991). The psychological foundations of culture. In *The adapted mind.* J. Barkow, L. Cosmides, and J. Tooby, eds. New York: Oxford University Press.

Turkle, S. (1997). *Life on the screen: Identity in the age of the Internet.* New York: Touchstone.

Vygotsky, L. (1978). *Mind in society.* Cambridge, MA: Harvard University Press.

Walker, G. (2002a). *Reflections of the International Baccalaureate.* Paper presented at the Retreat on Education and Globalization, Tarrytown, NY, April 2002.

Walker, G. (2002b). *To educate the nations.* Suffolk, NY: John Catt Educational Limited.

Wiske, M. S. (1998). *Teaching for understanding.* San Francisco: Jossey-Bass.

Notes on Contributors

Antonio M. Battro was Robert F. Kennedy Visiting Professor of Latin American Studies at Harvard University (2002–2003) and is a member of the Pontifical Academy of Sciences.

David E. Bloom is Clarence James Gamble Professor of Economics and Demography at Harvard University.

John H. Coatsworth is Monroe Gutman Professor of Latin American Affairs at Harvard University.

Howard Gardner is John H. and Elisabeth A. Hobbs Professor of Cognition and Education at Harvard University.

Henry Jenkins is Ann Fetter Friedlaender Professor of Humanities at Massachusetts Institute of Technology.

Sunaina Maira is Associate Professor of Asian American Studies at the University of California at Davis.

Desirée Baolian Qin-Hilliard is a doctoral candidate at Harvard Graduate School of Education.

Courtney Ross-Holst is founder and chair of the Ross Institute in New York.

Carola Suárez-Orozco is Co-director of the Harvard Immigration Projects and a Scholar in Residence at the Ross Institute.

Marcelo M. Suárez-Orozco is Victor S. Thomas Professor of Education at Harvard University and a Scholar in Residence at the Ross Institute.

Sherry Turkle is Abby Rockefeller Mauzé Professor of the Social Studies of Science and Technology at Massachusetts Institute of Technology.

James L. Watson is John King and Wilma Cannon Fairbank Professor of Chinese Society at Harvard University.

Index

Compositor:	Michael Bass Associates
Indexer:	Herr's Indexing Service
Text:	10/14 Sabon
Display:	Franklin Gothic
Printer and binder:	Malloy Lithographing, Inc.